THE DISCOVERY OF TEACHING

"The art of being taught is the art of discovery, as the
art of teaching is the art of assisting discovery."

MARK VAN DOREN

To Helen

THE DISCOVERY OF TEACHING

Cole S. Brembeck

MICHIGAN STATE UNIVERSITY

1962

Prentice-Hall, Inc.   ENGLEWOOD CLIFFS, N.J.

PREFACE

This book is built around living experiences in teaching and learning. It is a combination text and case book. The cases capture examples of teaching, learning, and educational problem-solving. The textual materials, in which the cases are set, help the student to probe the cases, examine them, and find answers to such questions as: "What do *I* think?" and "What would *I* do?" In short, the purpose of the book is to assist students in making their own exciting discoveries in the world of teaching.

The idea for this book grew out of my early experiences in conducting a course in "Introduction to Teaching." As we moved into the course, one thing became clear: the students wanted and needed something more than straight textual materials. Teaching, they sensed, is dynamic and alive, not easily reduced to fixed rules and principles. We needed materials which would present teaching for what it is, a living experience.

We began our search for cases which capture teaching and learning as it happens. We found them in many places—in the professional literature on teaching, interviews, autobiographies, essays, and letters. And we found them in the experiences of one hundred student teachers, whose discoveries in teaching are reported in section one.

As we proceeded to use the cases, we found that they were interesting, stirred lively discussions and argument, and provided inspiration for student projects. But something was lacking. The students wanted more "leads" and "tools" with which to work.

Finally a student suggested that I "build textual materials around the cases. Give us the tools we need for analyzing them. Then, pose some questions which will help us transfer our discoveries to our own teaching."

This book, then, is the result of that suggestion. It leads to the work of the instructor. It provides a readiness for his contribution. It raises more questions than it answers, and provokes more discussions than it settles. Its aim is to make the student more venturesome as the instructor directs him toward important discoveries in teaching and learning.

ACKNOWLEDGMENTS

The extent of one's debt to others when writing a book is manifest in the act of gathering their names into a single list. It is a good reminder of how one's efforts are dependent upon those of others. Since it is impossible to name all who have helped, I simply acknowledge my debt.

I wish to thank George Counts for reading Chapter Six and making valuable suggestions. Ernest Melby, who earlier taught the foundation course from which this book has grown, has always been generous with his help and inspiration. My running discussion with Floyd Reeves has extended around the world and touched upon diverse educational problems. The survey of student teacher opinion was made possible by Vern Hicks. Bernard Corman has always had a spare moment to contribute useful ideas about case materials and psychological approaches to teaching. Wilbur Brookover approved All-University research grants which helped to make possible the location of case materials and their testing in class use. Edwin Bailey, as graduate assistant, helped me teach the course while the manuscript was being developed, and provided useful insights and suggestions. Roger Holloway, Prentice-Hall editor, talks about the anatomy of a manuscript in such a way that the author sees new ways to improve it. My students have not spared me, and many suggestions have come from them. I especially thank those students whose papers are published here: Richard E. Anstine, Douglas G. Balogh, Marilynne A. Brown, Earlyn Byas, Sarah Litowsky, Doris Carole McCall, Alice Jan Ressler, Stephanie Walsh, and Samuel Webster. My debt to the one hundred student teachers will be clear to all those who read section one. Dean Clifford E. Erickson, who has never seen the manuscript, nonetheless contributed greatly to it.

The decision to use case situations was made possible by the many individuals and publishers who granted permission to reproduce materials. I wish to thank the following for permission to use excerpts from the indicated sources: American Universities Field Staff, "Education in Tepoztlan," by James Maddox. Cambridge University Press, *Desiderius Erasmus,* by William Harrison Woodward. Columbia University Press, *The Other Side of Main Street,* by Henry Johnson. Paul Cruikshank, *Memories and Opinions,* by Horace Dutton Taft. Doubleday and Company, *Up From Slavery,* by Booker T. Washington. Dryden L. Phelps, *Teaching in School and College,* by William Lyon Phelps. E. P. Dutton and Company, *Emile,* by Rousseau. The Epworth Press, *The Journal of John Wesley,* by John Wesley. Estate of John Dewey, *The School and Society,* by John Dewey. Harcourt, Brace & World, Inc., *Love Against Hate,* by Karl Menninger. Harper and Brothers, "Education Is the Balance Wheel of the Social Machinery," in *Living Ideas in America,* by Henry Steele Commager; *Jonesville,* by W. Lloyd Warner. Holt, Rinehart, and Winston, Inc., *Out of My Life and Thought,* by Albert Schweitzer; *Wisconsin Historian,* by Carl Becker. Houghton Mifflin Company, *The Promised Land,* by Mary Antin. Nannine Joseph, *Liberal Education,* by Mark Van Doren. Alfred A. Knopf, Inc., *The Prophet,* by Kahlil Gibran. *Life Magazine,* "Our Schools Have Kept Us

Free," by Henry Steele Commager. J. B. Lippincott Company, *Leap to Free-dom*, by Oksana Kasenkina. The Macmillan Company, *The Aims of Education*, by Albert North Whitehead; *A Goodly Fellowship*, by Mary Ellen Chase; *The Philosophy of Civilization*, by Albert Schweitzer; *A Son of the Middle Border*, by Hamlin Garland. New York *Times*, "Utopian Schools," by John Dewey. Oxford University Press, *Quintilian On Education*, by William Smail. Philosophical Library, *The Selected Writings of Benjamin Rush*, by Dagabert D. Runes. Charles Scribner's Sons, *Farmington*, by Clarence Darrow; "A Letter of Gratitude and Indebtedness," by Thomas Wolfe; *The Thread That Runs So True*, by Jesse Stuart. The University of North Carolina Press, *Notes on the State of Virginia*, by Thomas Jefferson.

Finally, I express deep appreciation to Helen, Beth, and Mark, who all must have shared little Mark's frequent question: "Why do you *always* have to go to the office?" and who tolerated my answers, even though they were not very good ones.

C. S. B.

CONTENTS

4. Experienced Teachers Speak (Cont.):

answer Kahlil Gibran, Socrates, Erasmus, and Whitehead. No; it is the art of putting something in the learner say Cicero, Quintilian, Arnold, and Phelps. What is your judgment? Test your position.

5. Two Classrooms: Two Answers 73

Visit the classrooms of Mary Ellen Chase and Henry Johnson. What do they believe about teaching? Learning? Students? Viewpoints influence practice.

III LIVING ISSUES WITHIN CLASSROOMS

6. Four Questions for the Teacher 89

John Dewey and Mark Van Doren debate four questions which confront the teacher: How do we learn? What shall we teach? How shall we teach? What is the proper focus for teaching? Teacher education is the process of developing answers to these questions.

IV LEARNING: REMARKABLE PRODUCT OF TEACHING

7. The Learning Around Us 109

A little boy announces a wonderful surprise: He can write his name. What makes learning possible? What factors stimulate learning?

8. Learning in Tomorrow's Schools 121

A field trip to John Dewey's Utopia stirs four questions about school learning: What is a good physical environment for learning? What qualities should teachers possess? How should learning be carried on? What should be the learning objectives?

V THE TEACHER AT WORK WITH STUDENTS

9. Non-directed Learning 145

Jean Jacques Rousseau got Emile "lost" in the forest, then asked him: "How shall we find our way home?" He taught astronomy by non-direction. How does the non-directive teacher view his students? How does he evaluate them? Is non-directive learning effective?

10. Directed Learning 162

Agassiz put a fish before Scudder and said: "Look at it." Scudder saw very little, until. . . . What view does a directive teacher take

10. Directed Learning (Cont.):

of teaching and learning? Compare Agassiz and Rousseau. How shall we judge directed learning?

11. Dominated Learning   175

Said Susanna Wesley about teaching her nineteen children: "First conquer the will." Her children learned rapidly, but unlearning took place. Mr. Jackman illustrates the use of the teacher-dominated method in a fifth grade classroom. How shall we judge dominated learning? What kind of leadership shall we employ?

VI THE SCHOOL AND COMMUNITY

12. What Is the Task of the School?   193

When Booker T. Washington founded Tuskegee Institute he spent a month traveling through rural Alabama studying the community Tuskegee was to serve. There are certain principles governing the relationship of a school and community. To test these principles we take a field trip to a village school in Mexico. Is this school living up to its part of the relationship?

13. The Teacher and Community   208

When Jesse Stuart catches students playing poker behind the school fence he poses a question: Whose responsibility is it? The teacher's or the community's? Significant ideas govern teacher-community relationships. Community participation involves some risks and problems. Here are some ponderables for teachers: How can I help the school become a tool for achieving desirable community goals? How can I help to weld together school and community to achieve better learning and living? How can I keep professionally aware of my ever widening responsibility for school-community leadership?

14. The Teacher and Parents   221

Horace Dutton Taft, who worked almost fifty years with parents, remarked: "Every parent has a tremendous prejudice in favor of his or her offspring." Working with parents is a part of teaching. Much depends upon the relationship. What do parents expect of teachers? What do teachers expect of parents? Here are six things a teacher can do to encourage wholesome relationships with parents.

THE DISCOVERY OF TEACHING

ONE HUNDRED STUDENT TEACHERS

CHAPTER 1

THE FIRST EXCITEMENT OF TEACHING

"A wonderful feeling of accomplishment comes when, one day, the class regards you as their teacher."

A STUDENT TEACHER

Most teachers remember the day they began to teach. New teachers like to talk about that first day, and prospective teachers look forward to it with mingled expectations and anxiety. Beginning to teach is a meaningful and remembered experience.

What is it like? Does the experience differ from the expectation? What are the first impressions? What part of teaching does the new teacher enjoy the most? Least? What baffles and startles the new teacher? Do students behave like he thought they would? How does the first experience affect his desire to teach? What suggestions does the new teacher make to others preparing to teach?

FOR THE NEW TEACHER, WHAT IS TEACHING REALLY LIKE?

The question is worth asking. The first reactions of the new teacher can help us in many ways.

First, the new teacher can help the college student who has not yet made a decision to teach but who wants to learn more about teaching. A realistic way to learn about a profession is to talk with people who are in it. From them we can gain a first-hand impression of what the work is like. Such experiences can help us make a wiser personal decision.

Second, the new teacher can help those who have already made the decision to teach. The new teacher is close to college preparation. He is

3

eager to try new ideas. What does he learn from the experience? The new teacher can test the adequacy of his preparation, and tell us what he finds most useful. His experience can guide us in our own preparation. First experiences are important. Good first experiences can have much to do with later success in teaching.

Third, the new teacher can tell us what it actually "feels like to be a teacher" and can share with us the joys and frustrations of his new status.

In the first three chapters of this book we shall listen as one hundred student teachers report their initial reactions to teaching. All were college juniors or seniors. They had completed, or nearly completed, their professional requirements for the teaching certificate. For their student teaching they left the campus for one term and most of them lived in the communities where they taught. The one hundred student teachers taught in twenty-two different public schools, both elementary and secondary. Each of them was assigned to a supervising teacher under whom and with whom they worked. After student teaching they returned to the campus to complete their requirements for graduation.

They were given actual charge of their classes for varying periods of time. Some taught for nearly all of the three months, others for shorter periods. Many took part in community activities, conferred with parents, attended P.T.A. and faculty meetings, worked on committees, kept student records, and generally assumed a teacher's responsibilities. Short of working as regular and full time teachers, these one hundred college students probably acquired as much teaching experience in a short time as is possible. What did they think of the experience?

Here are five questions to which they responded:

1. What do you find most rewarding in teaching?
2. Does teaching differ from what you expected?
3. What are the toughest problems in teaching?
4. How does teaching affect your desire to teach?
5. What suggestions do you have for other prospective teachers?

In this chapter we shall listen to the student teachers answer the first two questions about the rewards of teaching and the differences they encounter.

WHAT DO YOU FIND MOST REWARDING IN TEACHING?

The one hundred student teachers are almost unanimous in their answers. *Working with students* provides the most rewarding experience. The student teachers find great satisfaction in seeing learning take place.

The thought that they helped to bring this learning about provides the special reward for their work. One student teacher put it this way: "To see the 'light go on' after working hard with students is the most satisfying experience that one can imagine. I had heard from other teachers that this was truly satisfying; yet, it isn't until you see it on the faces of your own students that you really understand its meaning." Another agreed, "There are those moments when something special takes place. The class as well as the teacher feels it. You can almost feel the learning take place."

Working With Students Is Rewarding

Let us listen to the student teachers as they deal with the every-day learning problems confronted by almost all teachers.

Take, for example, the problem one student teacher encountered in teaching Sandra about fractions. She comments:

> I tried every method imaginable, every approach I knew to teach Sandra what a fraction is. For two weeks I tried. For two weeks I had little success. Sandra would say she understood, but I could see she didn't. We would start again and eventually end up in the same place—nowhere.
>
> One day during a class discussion of fractions I hit upon an idea of using a row of twelve children to represent one whole number. Sandra could visualize this. I pushed on. "Tell one-half of the boys and girls to sit down, Sandra," I said as I wrote the fraction $\frac{1}{2}$ on the board. Sandra told six of the children to sit down. Her eyes began to light up. In the next ten minutes we used various combinations of children to represent common fractions. Sandra learned what a fraction is.
>
> A little incident you say? Sure. Nothing earth shaking. But to me, rewarding beyond measure.

A high school student teacher in history discovered that his most rewarding experience came when his students suddenly grasped the full significance of an historical event.

> Suddenly on the faces you see interest and suspense. The greatest challenge is to awaken such interest.
>
> As an example I might cite our unit on the rise of European dictatorships in the 1930's. We dealt with the Nazi regime in Germany at some length, working with such concepts as the "totalitarian state" and the "master race." When the students began to ask minute questions about life under the Nazis and to draw comparisons between this and the present Russian regime (without

any coaching from me), I noted with gratification that they understood the concepts being used. They were seeing the difference between this type of government and the democratic way of life.

A fourth grade teacher found her most rewarding experience in teaching a science unit on energy.

> The enthusiasm and response of the children was very encouraging. We divided the class into eight committees, each having a type of energy for its topic. Each committee's assignment was to present a program on its type of energy with each child covering some phase of that type. The programs were excellent. One committee did its program in the form of a TV show. Another presented a science fair. A couple of committees presented plays covering their topics. Another presented a quiz program. The work the children put on the programs was a rewarding experience. Even more rewarding was what they learned about energy. They did excellent work for fourth graders.

A student teacher in English found her most rewarding teaching experience in dramatics.

> Let me illustrate. In dramatics we start with raw material. We first select a cast from inexperienced eighth and ninth graders. We try to develop each individual according to his ability in such things as speaking voice, stage action, and acting ability. The climax of all activity comes in three days of performances before a daily audience of 125 students and parents in the dramatics room. My reward came in watching the audience enjoy a good performance and observing the cast put into practice what they had learned during the year. Probably the most rewarding experience of all is exchanging comments on the performance with the audience immediately following the play and telling the cast they did a good job.

A physical education teacher found equal satisfaction in seeing his seventh grade tumbling class develop.

> My supervising teacher gave me twenty boys to teach "anything I wanted to." Since the facilities were available, I instructed them in doubles tumbling for four weeks. During that time they moved from the basic stunts to full routines. I got to know them very well and could see them profiting both physically and socially from what they were doing. I don't think I will ever experience again the pride which I felt when they demonstrated their new skills for my supervising teacher.

A home economics student teacher reports:

> My students were interested in foreign foods; so we spent a week learning all we could about foods from other countries. To complete the unit we had a buffet consisting of a variety of foods from other lands. We planned simple table decorations suggestive of foreign countries. It was a good learning experience for the girls and for me. Afterwards, the girls said, "This was great! We've never done things like this before." It made me feel good.

An elementary school student teacher remembered with satisfaction the unit her students did on "Our State."

> The children were so enthused with their work that they didn't want to take an afternoon recess, although the temperature was in the eighties. I had literally to push them out the door. (They would have been too wiggly and noisy the rest of the afternoon without recess.) They told me how excited they were to do the group work which they had planned.

These reports give us an accurate indication of the satisfaction which new teachers experience in working with students. Here are some brief additional comments which confirm those reported above.

> Mine was a seventh grade general music class. Did you ever try to get seventh graders to sing, especially the boys? When I finally got them to open their mouths and "let go," I realized a moment of true satisfaction.

> My students evaluated me. I came off better than I should have, but it was rewarding to read their comments. One of them said, "I like the way you taught us to use science." It made me feel that I had accomplished something.

> The most rewarding experiences have been in the music programs which I presented this year. One in particular I remember—a program of K-5 grades. When the children sang with so much enthusiasm, I wanted to cry.

> My third hour students gave a debate. They spent a lot of time preparing and it really paid off. They would have embarrassed some college debaters that day.

> Leading a student discussion can be very enjoyable. At first my students were reluctant to volunteer information. Finally, I was able to draw them out. They became anxious to show their knowledge of the subject.

Every year there is a city track meet in which both boys and girls participate. The competition is stiff and our students usually do poorly. Not this year! Our hard work really paid off.

Linda had trouble at first getting the concept of "carrying" in arithmetic. We worked for a long time on it. Finally! It was a great day for both of us!

Fred stays in his seat for more than five minutes at a time . . . Bobby finally writes something that is legible . . . Dick takes his time on some arithmetic problems and gets them all right . . . Eugene spells half of his spelling words correctly . . . Larry opens the door for (of all things) a girl . . . Jerry doesn't slam his bat to the ground after taking a called third strike—rewarding experiences all.

There Is Satisfaction In Working With Children
Who Have Special Problems

Some students have special problems in learning. In the previous examples the student teachers find satisfaction in the teacher's main task, working with children and youth. The examples deal mostly with the usual learning problems found in every classroom. Most classrooms, too, present difficult challenges: the child who doesn't want to learn, the slow one, the emotionally disturbed one, and the bright one who is bored. How do new teachers respond to these? Is working with such children also rewarding? Apparently so. It is harder and frequently more frustrating, but just as rewarding. In fact, many student teachers find the satisfaction of helping these children especially to their liking. Listen first to those who relate their experiences in working with slow students.

A high school student teacher reports:

> I have an extremely slow student in general math. He is a freshman interested only in boxing. His interest is certainly not in math! What to do? I finally devised a special problem set for him with mathematical applications to boxing, such as the area and perimeter of the boxing ring and the cost of ring canvasing and roping. He was so pleased that someone else had taken an interest in boxing. The problem set turned out to have 62 problems in it. (Not all the questions dealt with math; some dealt with diet, fatigue factors, and boxing form, including weight problems.) Three days later he turned in the whole problem set! Problem: He still isn't doing his homework assignment from the text. What do I do now?

A boy in a low ability general English class presented a problem for another high school teacher.

He lived in a dream world. One day when we were studying about the Wright brothers, I brought a model of their airplane, the "Kitty Hawk." I asked if someone in the class might like to build such a model. The boy came out of his dream world and shot his hand up. Later he asked for a pass to the library to get more information on the Wright brothers and "Kitty Hawk." He did a respectable theme on the "Kitty Hawk," and the model turned out all right, too.

Another new teacher expresses her satisfaction this way:

I was gratified to see some of my slow students working hard and really trying to get ahead. One boy in particular gave me encouragement. He had been flunking all along and I had thought he just wasn't very bright. After a couple of weeks, however, he really started to work. Then one day another fellow in the class had a tough question for me. Before I could answer his question, my "problem" boy gave him a wonderful explanation. He has done this several times on varied material. I have found out that many of the people I thought were not very bright were just lacking motivation. Once they became interested they did a fine job.

An elementary school student teacher found satisfaction in working with a slow reading group.

We have one reading unit on "Old Tales from Different Lands." Seven children in my fourth grade group each told the whole class a tale from a different land, each chosen outside the stories in our own book. They read other books and made their own selections. Some of them were excellent story tellers. They surprised both the class and me.

That the student teachers find deep satisfaction in working with students with special learning problems is clear.

Let us now turn to some examples of other kinds of problems confronted by student teachers. These deal mostly with problems of attitude and behavior. Here, too, the new teachers find satisfying experiences. Notice how attitude and behavior problems influence learning.

A physical education teacher reports:

I like to see students begin to become better individuals because of something we've been able to do for them. One student in particular gave me a bad time. All he said he wanted to do was to quit school and join the Air Force. He had natural ability in track, especially as a long distance runner. I showed him what he could do if only he wanted to. I encouraged him to go out for track and contribute his ability to the team. This encouragement seems to have taken root. He has just told me that he plans to stay in school. Every night he has run and is working hard. I thing this "dead-end kid" is getting a new outlook and I hope he carries through.

A home economics student teacher reports success with a classroom behavior problem:

During the first day of clothing laboratory, the girls were as noisy as could be. The classroom was bedlam. I had to cope with the problem. But how? I didn't want to hurt their feelings, yet I wanted to make a point. Finally, I decided to put my art experience to work. I made a bulletin board depicting their actions in class. The caption across the top read: *The Latest Thing in Clothing*. Then below I sketched a number of stick figures, each saying things the girls had said in the classroom the day before. One stick figure pictured a girl seated at her sewing machine with her mouth wide open. "Say, Jan, guess what I'm doing Saturday night?" Another stick figure depicted a girl doing some hand sewing and not paying any attention to what she was doing. She was saying, "Oh, I'm so excited. Jerry asked me to go steady." There were more stick figures with similar conversation.

I placed the bulletin board near the door where everyone could see it, and I waited. Everybody looked at it and soon the girls were buzzing good naturedly about it. This led to a serious discussion of how we should behave in clothing laboratory. It worked. I had no more trouble. It doesn't sound sensational, but to me the experience was most rewarding.

A kindergarten teacher found satisfaction in learning how to handle a group of spirited five year olds.

When I first started, for instance, we would wait, morning and afternoon, for over half the children to settle down for class to begin. Now, after praising those quick to respond and giving friendly reminders to those who kept us waiting, I got them to come over to me immediately, sit down, and be quiet.

Another problem with kindergarteners is to get them to raise their hands when they want to speak. We finally obtained splendid results, though it took a long time. They are so anxious to speak that they forgot about others. It is a great source of satisfaction to me that almost all of the youngsters are now cooperating on these efforts to be thoughtful of all those in the group.

A case of cheating was reported by a commercial teacher.

> The most rewarding experience I believe I have had this term was when a girl came up to me and said she had cheated on a test. It was in shorthand class and she had asked another girl what a few words were when she was transcribing shorthand notes. I had not seen her cheat and I was at a loss for words. But she had such a relieved look on her face that nothing needed to be said. I was pleased at the thought that she would tell me.

The following random comments are also from student teachers who found satisfaction in working with students with special problems:

> My most rewarding experience has been to stimulate the interest of several students in science who had previously shown no interest.

> I had a rewarding experience in giving a slow reader individual help. He didn't like to read, nor did he wish to improve his reading. I worked with him alone every day for about a month. After about a week he began to show real interest and started to work very hard.

> I have found that getting a lazy student to produce some good art work is a most thrilling thing.

> This little boy would read all the time and never turn in any work. Now he does both.

> This little girl was all mixed up. She couldn't remember from one day to the next how to add and subtract. I worked with her every day for weeks. My happiest day came when she got an "A" on her arithmetic test.

> A boy who was retained was unsociable and hostile. In addition, he was dirty. He's no honor student yet, but now he takes part in activities, wears clean clothes, and scrubs his hands.

> One of my slow second grade readers had trouble with words starting with *wh, th,* and *ch.* After two weeks of special help this child suddenly came through. His growth in reading is remarkable.

> One of my most rewarding experiences has been with one of my bright children. It's a great challenge to keep him interested. Finally, I've gotten him so he will go ahead on his own.

When new teachers consider the rewards in teaching, their thoughts turn to students and to the accomplishments in which the teachers share. These experiences are quite representative of the one hundred student teachers. Their greatest rewards come in seeing students grow and develop, surmount difficult problems, and make progress on the road to maturity.

1. Have you had an opportunity to work with children or young people? Do the experiences related by the practice teachers call to mind any of your own? If so, what was your greatest source of satisfaction?

DOES TEACHING DIFFER FROM WHAT YOU EXPECTED?

Does the first experience of teaching hold some surprises? Or is it about what the new teacher expects? The great majority of these beginning teachers find the experience considerably different from what they anticipated. Only fifteen of the one hundred report that teaching holds no surprises. Twenty-five of the new teachers discovered that teaching is easier than they expected. They are pleasantly surprised at their ability to cope with their first teaching experiences. Sixty of the student teachers were jolted by the size of the job. They feel that for a number of reasons teaching demands far more of them than they expected.

For A Few Beginners Teaching Holds No Surprises

"My real experience of teaching does not differ much at all from what I expected," reports a beginning science teacher. An elementary practice teacher adds, "I expected teaching to be a lot of work and fun. It's been exactly that." A confident junior high school teacher replies with the question, "Why should the actual experience differ? We prepared for it, didn't we?"

These new teachers who experienced few surprises took a calm and realistic view of their future responsibilities. This reaction is representative:

> I feel that teaching is just what I expected it to be. There is lots of work to do before hand in preparing lessons and activities. There's the problem of keeping the class busy and interested at all times. Then there's the work to be done after school—preparation for the next day, tests and homework to correct. A teacher must attend outside activities. The students like teachers who can take an interest in their activities outside the classroom. All this is what I expected.

2. Can you make an "educated guess" as to why teaching for this group of practice teachers was about what they expected?

For Some Beginners Teaching Is Easier Than Expected

The twenty-five new teachers who found teaching easier than they expected report a number of different reasons for their reactions. Most, however, are gratified by their ability to handle teaching problems.

Being proficient in subject matter concerns a number of the student teachers who found teaching easier than expected. "When I was on campus," states one, "I worried about my knowledge of subject matter. I found that by keeping up on my daily lessons I can master the subject." Another student teacher said, "I was scared of not being competent in my subject, but I found that I had plenty of time to prepare and practice before presenting a lesson to the class."

These teachers find that working with students is an interesting rather than forbidding task. They find students cooperative, willing, and even eager to please. As an elementary school teacher put it, "Helping children to learn is actually fun." A high school teacher commented, "I expected the worst in discipline problems. Much to my surprise, there has been absolutely no trouble in this area."

Communicating with students concerns others in this group. "I was afraid," states a junior high school student teacher, "that I wouldn't be able to express myself adequately in front of a group of students, but they almost pushed me into overtime!" A high school teacher remarks, "I was afraid that I might not be able to hold attention and command student respect. However, I just acted as if I expected their attention and respect and I got them. It turned out to be much easier than I expected." Another high school teacher says, "I was surprised at what I could do in the actual classroom. I had a great fear of standing and speaking before a group, but soon this came as natural as breathing."

Working with the school administration is an important part of teaching. One student teacher observed, "I expected the principal and supervisor to be demanding and critical, but I found, on the contrary, that they were more interested in my getting a good impression of them and the school."

These new teachers are fully aware that teaching is demanding work. They are gratified that they are equal to the job, though one half-humorously warns, "You can't stay up half the night like you can in college and expect to do a good job the next day."

Taken altogether, this group of student teachers finds teaching to be much easier, more exciting, and more interesting than they had expected.

These teachers who find teaching easier than they had expected are quite realistic in their appraisal of it. They expected certain problems. When they began to teach, they either discovered that the problems were not as great as they had anticipated or that their ability to handle them was more than adequate. They were not taken unawares by what they found in the classroom.

3. Do the experiences of this group suggest anything to you about good preparation for teaching?

Many New Teachers Are Jolted By The Size Of The Job

The sixty student teachers who find teaching more difficult than they anticipated are somewhat less realistic in their attitude toward it. Most of them eventually find the same satisfaction in teaching. The initial surprises, however, are greater and more adjustments are necessary. Once the adjustments are made these practice teachers are able to report rich rewards from teaching.

There are three main reasons why these new teachers feel teaching is much more difficult than they anticipated. First, some of them feel that they over-idealized teaching and were not ready to deal with its realities. Second, most of them are surprised at the hard work involved in teaching and find it much more physically demanding than they expected. Third, they are amazed at the know-how required to work successfully with students.

(1) A beginning teacher may over-idealize teaching. A high school practice teacher says, "The big change I had to make was from the idealistic to the realistic. You must adapt your ideas to actual conditions—materials, equipment, students. It's a big leap from campus theory to classroom practice."

A fourth grade practice teacher complains that her college work had not prepared her for the realities of classroom teaching:

> I am afraid too often during my stay on campus I was presented with an ideal picture of teaching. We were led to think that everything runs like clockwork if we are careful enough to plan correctly and keep children occupied. This is not true. The new teacher stepping out of the world of ideal theory and into the real situation is completely unprepared for making a class function as it should. Many of the children are not "ideal"; they are "problems." There is still a need for making children sit in the corner and do their work.

(2) A beginning teacher may underestimate the work. The second reason these student teachers find teaching more difficult than expected is the hard work involved. Those who think that teaching is easy soon discover that there is lots of work for the teacher both in and out of school.

Why is teaching hard work? The student teachers furnish us with a long catalogue of items: lesson preparation, making plans, collecting materials, marking papers, taking role, keeping records, supervising after-school activities, club meetings, staff meetings, committee meetings, talking with parents, social affairs, and just plain teaching.

This student teacher speaks for many others when he sums up his own experiences this way:

> College instructors will tell you that teaching is a 24-hour job. Believe them. You will discover it for yourself. You'll fall asleep nights wondering how to motivate Danny, how to discipline Fred, how to get Bonnie to talk, and how to keep Billy quiet. You'll be sure it was a teacher who first said, "Thank God it's Friday!" Then you'll spend the week-ends correcting papers, thumbing through magazines and the Sunday paper for pertinent articles. You'll monitor television shows and plan next week's lessons. Then on Sunday you'll remember that you forgot to collect the milk money on Friday. Oh yes, and how am I going to keep Paul in his seat?

(3) Working with students requires know-how. Let us turn now to the third reason these new teachers find teaching difficult. They discover that working with students differs in a number of ways from what they had expected. First, they discover that students are real human beings. They are not the same as the textbook children they had been learning about. Second, they discover that students are individuals and are all different from one another. Teaching has constantly to be adapted to their individual interests and levels of comprehension. Third, they are surprised at how apathetic some students can be toward learning. They discover that motivation can be a big problem for the teacher.

Students are real people. Let us look at the responses of the first group who discover that students are real human beings and not the clinical specimens discussed in class.

A sixth grade student teacher comments:

> Children were represented in my teacher education courses as subjects of clinically worded case studies. You taught these children by using proper methods. In my classroom, as I began to teach, the children suddenly became real, living, needing people. The problems were to motivate, get-through, challenge, satisfy and help. These real children, in spite of everything I had learned in educational psychology, are continually frustrating, challenging, interesting and seemingly imponderable.

A third grade student teacher reports: "I tried not to have many preconceived ideas that might hinder me when I started teaching. I discovered quickly, however, that students are human beings and not clinical specimens that we discussed in our classes."

A high school teacher says: "The actual teaching experience has been quite a revelation. I had preformed ideas as to what was involved. I feel now that the college student cannot possibly realize what high school pupils are like if he depends on textbook information alone. The biggest difference I found was that I am working with real human beings."

4. Some student teachers feel that their college courses give them only an "idealized" picture of "clinical" and "textbook" children. Then they discover that "real" children are not "ideal" at all; they are "problems." Yet, it is probably accurate to say that most college courses and textbooks dealing with child psychology, growth, and learning are quite realistic, even brutal at times, though sympathetic, in presenting the child. Yet, the point is missed by some students, and they are jolted by their first teaching experience. Are you able to account for this? How can a prospective teacher avoid this miscalculation about the nature of real children?

With these real human beings teachers must work very closely. This close relationship comes as a surprise to some beginning teachers. "The teacher develops a closer relationship with the student than I ever realized," said one surprised student teacher. "One has to deal with the student as a person much more than I had thought. Subject matter is important, but the student is even more important. The problems which he brings with him from home profoundly affect his ability to do work."

Students are individually different. Not only are students real people with whom the teacher works closely, but also they are all individuals. To these differences a teacher must constantly adapt his teaching. One elementary school teacher uses his class to illustrate the great variety of individual differences:

My biggest, toughest problem arises from the fact that children are individuals, that each child behaves in his own way, that each child learns at his own rate, likes different things, and has special needs.

No text book can possibly drive this point home as well as my class of children:

Ken—unable to do almost anything except draw.
Kay—able to do everything except draw.
Eugene—four feet two inches tall, thirteen years old.
Ted—five feet nine inches tall, ten years old.
Bonnie—never (I mean *never*) talks.
Larry—never stops talking.

Fred—never sits still.
Cliff—always too tired to move.
Joanne—writes beautifully.
Jerry—can't print.
Ken—unable to read "Look, Jane, Look."
Mary—reads and understands, "When in the course of human events . . ."
Bob—tremendous talent in all areas.
Larry—almost retarded.
Dick—horrible monotone.
Cheryl—sings beautifully.
Gale—mother gave him away when he was born.
Fred—father in prison for armed robbery.
Jerry—six brothers, four sisters.
Gloria—an only child.
Mary Jo—lots of ability, little desire.
Paula—lots of desire, little ability.

This could go on forever . . .

These individual differences must be reckoned within teaching. Student teachers soon discover that they cannot be ignored. "I thought as a teacher I would plan my lessons and go into the classroom and teach this planned information. But it doesn't work this way," reports a practice teacher in science. Another says, "I believed that I would prepare my lessons and they would go smoothly. I soon found out differently. Things do not go as you plan. Instead, children have their own desires, and the teacher must hold their interest and make them a part of everything he does." This means that the plan for the day may not be followed by the entire class. Some students are very slow, others just average, and a few very fast. You have to have extra ideas and activities to suit all groups.

Not only do children's interests and abilities differ from one another, but their interests also change from day to day. The teacher must adjust to their changing moods. A student teacher in English gives us this example:

The children came to my class after a physical education class. They were really excited after the gym class. It usually takes five to ten minutes to quiet them down, but they were not in a mood for any concentrated study of subjects and verbs. I finally ended up reading them a story. Was the period wasted? Not necessarily. Sometimes the mood of the class is such that nothing else will interest them, and a good story can sometimes give something more valuable than subjects and verbs.

Some students are apathetic toward learning. New teachers discover that some students are very indifferent, do not have a desire to learn, and just fill a seat. "I had previously thought," reports a high school student teacher, "that if I were enthusiastic about my subject, the students would be also. It isn't necessarily true. Such indifference makes it a real job to stir up and maintain interest. It's one of the teacher's most difficult challenges."

> 5. This group was jolted by the size of a teacher's job. Do you think that people generally may underestimate the size of the teacher's task? If so, can you explain why?

How is teaching different from what these practice teachers thought it might be? For a few, 15 per cent, it doesn't differ at all. It is exactly what they expect. For another 25 per cent teaching is a pleasant surprise. They feel more equal to the task than they thought they would. Before entering the classroom they had projected themselves quite accurately into it, and were pleased with their estimate of the situation. Sixty per cent of the student teachers find that teaching holds some shocks. A few discover that their attitudes are too idealistic. Many are surprised by the hard work demanded by teaching. Most of them are surprised at the knowledge and skill required to work successfully with students, for students must be understood as individual human beings. The individual differences among students comes as a challenge, requiring on-the-spot adjustments in well-laid plans. Teaching, they discover, is more than talking. It requires motivating and interesting all kinds of students, including those who are apathetic toward learning.

> 6. This question will help you make a self-appraisal. If you were to project yourself ahead to student teaching, into which of these three groups do you think you would fall? Into which one would you *like* to fall? Does this suggest anything to you in terms of your own personal preparation for teaching?

Rewards are important in any profession. These student teachers found their greatest rewards in working with their students and in seeing them grow and mature.

Expectations are important. Wholesome expectations can lead one to prepare well and improve his chances for success in teaching.

In Chapter 2 the student teachers answer another significant question: What are the toughest problems in teaching?

Good Follow-up Reading and Viewing

BOOKS

Chandler, J. B., *Education and the Teacher,* chap. 16, "Satisfaction in Teaching." New York: Dodd, Mead & Co., 1961. A fine statement of the professional and personal satisfactions in teaching.

Gross, Cordelia B., *et al., I Am A Teacher.* Pleasantville, N.Y.: Reader's Digest Services, Inc., 1957. Six excellent articles about teachers.

Lloyd-Jones, Esther, and Mary V. Holman, "Why People Become Teachers," in *The Teacher's Role in American Society,* ed. Lindley J. Stiles, pp. 235-46. New York: Harper & Brothers, 1957. A review of the research literature which deals with the question of why people choose to teach.

McCloskey, Gordon, *et al., Introduction to Teaching in America,* chap. 1, "So You Want To Teach?" New York: Harcourt, Brace & World, Inc., 1954. A lively discussion of the importance of teaching in America, opportunities and obligations of teachers, and what teaching involves.

Phelps, William Lyon, *The Excitement of Teaching,* pp. 60-71. New York: Liveright Publishing Corp., 1931. A distinguished teacher relates the personal problems and the professional rewards of teachers. Teaching is one of the most mentally and spiritually rewarding professions in the whole world. At the same time it is one that is "almost forgotten by the public."

Sharp, D. Louise, ed., *Why Teach?* New York: Henry Holt & Co., Inc., 1957. This excellent collection of essays about teachers and teaching was written by distinguished Americans. Excellent reading for all who are considering teaching as a profession.

Weber, Julia, *My Country School Diary.* New York: Harper & Brothers, 1946. This engaging diary shows the teacher and children planning, working, and living together. As a wise counselor and guide, the teacher works with the students in deciding what should be done and how it should be done.

PERIODICALS

Flaum, Laurence S., "A Credo For Teachers," *The Journal of Teacher Education,* Vol. 10, No. 4, December, 1959, pp. 422-28. A personal and moving statement of why a teacher teaches. "We teach because we believe each child is a world in the making."

Hines, Vynce A., "Why Do Teachers Keep Teaching?" *National Elementary Principal,* Vol. 37, February, 1958, pp. 37-40. The author reports a series of interesting interviews with teachers in a Florida school.

McLaughlin, W. J., "Wear the Mantle Proudly," *NEA Journal,* Vol. 48, April, 1959, pp. 35-38. The true story of a high school teacher's busy and rewarding life, inside and outside of school.

Merriken, Ruth, "Needed, Wanted, and Welcome," and (Anonymous) "I Don't Know How I'll Stick It Out Till June," *NEA Journal,* Vol. 47, May, 1958, pp. 297-99. Two student teachers have radically different experiences, one happy, one sad.

Star, Jack, "Comeback of the Male Teacher," *Look,* February 17, 1959, pp.

84-89. An interesting picture story about the increasing number of men entering education. Explains the reasons and the results.

Stier, Lealand D., "Orientations of Prospective Teachers," *The Educational Forum,* Vol. 25, January, 1961, pp. 167-73. Seven hundred and eighty-two prospective teachers write on these topics: "Why I Selected Teaching as a Profession," and "My Philosophy of Life." The article is a revealing analysis of the statements, showing interesting differences between elementary and secondary prospective teachers.

FILMS [1]

Adventure in Teaching

Here are portraits of prospective teachers in metropolitan classrooms. A treatment of their interests, needs, and problems. (Harmon Foundation, color or black and white, 25 minutes.)

And Gladly Teach

The deep satisfactions of teaching—its responsibilities and opportunities. (National Education Association, Agra Films, Inc., color, 28 minutes.)

Introduction to Student Teaching

The activities of three seniors during the early weeks of their student teaching. Demonstration of four fundamentals: getting acquainted with the school; becoming accustomed to handling routine classroom matters; becoming familiar with a wide variety of instructional materials; and becoming acquainted with the pupils. (University of Indiana, black and white, 19 minutes.)

What Greater Gift?

A high school girl is fascinated by her work with children at a play center and decides that she would like to teach. (National Education Association, color or black and white, 28 minutes.)

---

[1] The films listed at the end of each chapter in this book are 16-mm sound films. The director of the film library or audio-visual department in your college or university can tell you where these films may be rented or purchased.

CHAPTER 2

THE TOUGH CHALLENGE OF TEACHING

You don't know how much it hurts to be talking about the Bill of Rights and have some little kid stand up and say, "What do we want this jazz for?"

A STUDENT TEACHER

Teaching, we discovered in chapter one, has its rewards and surprises for those who enter it. It also has its problems. Most professions do. Anyone thinking of teaching should consider the challenges which lie ahead. Sometimes these challenges are especially difficult for the beginner to handle.

WHAT ARE THE TOUGHEST PROBLEMS IN TEACHING?

On this question there is considerable agreement. The new teachers name three problems: (1) handling discipline problems, (2) motivating students, and (3) gaining professional competence. Let us examine them.

Discipline Problems

No single problem is mentioned more frequently by these student teachers. No other problem made greater demand upon their growing skill; yet, they demonstrated their ability to learn fast, and most of them emerged from student teaching feeling confident to handle most problems in classroom control.

The problem is real. The new teachers agree that most students are easy to deal with. There are those few, however, who have the power to cause endless conflicts and frustrations in the classroom. These few cause more than their share of troubles and can be purposely vicious at times.

21

Some beginning teachers accept the reality of this situation only after some hard experiences. One teacher says, "I had been told that establishing discipline in the room is the toughest problem. But the warning held little meaning for me until I made mistakes and suffered the consequences."

Discipline problems can be especially acute for the beginning teacher. The beginner is unusually sensitive to student feelings. This attitude is good, but because the beginner wants very much for students to like him, he is reluctant to give guidance. One fourth grade teacher remarked, "I wanted so badly for the children to like me that at first I wasn't firm enough. The turmoil in the room was unbearable." A high school teacher said, "One of the biggest pitfalls for the beginning teacher concerns his desire to be liked by students. Too much chumminess destroys authority and respect for the teacher. It is difficult to create a healthy atmosphere once it has been destroyed."

Further, students like to test a new teacher to see how far they can go. Observe these representative opinions of the matter:

> The big problem I had to face was this idea of the students: "What will he let me get away with?"

> The students will always know the ropes better than the new teacher and will usually try to get away with things that they would not try otherwise.

> The children realize that the new teacher is a greenhorn, and even though she is accepted as a person, she isn't completely accepted as a disciplinarian.

Discipline problems are real and the new teacher must prepare to meet them.

Let's turn now to some actual discipline problems which the student teachers confronted. This one is reported by an art teacher:

> On the senior level you just have to maintain a certain amount of order. An art class is quite a free type of class, but if you have no order, no discipline, students won't get a thing done. And you've got to be prepared for anything that might happen. Take the example of something that happened to me last week. This was a real problem as far as I was concerned. A group of senior boys had taken a large sheet of paper and had drawn some pornographic pictures on it. I said to myself, "What do I do in this case?" So I more or less handled them the way I would like to have been handled had I been in their place. I just went over to them and said,

"I'm glad you're so socially minded. Now how about putting it in the wastebasket and let's not have any more." Without hesitating, they did it. I'm getting along fine with the fellows now and have no trouble with them. Had I made an issue out of the incident, it would have been that much more hilarious to them and they would have made a spectacle out of it.

A junior high school teacher reports the following incident:

One group of students planned a little surprise for me one day. They all turned up in class wearing dark glasses. It was obviously prearranged. I had to do some fast thinking. I decided to be both casual and firm. I commented first upon the unusually large number of the members traveling incognito. This they seemed to enjoy. Then I asked them to take the glasses off, and threatened them with E's should it happen again. It seemed to work.

1. This student teacher uses a threat in order to secure better classroom behavior. And in this instance it seemed to work. Still, many authorities question this approach to behavior problems. The selected reading references and the films listed at the end of this chapter open a whole range of new ideas about human behavior and motivation. Study two or three of them carefully. Then put yourself in the position of the student teacher facing a room full of dark glasses. Can you suggest a better way to handle the problem?

A teacher whose student refused to obey had this story to tell:

Once I told a student to take his seat. (He was wandering around the room while everyone was doing an exercise.) He walked up to me and said, "I don't feel like taking my seat." "What do I do now?" I thought to myself. I was about ready to tell him to leave the room when I was saved by one of the boys in the back of the room. "Take your seat, Frank, and behave yourself," he said. Frank took his seat.

Some discipline problems cause a teacher to ask searching questions about a student's welfare:

If a student gets expelled from school, what happens to him after this? Have you really helped him? Or have you dodged the issue by getting rid of him? On the other hand, if you permit the student to remain in the classroom, you are letting one person spoil things for everyone else.

This experience will illustrate what I mean. I asked a student to leave the classroom and stand in the hall. He refused to go. I did not attempt to make a big thing of it or throw him out bodily. Later I asked the supervising teacher to help me talk with the boy. As it turned out he felt I was picking on him. After that I went out of my way to see that he did not retain this feeling. However, this past week another incident came up. This time he left the classroom when I told him. However, he refused to come in after class, even for a minute. I then sent him to the office, with the supervising teacher's consent, and he was expelled from school for an indefinite period of time. He had, I discovered, been expelled from school once before. Basically he's not a bad fellow, but he's extremely defiant and that is his downfall. But I feel badly. Had we really helped him? I don't think so.

2. Do you agree with the way the student teacher handled this case? Would you have handled it differently? If so, what would you have done?

What factors influence classroom behavior? The beginning teachers were quick to observe that behavior problems are related to other matters. They do not exist by themselves. Some factors will lessen such problems; other factors will increase them. They specifically mentioned three strong influences upon classroom behavior: (1) the teacher, (2) the physical surroundings, and (3) the home and community.

The teacher is the key influence in setting the classroom tone. He must be fair and forthright with his pupils, making sure not to show favoritism. Yet, he must treat individuals differently. A beginning teacher comments:

> One boy cried if I raised my voice at him. One boy had to be firmly told what to do. It is difficult to discipline the class as a whole, knowing these extremes exist.
>
> The teacher can set the limits and give the students the security of knowing how far they can go and how free they can be. Most of all, the teacher must show genuine concern for students, go out of his way to be helpful, and plan a class full of challenging activities. Good teaching is still one of the best ways to produce good classroom behavior.

Physical surroundings have much to do with the way students behave. A large, airy, bright classroom seems to encourage good behavior. On the other hand, a cramped and unattractive classroom can foster bad behavior. A fourth grade teacher remarks:

> I once had forty-five fourth graders in one classroom built for twenty-five. We were cramped for room and had little teaching

space. The children were so jammed together that behavior became a real problem. In the class there were many individual differences. Yet, the lack of space made it practically impossible to work with the children in groups.

Teachers see in students the influence of the home and community. Students bring with them to school the values and attitudes which they have learned through primary contacts with parents, close friends, and neighborhood groups. The child does not come to school as a "clean page but rather as a continued story." Important events have gone before. Others are to come. Some children have been taught regard for the teacher and school and the importance of education. These students may become troublesome at times but for the most part they will behave themselves.

On the other hand, some students come from homes which are unconcerned about education. They don't share the values of the school and find nothing in it of interest to them. These students may revolt against what the school is trying to do. A high school student teacher who had experience with such students says:

> Most of these students are from families which don't care for education. Only two of the mothers of children in this class graduated from high school. The majority of the parents went only through the sixth or eighth grade. Several have no schooling at all; so they don't place much value on education. This attitude has been communicated to the children. Their parents didn't go to school. Why should they? They get their unfavorable attitude toward education honestly.

The teacher, the physical surroundings, and the home and community are all important influences in the behavior of students.

3. Can you recall a discipline case from your high school or elementary school days? Do you think any of these three factors may have been a contributing cause? If so, which ones?

What can the teacher do to stimulate good behavior? Out of their personal experience, the beginning teachers developed some guide lines:

(1) Accept the fact that discipline can be a problem and prepare to meet it. Those beginning teachers who viewed discipline problems realistically were better prepared to handle them. They had studied and asked questions about discipline. They fully recognized that dealing with

discipline problems can be a hard job and require a great deal of understanding and thought. Take all the courses you can get which deal with child and adolescent behavior.

(2) Get to know children as individuals and as real human beings. Good teaching begins in an understanding of children. Look for situations which will permit you to work with children and youth. "You must consider each child as an individual and discover the proper way to handle him," counsels a high school student teacher.

(3) Establish a personal relationship with each student. It is important to have a good relationship with the group. Equally important is the teacher's individual relationship with each student. The importance of a good personal relationship is illustrated by this high school teacher:

> I had a boy who continually disrupted the class and caused trouble. I discovered that it was best to get him away from his followers occasionally and establish a personal understanding. We talked several times alone, and each time I could see our personal relationship improving. Once we reached a real understanding the behavior problem disappeared.

(4) Encourage the class to set its own standards of behavior. Group sanctions are important in maintaining good classroom behavior. A child is as sensitive as the teacher to the feelings of his fellow students, frequently more so. A number of new teachers learned to use this group pressure to foster good behavior. A fifth grade teacher relates this experience:

> I found it best to talk about misbehavior with the class before problems actually arose. They agreed how we should act and what should be done "just in case." This way the decision was the children's and not mine. Since they made the decision on the type of punishment, there were no arguments about whether or not the punishment was fair. Of course I had to see that the agreements were carried out, but the class took the initiative in keeping good conduct.

(5) Take a positive approach to conduct. A third grade teacher reported: "My first inclination was to say, 'Don't do that!' Later I discovered that it was better to say, 'Paul, let's save that for recess. It would be more appropriate then, don't you think?' "

(6) Recognize that discipline problems are complex and some may seem impossible to solve. Beginning teachers may get discouraged when they confront a discipline problem for which there seems to be no solu-

tion. Human behavior is seldom simple or easily diagnosed. If we begin with an awareness of the complexity of child and adolescent behavior, we can have a healthy respect for discipline problems without being overwhelmed by them. A certain amount of frustration in the face of difficult situations is probably a normal, even wholesome, reaction. This student teacher spoke the feelings of many others when he said:

> It seems as if there are students who always want to start a fight, throw chalk, and bother other students. I have one student who does all of these things because he knows it disturbs me. As far as the solution is concerned, I haven't found one. Generally I do the first thing that comes to mind. One thing I've learned—yelling doesn't help. If there's a real solution I haven't found it.

While some discipline problems seem beyond solution, beginning teachers learn to handle most of them. Discipline problems are real, and those who accept them as real and prepare to handle them usually discover they have the ability to do so. It is helpful to understand the importance of the teacher, the physical surroundings, and the home and community in children's behavior. Beyond understanding, the teacher must develop specific skills and techniques in establishing wholesome classroom behavior.

4. Suppose, before reading these experiences, you had made a list entitled: "The Five Toughest Problems of Beginning Teachers." Would you have placed discipline on the list? Where? What do the experiences of these student teachers suggest to a person who is planning to teach?

Motivation Problems

Next to discipline, motivation is reported by these new teachers to be the toughest problem. The two are closely related. Students who are motivated to learn are not apt to be discipline problems. They are attentive, interested, and challenged by the tasks at hand. When attention turns into inattention and interest into boredom, behavior problems begin.

Motivation is a requisite for learning. The teacher's first task is to motivate students to do good work, find interest and enjoyment in their activities, and take pride in their accomplishments. Students thus motivated will learn.

Motivating students is not always an easy task. Listen to the testimony of these high school teachers: (1) "How can I get a student who is plainly not interested to sit up and take notice?" (2) "My toughest problem is to motivate the unmotivated." (3) "What do you do when your students just want to talk among themselves or gaze out the window?" (4) "My students are neither interested nor concerned with anything but teen-age problems." (5) "Convincing some students that the subject matter and school in general are worthwhile is tough." (6) "Certain students refuse to accept the responsibility of studying."

The problem is not confined to high school. Elementary teachers face it too: (1) "Children are usually willing to learn, but they still go through periods of being bored. When they are, watch out." (2) "Most of my children want to learn, but that doesn't mean that they will. The atmosphere for learning must be well established. Motivation is very important." (3) "First graders' attention spans are very short. If you keep them interested, everything is fine. The minute you lose their interest, problems begin."

Clearly, learning depends upon motivation. A student teacher in art reports:

> I found a wall of apathy and indifference between myself and certain of my students. One of the boys did a very good sculpture of wrestlers. He couldn't think of what would be the best way to finish it, so he just painted it all red (a most unfortunate choice). He had no interest in finishing the job right. He just said he wanted it that way.

A home economics beginner relates:

> We were studying fabrics, weaves, and coloring methods of many materials. I just couldn't interest the students in these matters. I tried various ways and techniques and finally came to the conclusion that I was expecting too much of them. The need just wasn't there. I still feel that I've got to do something to demonstrate to the girls the need for studying and learning about fabrics.

A social studies teacher discovers:

> My biggest problem is keeping the attention of a bored class. I had this problem especially in my last hour class, where the students were tired of sitting at the end of a long day. Added to this was the rather difficult composition of the class, a strange mixture of some of the fastest students in the Junior class, as well as a large percentage of the very slow ones. How do you hold the interest of the better students without losing the poorer ones?

A sixth grade teacher reports this experience with one of her girls:

> P. L. is interested only in horses. She says she is going to live on a horse ranch (an idea she obtained from a cousin) so why study? In talking with her parents I find that this attitude developed only recently. Her grades fell about one mark in every subject since. She is the oldest of several children. In dealing with her, threats and temporary restrictions have helped some, but so far I feel I have gained very little. Both her parents and I hope that the new interests accompanying junior high school will bring her out of it.

A ninth grade English teacher reports:

> My class is near the bottom in grouping. There is no motivation in the group. It consists of students who just can't wait until they are 16 and can quit school. Teachers who expect to teach in a graded system must be willing to face this problem in the lower sections. These students try every excuse in the book to get out of class. The prospective teacher must make special preparation for these low sections, find something that will keep their interest, and motivate them to learn. One thing I have found rather successful with this group has been our unit on short stories. The students like these stories and you can really keep yourself on top as teacher if you read these stories aloud to them.

5. Perhaps you can remember cases like these from your own school experience. Take a real-life case. Put *yourself* in the position of the student—for example, the boy with the sculpture of wrestlers, a girl studying fabrics and colors, a social studies student tired and restless at the end of a long day, a sixth grader who loves horses, or a sixteen year old English student who wants to quit school. From the *student's* point of view, what should the teacher do to meet your need for motivation? Again, you'll find the references at the end of the chapter helpful in seeking an answer.

Effective motivation is geared to individual needs. We have spoken of the great variety of individual differences which the new teachers find among the students in their classrooms. These students have different abilities, interests, and backgrounds. What will motivate one of these children may not motivate another. Indeed, what will motivate one may repel another. Ideally, each child should be taught separately. That, of course, is impossible, yet effective motivation depends upon individualized instruction. For example, some students work so fast that it is hard to keep them busy. Others work at a very slow rate of speed. The interest span of students differs so widely that a teacher must often have two, three, or even four activities going on in the room at the same time.

The teacher has resources for motivating students. Difficult though it is, motivating students can be the teacher's most rewarding task. New vistas open to the student who discovers new interest and excitement in his work. Learning advances as our interest in it enlarges.

For this task the teacher has available resources. The first is his sympathetic appreciation of the student and his problems. The second is a rich program of instruction.

The teacher is a counselor. These new teachers discovered early in their experience that they were more than teachers of arithmetic, reading, history, or any other subject. They were counselors who had to be deeply concerned about the students who were to learn arithmetic, reading, and history. Unless the students want to learn, and can, teaching is futile business. They discovered that ten and eleven year olds can have emotional problems as great as those of the teacher. Some students have homes that are broken; others have parents who nag them and brothers and sisters who beat them. They have problems with their friends at school, wondering whether or not they are accepted. One student teacher says:

> You've got to help them take care of these problems as you are teaching or you don't get through to them at all. They're not thinking about how many times four will go into twenty-four. You can't come right out and tell them what their problems are, because often they don't want you to know. You must realize from a psychological point of view how you can help them.

This description of ten and eleven year olds could be extended to almost all public school age groups: "You've got to help them take care of these problems, or you don't get through to them at all." The teacher is, indeed, a counselor. He finds that understanding students and their problems is a prerequisite to teaching them.

An elementary teacher relates:

> One student was told at home not to "do" his best, but to "be" the best. He hasn't the ability, but his mother won't let him rest. If we judged his work like that of everyone else, it would be very poor. We realize that he is striving so very hard to be perfect, that he isn't even doing as well as he could were he not under pressure. This is the kind of thing you can learn if you take a special interest in understanding students.

Another elementary teacher says:

> I have a little girl in class who is pretty and intelligent, but she
> is not well liked. I thought she was quite cute the first day or two,
> but then I began to realize that she was a nuisance. She broke up
> other girls' games and lorded her intelligence over everybody else.
> I thought there must be some explanation, either in her home or
> in herself. The next day we were square dancing and I happened to
> look at her feet while she was dancing. She had a lift about two
> inches high on her shoe. I learned later that she had had polio and
> that at first the lift was six inches high. I am sure that even though
> she may not think about this, she often has the feeling that she is
> physically inferior and must therefore flaunt her mental superiority.
> Understanding this, I don't feel quite so irritated when she is
> showing off her intelligence in class. Perhaps I can help her.

We may think the teacher's counseling is confined to students who
come from underpriviledged homes or who have special physical or
emotional limitations. Such is not the case, as this high school teacher
illustrates:

> I'm in a school where most of the children are privileged. They
> are children of college professors, prominent lawyers, other profes-
> sional people, and successful business men. Their homes have
> libraries and all kinds of opportunities. These students have been
> places; they've read many books; and they can talk about a lot of
> things. To teach these children you've got to know a great deal
> about them. They have their problems too. You don't want to talk
> down to them, nor do you want to talk over their heads. You've
> really got to go out and find out about them.

The good teacher is a counselor, understanding of students and their
problems. Such understanding is a resource for motivating students.

Motivation is stimulated by a program of rich instruction. In addition
to understanding students, the practice teachers find another item to be
important in motivating students—good classroom instruction. They
discovered that talking was not enough. They had to have some interesting things for their students to do. Here are two typical comments:

> I found that you cannot keep the students motivated by lectur-
> ing. You've got to have a well-prepared lesson plan with interesting
> activities. I involve the students a lot, and they just about operate
> the class. I simply add comments where they seem appropriate.

To plan 50 or 55 minutes of reasonably interesting learning activities requires more work than what one might ordinarily think. The students must be occupied with tasks during this time that will be both interesting and profitable.

It must be obvious from their comments that the student teachers came to have a realistic appreciation of the problem of motivation. They lived with it and struggled to master it. They drew some conclusions about motivating students. Since students differ widely in their abilities, interests, and backgrounds, the teacher must do everything he can to understand students. He must know all he can about them and counsel them. Beyond this he must prepare his classroom work thoroughly, having projects, activities, and aids to motivate and reinforce the learning.

Problems Dealing With Professional Competence

Here the practice teachers mention a galaxy of matters. We shall deal with five. First, some beginners, being young themselves, find it difficult to assume a teacher's role. Second, many lack self confidence. Third, some new teachers discover that they didn't know their subject matter well enough to teach it and that their day-to-day lesson preparation is inadequate. Fourth, they must learn to talk to students. Fifth, they find some of the detail work of teaching to be tiresome.

Teacher and student roles differ. The following high school teacher spoke for a number of others who were assuming a teacher's role for the first time:

The big job is to change from a student to a teacher. I had to draw a line between myself and my students. It wasn't easy to separate myself from the students. I am 21, just 4 years out of high school, and some of my students are 18 and 19. This is my problem, an individual one perhaps, but it has been a problem to me.

Another new teacher pondered:

I'm not sure how to strike the right relationship with students. It's hard for me to know when I am becoming so friendly that the students no longer regard me as teacher. It's equally difficult to know when I'm remaining so aloof that they don't think I'm human. I have attempted to solve this problem by freely discussing such things as baseball and TV shows before class, and then attempting to remain as businesslike as possible during class. This doesn't mean that I don't laugh if something amusing happens during class.

Self confidence grows with experience. The feelings of insecurity which go with a new position were experienced by some of the new teachers. An elementary teacher expressed the problem this way:

> In the beginning you enter the classroom knowing really very little about these boys and girls. You do not know what actually will or will not go over successfully in your teaching methods. You have to go slowly the first few weeks and feel your way! It helps them if they know a little bit about you, just as it gives you confidence to learn about them. Slowly you gain their confidence and your own.

A high school teacher concurred:

> One of the worst problems is to gain self confidence. I worked hard on my lesson plans, and I was well prepared. But when I stood before my first class to teach I was very self-conscious. I would stress, however, that one should not get discouraged. Each time that you stand before the class, you find that it comes much easier.

Mastery of subject matter and solid preparation are vital. To teach subject matter, it must first be fully mastered. Know the subject matter well. Further, subject matter needs to be "known" in a different way. It must be simplified, broken down, and thoroughly understood. One beginner noted that he had to know the subject matter well enough so that he could change plans at a moment's notice and concentrate on helping students without worrying about the subject matter or himself. In a similar view a high school mathematics teacher commented that the actual use of subject matter in a classroom is far different from knowing it well enough to pass an examination on it in college. He remarked that passing a college examination is easy by comparison.

Subject matter has to be translated into daily classroom programs. This can be a sizeable task. An arithmetic teacher said:

> Being able to organize material and present it to pupils is one of my toughest problems. For example, an arithmetic lesson failed because I had not collected all my materials. I learned from this that I had to do a lot of planning and organizing before class. I discovered that unless my lesson is well planned and organized the students will pull away from me. They seem to sense it when I haven't fully mastered the lesson.

Then there are the details of planning. The student teachers asked questions such as these: (1) How much time should I allow for this? How much for that? (2) How much work can they do? (3) How small must a group be to function well? (4) How do you plan far enough ahead and make decisions fast enough? (5) How much work should I plan for a certain period?

Effective communication is essential. In addition to day-to-day planning the new teachers spoke of the problem of pitching their teaching to a level of the students, of being able to explain problems or concepts in a simple manner. The teacher's language must be made up of small words, words that the students are acquainted with and recognize.

One teacher related this experience: "I was telling a student that he shouldn't treat teachers as *peers.* He gave me a look that had written all over it, "Why, I don't treat them like *piers.*" Another reported: "I had a tendency to use college terms in explaining some of the principles of biology. I had to find simple terms. Then, too, I had to repeat materials in many different ways before the students understood. On tests I must use words which are understood by the whole class or the questions are of no value." An elementary teacher agreed: "It's hard for me to remember that they are children. Things must be emphasized over and over again; once is never enough."

The teacher is a record keeper. Some new teachers found the clerical details of teaching to be difficult. An elementary teacher observed that most prospective teachers don't realize the administrative details involved, particularly in elementary schools. Another warned that keeping up with the paper work is a full-time job. A high school teacher reflected upon her own training and commented that she heard only plaudits for the teaching profession, and that the instances of petty bookkeeping and dull routine were only rarely mentioned.

A new teacher has sizeable professional problems. To move from a student's to a teacher's role is not always easy. The teaching situation is new and self confidence must be built up. Subject matter must not only be thoroughly mastered; it must be translated into lively classroom teaching. Daily lessons must be carefully planned. Communication with students is important. One must learn to pitch what he says to their level of understanding. Finally, dealing with students is not the teacher's only task. Records must be kept, reports prepared, and papers graded. These professional tasks add up to a busy position, full of demands and responsibilities.

6. You now know the problems which these new teachers found to be tough. How do they strike you? Are they about what you expected? Or do they present a side of teaching which you had not thought about before? Now prepare a short report on what the experiences of these student teachers mean to you personally.

Discipline, motivation, professional problems—these the new teachers found to be their toughest. How they react to these tough problems and what they suggest for others who are considering teaching we shall discover in the next chapter.

Good Follow-up Reading and Viewing

BOOKS

Association for Supervision and Curriculum Development, *Growing Up In An Anxious Age*. Washington, D.C.: National Education Association, 1952. This book deals with the problems and anxieties of children and youth, and relates how teachers can help them grow up in an anxious age.

Eggleston, Edward, *The Hoosier School-master,* chap. 1. New York: Grosset & Dunlap, Inc., 1892. This literary classic continues to be a worthy source of pleasure and study. Chapter one is a case study in the psychology of handling a youthful prank.

Holman, Mary, *How It Feels To Be A Teacher*. New York: Bureau of Publications, Teachers College, Columbia University, 1950. An excellent statement of the satisfactions and concerns of teachers.

Jenkins, Gladys E., Helen Shacter, and W. W. Bauer, *These Are Your Children*. Chicago: Scott, Foresman & Company, 1949. An excellent discussion of the factors determining children's behavior. Valuable suggestions on how teachers and parents can work with and enjoy children.

Kane, Harnett T., *Miracle in the Mountains*. New York: Doubleday & Company, Inc., 1956. A story of the life of Martha Berry and of her long record of usefulness in the schools which bear her name.

Sheviakov, George V., and Fritz Redl, *Discipline*. Washington, D.C.: National Education Association, 1956. This sixty-four page pamphlet concentrates on the teacher's role in educating for self-discipline. Good individual behavior is fostered by the teacher's group leadership.

Snygg, Donald, and Arthur W. Combs, *Individual Behavior,* chap. 11, "The Task of the Teacher." New York: Harper & Brothers, 1949. This entire book is valuable for its promising approaches to human behavior. Chapter eleven provides fruitful information for handling behavioral problems similar to those confronted by the student teacher.

Wittenburg, R. M., *So You Want To Help People*. New York: Association Press, 1947. An interesting discussion of the psychological factors involved in working with groups of adolescents.

PERIODICALS

Anderson, Paul S., "Discipline in The Classroom Today," *Phi Delta Kappan,* Vol. 41, pp. 114-115. The writer offers a "short course" in classroom control and points out that "the difference between what the school desires some children to do and what these children seek to do seems to expand as we go through the school years."

Berlin, I. N., M.D., "Teacher's Self-Expectations: How Realistic Are They?"

The School Review, Vol. 46, Summer, 1958, pp. 135-43. Berlin states that a young teacher may have unrealistic expectations which produce self-defeating attitudes toward children and their parents. Excellent suggestions to help the new teacher understand the role he plays in the child's growth and development.

"Discipline," *NEA Journal,* Vol. 47, September, 1958, pp. 367-81. A series of valuable articles on different aspects of discipline, including one entitled "Tips for the New Teacher."

Dodge, Ruth Emelie, "Classroom Control in the High School," *NEA Journal,* Vol. 47, March, 1958, pp. 180-81. An experienced English teacher writes of her first days in the classroom and of her feeling of unpreparedness to cope with problems of classroom behavior. She relates how she devised her method of controlling the classroom by not allowing problems to develop.

Krastin, Alexandra, "Don't Tell Me Teaching's a Soft Job!" *The Saturday Evening Post,* May 8, 1954, pp. 22-23. A teacher describes the hazards of teaching, then relates the qualities which enable good teachers to surmount the hazards and enjoy their work.

Manning, John, "Discipline in the Good Old Days," *Phi Delta Kappan,* Vol. 41, December, 1959, pp. 94-99. The ways of dealing with behavior problems in school have changed. An interesting study of discipline methods of past years.

Martin, John E., "Discipline, The Student Teacher's Nemesis," *The Educational Forum,* Vol. 25, January, 1961, pp. 213-14. Valuable suggestions on discipline for the student teacher, with special emphasis upon the importance of self-understanding.

Mayer, Frederick, "A Letter to A Teacher," *Phi Delta Kappan,* Vol. 40, February, 1959. The author appeals to a young man who is thinking of leaving teaching. An eloquent statement of one teacher's faith.

Menninger, William C., "Self-Understanding for Teachers," *NEA Journal,* Vol. 42, September, 1953, pp. 331-36. A famed psychiatrist discusses the mental health of the teacher and offers suggestions for achieving emotional maturity.

FILMS

Appointment with Youth

A dramatic presentation of the professional work of the teacher and of the resulting personal satisfactions. Includes information on salaries and working conditions. (Crowley, black and white, 26 minutes.)

Emotional Maturity

A dramatization of a high school boy's behavior, showing some of the consequences of an adolescent's failure to channel his emotions into positive actions and feelings. Illustrates importance of adult understanding. (Young American Films, Inc.; McGraw-Hill Book Co., Inc., black and white, 20 minutes.)

First Lessons

Adjustment problems of a new aggressive pupil in a class of second graders. How the teacher helps children gain insight into feelings that lie behind behavior. (National Association for Mental Hygiene; International Film Bureau, black and white, 21 minutes.)

Maintaining Classroom Discipline

Positive approach to the teacher's role in controlling class conduct and attitude; contrasting methods of handling a class. (McGraw-Hill Book Co., Inc., black and white, 15 minutes.)

School and the Teen-Ager (Kinescope)

Relationship of the teen-ager to the school. Why adolescents like some classes and teachers while disliking others. Teen-age attitudes. (University of Michigan, black and white, 30 minutes.)

CHAPTER 3

HOW TO PREPARE FOR TEACHING

If you enjoy children and young people and are willing to work
hard, be prepared for the time of your life.

A STUDENT TEACHER

We have just reviewed the tough problems confronted by the one
hundred student teachers. How does experience with these problems
influence their desire to teach? Does it weaken their desire to teach?
Considering the knotty problems confronted by a number of them, this
reaction would be understandable. Or, do these experiences have the
opposite effect? Do they strengthen the desire to teach? Let's ask the new
teachers.

HOW DOES TEACHING AFFECT YOUR DESIRE TO TEACH?

For the great majority of the new teachers the desire to teach is increased by teaching. Eighty of the one hundred beginners are enthusiastic
about the experience and report that they look forward more eagerly
than before to full time teaching. Ten of the one hundred have some
difficulty in evaluating the experience. In some ways it strengthens, in
some ways weakens their desire to teach. Five of the one hundred believe
that the experience did not change their desire to teach one way or
another. They remain unchanged by the teaching experience. The remaining five student teachers find that the experience weakens their desire to teach. They are less sure that they want to teach.

38

For A Few Student Teachers Experience Weakens The
Desire To Teach

These people give different reasons for their reactions. For the most part, however, they find that teaching simply does not live up to their expectations. "Before teaching I was idealistic," states one. "During student teaching one faces reality, and one has to cope with it. If anything, this weakens my desire to teach." A high school teacher expresses the same thought in another way:

> In education courses teaching is presented generally as an ideal, a bundle of inspiring ideals that will make you a good teacher. In student teaching you climb down from the clouds and get your feet wet. The experience can make the 'natural' for teaching more eager than ever to teach. Or, it can repel one who got several false ideas about the profession during his preparation for teaching. I am in the latter group.

The teaching experience weakens the desire of an elementary beginner because she felt so terribly inadequate. "When I did begin to feel confident," she says, "the routine became so routine that it was a bore." Another said, "It is more trouble than it's worth."

> 1. As in Chapter 2, several student teachers state that they were led to over-idealize teaching. They feel let down in actual practice. Do you think idealism has a place in teaching? If so, how would you describe the right kind of idealism necessary for teaching?

A Few Student Teachers Remain Unchanged In Their
Desire To Teach

Five student teachers remain unchanged in the desire to teach. A high school teacher speaks for the group when he reports: "A great deal depends upon the kind of experience you have in student teaching. As for myself the experience neither increased nor decreased my desire to teach. I did find that my work with students was a pleasant experience."

For Some The Experience Both Weakens And Strengthens
The Desire To Teach

These people find the question a difficult one to answer. As one said, "There is no one answer to this question. It depends on the individual, what he desires out of teaching, and how his teaching experience meets these expectations. Then, too, in my own case it sometimes strengthened, sometimes weakened my desire to teach." Another student teacher catalogues specifically the factors that cause his desire to teach both to increase and decrease:

> I would say many factors increase my desire to teach. Teenagers and their problems are a challenge. Each day brings a new situation. You must keep well informed in several areas. It's fun to try out ideas and see them in action. On the other hand, several factors decrease my desire to teach: (1) little appreciation is shown for personal time and effort; (2) weak administration; (3) some faculty attitudes I think are unprofessional.

For Most Student Teachers The Desire To Teach Is Strengthened

First, it should be said that these eighty student teachers do not have their desire to teach strengthened because they find teaching easy. On the contrary, their desire to teach is strengthened because of the opportunity to experience teaching as it really is, to see some of the good and some of the bad points of the teaching profession. A representative student teacher from this group says:

> If you've studied education thinking it would be a snap and an easy way through college, your student teaching experience will open your eyes and show you that teaching is not a snap, and that it involves a great deal of work. This may weaken the desire of some to teach. Among the student teachers I know, however, it's had the opposite effect.

Another teacher concurs:

> Some people believe teaching is an easy life. Actually, this is not true. If a person enters teaching under this false impression, his desire to teach may be weakened. On the whole, though, I think teaching strengthens your desire to teach. In my own case I like children, and teaching puts you in a position to help them fulfill their objectives in life.

Second, most of the new teachers in this group agree that student teaching provides a golden opportunity to make an intelligent decision about teaching. "It's a good time for those who aren't sure about teaching to learn it and get out if they want." One male puts the idea in masculine terms: "If the decision to teach was made haphazardly, the experience might weaken one's desire to teach. If it does, student teaching might be justified as a process for separating the men from the boys."

All agree that the experience gives them an almost real indication about their decisions to teach.

> **2.** Let's agree that practice teaching is an excellent way to test one's decision to teach. But what if you do not wish to wait that long and risk wasting the time in teacher preparation? Can you suggest other ways to test the decision to teach?

Why is the desire to teach strengthened? Why does the teaching experience strengthen the desire of this group to teach? A variety of reasons is given, but most of them can be grouped around two large factors. First, in teaching the student teachers find satisfying personal fulfillment and growth. Second, and closely related, they genuinely enjoy working with children and youth.

(1) Teaching yields personal satisfactions. A large number of practice teachers experienced growth in themselves as they encouraged it in the others. Teaching, they found, stimulates personal discovery and leads to new levels of achievement. Let's listen to them talk about this personal factor in their teaching experience:

> Now that I'm almost finished with student teaching I feel fully confident to teach on my own.

> I really had a chance to see the product of my efforts. I learned my faults and good points through direct experience and I could profit by them. I got a chance to become a genuine part of the class and learn what its like to be a teacher.

> I became enriched by the human contacts, and had my knowledge of subject matter deepened. Nothing could be more encouraging or satisfying.

> I can hardly wait to have my own classes. I know there will be many disappointments; yet I feel now that I'm equal to them. I think I can be a good teacher.

> It seems that I am finally fulfilling a dream. I have always wanted to be useful to young people and I feel that I'm finally accomplishing this through teaching in high school.

> While serving as an officer in the army I was a battalion instructor. That started it. I re-entered college for the sole purpose of getting a teaching certificate. My student teaching experience has been wonderful. It has definitely convinced me that my life's work will be devoted to teaching youth.

> When I started to teach, I'll admit I was just getting a life insurance policy. However, I love teaching. I'm having a wonderful time and can't wait for next September to begin full time teaching.

The person who teaches becomes alert to what he may do to contribute to young people. If one feels that he can do something to help young people he will be happy in his work. I find myself looking forward very eagerly to my first teaching assignment. I don't plan on being disillusioned! I want to do my part to help as many young people as I can.

(2) Personal satisfaction derives from working with children and youth. In chapter one we discussed the rewards experienced by the student teachers in working with students. No further analysis is necessary. Here, however, are just a few representative comments from teachers who attribute their strengthened desire to teach to the satisfactions which derive from working with children and young people.

When you see students grow under your guidance, your desire to teach is definitely strengthened.

You don't realize the importance you play in a child's life until you actually work with him. The human element is a very important one.

Student teaching gives one the satisfaction of seeing how students change, even in a brief period of ten weeks.

Seeing a student's face light up when he or she understands a point you have been trying to get across is what makes teaching, as far as I'm concerned, the best profession in the world.

I found how interesting and refreshing students are and how you can do so much with them.

Students are basically eager to learn. As a teacher I became personally interested in every child and wanted to see each of them develop new learning and attitudes.

The great majority of the new teachers find that experience strengthens their desire to teach. They take a calm, realistic view of teaching, weigh both the work and the satisfactions, and come out with a strengthened desire to teach. A few of them discover that teaching strengthens their desire to teach in some ways, but weakens it in others. A small group is unchanged. Similarly, a small group is discouraged by the experience. Their desire to teach is weakened.

All groups agree that the teaching experience provides a realistic opportunity to test the decision to teach. It will likely turn one toward or away from teaching. The results of this survey confirm this conclusion.

Only five out of the one hundred student teachers are unchanged in their desire to teach. The eighty new teachers whose decision to teach is strengthened agree that the teaching profession makes high demands upon those who enter it. They are challenged by those demands. They find personal fulfillment in teaching, mostly because of the satisfaction they find in working with children and young people.

> 3. Using the experiences of these one hundred student teachers, make a personal inventory of your own assets for teaching. In what qualities are you strongest? Weakest?

WHAT SUGGESTIONS DO YOU HAVE FOR PROSPECTIVE TEACHERS?

What suggestions do new teachers make to persons who are planning to teach? Since the teaching experience for them is a moving one, we would expect that they would have some valuable advice. They do. Their main suggestions are five in number: Gain as much actual experience as you can in working with children and youth; reinforce this experience with appropriate studies in psychology and in child growth and development; master the subject matter you plan to teach; begin at once to gain a working knowledge of teaching methods; and take stock of yourself. Let's look at each of these suggestions.

Gain As Much Actual Experience As You Can In Working With Children And Youth

Almost without exception the student teachers stress the importance of working with children and young people. Those who had such experience prior to student teaching find it invaluable. Those who did not, wish they had. Let's listen to some representatives speak about the value of such experience: "Get all the experience you possibly can with children." "Work a lot with children—baby sit, teach Sunday School, lead Boy Scouts, be a camp counselor, direct a recreation program—anything to broaden your understanding of children. It will pay off." "Work with children the same age as you intend to teach. See how they think and act and why they do the things they do. See what interests them and why." "The most important thing is to have experience with children in a supervising capacity. Take opportunities to handle many kinds of children, work with them, talk to them, play with them, use materials with them. Many materials which fascinate adults leave children cold. Much adult vocabulary is meaningless to youngsters. You find these things out when you work with them."

4. Have you had opportunities to work with children and young people? Can you think of additional opportunities for gaining this valuable experience?

Reinforce This Experience With Appropriate Studies In
Psychology And In Child Growth And Development

In addition to practical experience secure a sound academic background in child and adolescent studies. The new teachers emphasize especially such areas as "child and adolescent psychology, motivation, emotional problems, mental hygiene, and child guidance." This practice teacher speaks for many others when he says:

> If I could do it over I'd take every course I could which deals with the growth and problems of young people. A prospective teacher can't get too much of this work. A course in child or adolescent psychology should be required of all teachers before they receive a teaching certificate.

5. Here is an opportunity to learn more about the teacher preparation program in your college or university. Does it include such valuable studies?

Master The Subject Matter You Plan To Teach

On few other topics are the new teachers more unanimous. "Don't simply assume that you know your subject matter," warns one. "Know it so well that you don't need to think about it as you teach." "Know it deeply; have more than a superficial knowledge," suggests another. One student teacher, stressing the consequences of not knowing the subject matter, says, "One cannot know too much about his subject. Students are quick to sense that one is unsure of his ground. Don't try to bluff. They know."

A number of new teachers underscore the importance of knowledge of the minor field, where demands are just as great as in the major field. One of the new teachers states, "A teacher cannot expect to be respected if he does not know anything; that includes his minor field. One student teacher worked in our school in the vocal music department. He had minored in music and his knowledge of it was slim. He had a very rough time."

A deep interest in the subject must accompany knowledge. A high school teacher said:

> Be sure you are deeply interested in your field. Whether it is English, economics, history, social studies, or whatever, be enthusiastic about your teaching area. If you are not interested, your

students will not be interested. This probably sounds obvious; yet after watching some teachers in action, I'm sure that it must be stressed.

6. Are you confident that your program of preparation will give you mastery of the subject matter you intend to teach? This might be a good question to discuss with your faculty advisor.

Begin At Once To Gain A Working Knowledge Of Teaching

Successful teaching does not begin with student teaching. It begins much earlier in intelligent preparation and planning. Many of the new teachers, looking back, wish they had made fuller use of their college preparation. They wish they had taken many opportunities which went unused. A number of teachers who took these opportunities find how helpful they are.

With special reference to developing teaching skill, the new teachers find that they could learn a great deal by observing and by putting to use what they were learning as they learned it. Here are their specific suggestions: Look for the practical applications of what you are studying and observing: Gain experience in group leadership. Observe teachers and students in action, and collect teaching materials and aids. Let's examine these.

Look for the practical applications of what you are studying and observing. The new teachers regret the amount of "just listening" they did in their college classes. One new teacher comments:

> I was a sponge, soaking up information in order to pass the tests. When I began to teach I discovered that the teacher must be more than a sponge. He has to *do* things with what he knows, and *use* ideas in such a way that the students learn them. Instead of being a sponge, I should have been asking questions such as, "How will I use that with my students?" and "Where can I try out this idea?"

An elementary teacher says:

> My training was unduly removed from actual practice. Why wait until student teaching to put theory into practice—it's too hard then. The prospective teacher needs experience in putting theory into practice while learning her theory and methods. One class I took required a lot of practical work with children outside. It was work, but I feel most confident in that area now.

These new teachers made the plea that all of one's training be related to "use," to "practical applications," to "actual situations" which come as close as possible to real teaching. They stress the value of taking an active rather than a passive attitude toward one's training, realizing that the day of action will soon come. Early preparation will pay rich dividends.

Gain experience in group leadership. The teacher is a group leader. Sometimes he works with large groups, sometimes with small groups. Skill in group leadership is vital to success in teaching. "Get before groups as much as possible," advises one new teacher. "Get experience in handling small groups," suggests another. "Make sure that future teachers are equipped to speak in front of a group," adds a third.

Several student teachers point to the importance of specifics in group leadership. One high school teacher says, "I would suggest that future teachers know ways of getting a class started. It's important, because if you don't get the attention of the whole class at once you won't have their attention through the class period." Another advises, "Learn how to get a point across."

Many student teachers wish they had more training in presenting materials and in using audio-visual aids. This chemistry teacher speaks for many others when he remarks, "In the field of chemistry it's important to present different concepts visually. My students have to see things before they understand them. Demonstrations are very important. Charts, graphs, and objects help. It's vital to know how to handle these."

Others call attention to the importance of being able to communicate with particular students. An elementary teacher says, "Learn how to talk to children. There is a definite art to it. Many student teachers make the mistake of talking in too general terms, or above the age level of the children. A good clear voice and a sparkle in personality are tremendous assets to a teacher." A high school teacher underscores the importance of studying how to get subject matter across to pupils. He says, "I regret that I didn't have to take or didn't take more courses in speech, psychology, and audio-visual aids. These I feel would have helped me make explanations and instructions clear and interesting."

Some beginners wish they had the opportunity to teach lessons before fellow college students in class. This one speaks for others when he advises: "Before going into full time student teaching each education student should have the opportunity to prepare and teach a day's lesson at the level he intends to teach. This would bring home a lot of ideas that are touched upon in readings and lectures, but don't really make sense until you face thirty students and come to the dismayed realization that the lesson you thought so simple and self-evident wasn't soaking in at all." To gain experience in handling small groups, another student teacher suggests that members of the college class harass the prospective teacher, ask him questions, and let him defend his way of teaching.

Whatever their specific recommendations, many practice teachers believe in the importance of early experience in working with groups, speaking, demonstrating, and "getting across ideas." These are the teacher's stock-in-trade, they discover, and the prospective teacher would do well to extend his experience with them.

Observe teachers and students in action. "Get a close-up view of schools and classrooms," recommend a number of practice teachers. This comment is representative:

> In order to give the prospective teacher more realistic images of what teaching is really like, he should be encouraged to visit classrooms and find out just what is involved. All this should be done in the freshman, sophomore, or junior years, or at least before actual student teaching begins. If college students would take this opportunity, they would be much better prepared to teach.

The following comments, taken at random, support the above viewpoint:

> If possible, visit schools and try becoming familiar with various developmental levels of high school students.

> Observe children in school as much as you can. They're different in school from what they are at home.

> Observe teachers at work and talk to them about their work. You can learn a lot from them.

> Observe classes in your own field every chance you get.

> Actual observations in classes are the best way for prospective teachers to learn.

> Observe a class for one hour for one week; analyze the teacher's lessons, the discipline problems, and the children's actions.

The value of firsthand observation as preparation for teaching is underlined by these new teachers. Books, lectures, and discussion all have their place, but the actual observation makes talked-of matters real and vital.

Collect teaching materials and aids. New teachers learn the value of having a bountiful supply of teaching materials. They strongly recommend that prospective teachers start a material file early and keep adding to the file as preparation progresses. "I think the prospective teacher should be warned," states one, "to look for interesting and clever materials with which to demonstrate lessons. The real need is for new ideas and you can't have too many." Another comments, "Such teaching aids attract attention and create interest. They should be at your finger tips."

What kind of material should go into the prospective teacher's professional file? There are many suggestions: pictures, free materials, class notes, instructional games, book lists, film lists, audio-visual aids, ideas for bulletin boards, ideas for student activities—and all good ideas which come along. One teacher puts the matter this way: "Teaching aids are so valuable and they make teaching such an easier and happier experience that one can afford to spend some time on them. Collect or make as many aids as you can because you'll be able to use them."

The importance of beginning such a file early is stressed by a teacher who reports, "The best thing I did was to gather a lot of materials before I began to student teach. They came from all sorts of places: books, magazines, teachers, class notes, newspapers, and discussions. I would suggest that in each methods course, students collect teaching aids and exchange them."

> 7. Can you name six specific things you can do to help you get a working knowledge of the skills of teaching?

Take Stock Of Yourself

The decision to teach should not be taken lightly, new teachers urge. It calls for some self-inventory. A high school teacher says, "Though there are many satisfactions obtained from teaching, take stock of yourself. Ask yourself whether you're willing to pay the price of dedication. If your answer is a whole-hearted "yes," then be a teacher. If your answer is filled with reservations about teaching, then don't teach." An elementary student teacher adds, "In teaching, dedication is a necessity, not an optional requirement."

To dedication must be added hard work. Be prepared to work as you never worked before, and expect twice as much work as you had in mind. Also be prepared to assume responsibilities.

"But the work is worth it," states one teacher. "Student teaching is a meaningful experience, the best of your college career. You cannot help but benefit in some way from such an experience. Teaching has unexpected compensations. The rewards will be many in helping others to grow and develop a healthy view of life and to acquire the necessary tools and skills to solve the problems that lie ahead of them." A high school practice teacher speaks for himself and many others when he sums up the experience this way. "It's wonderful, and I'm reluctant to leave teaching and return to the campus. Next fall I'll have my own classroom and I'm eager to get on the job. To the prospective teacher I can only say, 'Relax, enjoy yourself; it's a memorable experience which you'll never forget.'"

8. You have now read the reactions of one hundred student teachers. Here is a project which can give you a still more personal understanding of what teaching is really like. Interview an experienced teacher on the topic "What does it mean to teach?" You may wish to include in your interview some of the questions which were put to the student teachers. Contrast and compare the reactions of the experienced teacher with those of the student teachers.

To assist you in developing questions for your interview, here is the report of such an interview conducted by a student who is preparing to teach.

A STUDENT REPORTS AN INTERVIEW WITH A TEACHER

Miss S. Warned That When You Decide You Are Going To Teach, Learning Course Material Just To Receive A "B" Or An "A" Grade Will Not Benefit You.

Interviewed by
ALICE RESSLER

For the purpose of my paper, I shall call her Miss S. Miss S. is about twenty-five and has been teaching nursery school for two years. In the course of my interview I asked her questions on topics ranging from discipline problems, to married teachers, to handling parents, and finally, to preparing for teaching.

I began my interview with the basic questions that concern us in our education course. I asked Miss S. why she had chosen the teaching profession. "I have always enjoyed working with young children," she said. "They have an honesty that unfortunately becomes stifled by external pressures in our society by the time they are older."

I then inquired about Miss S.'s highest satisfactions throughout her teaching experiences. She replied by relating a situation that occurred in her nursery school classroom: "I had read the class a story about Mr. Blue and Mr. Yellow. The tale describes how the two men met and together formed a Mr. Green. The next day the class was busily painting at the easels. I went around to watch the children, and noticed that Terry was mixing colors. I asked her what she was doing with her paints. She proudly answered, 'Mixing blue and yellow to make a green for my painting.'" The background to this situation has some significance. Miss S. informed me that in the beginning weeks of school Terry was extremely inhibited and unreachable. When a teacher reaches an understanding between a student and herself, it is truly an achievement. "Another gratifying situation occurred after a week of my teaching," she continued. "I had noticed Peggy observing me all week. She watched every move attentively. Finally, at the end of the first week, she skipped over to me, threw her arms around me and said, 'I have decided I like you.'" This is a simple statement but a rewarding one to a teacher.

I then questioned Miss S. about her disappointments in teaching. "People aren't interested in learning new things," she said. "Even four-year-old children have already become inhibited."

As to discipline, Miss S. offered these suggestions: "I set up definite limits. Not many. But the few I do choose I enforce strictly. I find it most difficult to control the class during juice and story time. I found that by splitting up certain cliques during story time, I could avoid inattentiveness or distractions. I also found that by suggesting various things for the children to do, I could keep them occupied and interested."

I proposed the question concerning the type of relationship you should establish between the teacher and the class. "Your relationship should depend on the situation," replied Miss S. "Most children do not want another friend. They have their own peer group for this. They are looking for guidance in an older person. However, some situations might call you to step in as a friend for a specific instance. I do not teach the class on a formal basis."

I was also interested in the diplomacy involved in handling parents. "That is one of my difficult problems," said Miss S. "I am younger than the parents, which puts me in a bizarre position for suggesting improvements. I find that I must be honest but utilize great tact. You can suggest things more critically if you know the particular people or if they accept suggestions more readily." Miss S. had one situation with a boy named Tony, who was terribly aggressive in school. "I finally had to call a meeting with his parents," she said. "I discovered there had been some recent friction at home, and Tony's behavior was evidently a reaction to it." With co-operation between parent and teacher Tony has been able to adjust to school and his peers. "A teacher must use her discretion as to how much she can tell a parent."

I was interested in finding out what had prepared Miss S. best for her vocation. "I found that graduate work helped me most in my teaching career. Experience is also a great teacher. I did have a special teacher who provoked much thinking on my own part. This enabled me to stand independently in the classroom." When I questioned her further as to her first days of actual teaching she answered, "The first day in front of the class, I had that awful sinking feeling. I did feel more confident as the term progressed along with my students' accomplishments. I convinced myself that there was so much I must do and learn, that I had to measure up to what was expected of me. I enjoyed the strong challenge teaching offered. As you teach, you find yourself wanting to know more in many fields."

I then asked Miss S. what would help me to understand my students. "I cannot emphasize how pertinent it is to study your subjects for content. Absorb all the material; do not just cram for one examination." She advised me to take all the psychology courses available, because I would always be referring to them in classroom situations. "When you decide you are going to teach, learning course material just to receive a B or an A grade will not benefit you. Get all you can from each class, and take excellent notes on all your readings. Keep a record as to where you got your facts, so you may refer back to them if necessary. There are also certain things you will learn on your own."

I was curious to learn if teaching ever became boring. "A day-in and day-out job can become tedious. It is up to the teacher to keep herself interested. I do this by changing my methods and patterns of teaching. Use your imagination to think of novel ways to present material to the class."

I asked her who she thought was qualified to teach. "Not everybody should teach. A person who enters this vocation should be content with mundane tasks which are means to a bigger goal." After I asked Miss S. this question, I noticed a large stack of colored paper on her desk. I questioned her further as to its purpose. She was bordering each piece of paper with tape. Miss S. was then going to punch holes in it and make an individual story book for every child in her class. She planned to paste pictures of animals on these pages with fur, cotton and other attention-attracting elements for her children. This is an example of a mundane task for the fulfillment of a larger goal. I asked Miss S. if all her days seemed routine. "Some days don't go as well as others," she replied. "When this happens I look to myself and not to the children. It is up to the teacher to motivate her students." She also said that a prospective teacher must like the academic world, for there is where her life will center.

With a natural feminine curiosity, I asked Miss S. her opinion on teaching while raising a family. "I honestly feel that the most important thing for a woman is to marry and have a family," she said. "Attending both your home and teaching, if you are fully devoted, can be a full-time job. It depends on how much time you plan on devoting to your particular choice. If teaching helps you and your family financially and socially, then I feel you should, by all means, pursue this vocation. I do feel you should be aware of reality and certain obligations before you make your decisions." Miss S. discussed an idea she had for the future: "When I marry and move to a larger home, I want to open a private nursery school of my own, possibly just for the neighborhood children. This is not necessarily for money, just for the challenge and marvelous rewards of the teaching profession."

Miss S.'s desire to teach was definitely strengthened once she began her teaching profession. "When you are observing, it is not the same as experiencing the profession for yourself," she commented. I asked her if she had always wanted to be a teacher. "No," she said, "I developed this interest suddenly in college when I realized how much I enjoyed working with children. I also felt by having summers off, I would be able to pursue another vocation if it was financially necessary. I would also like to travel during my vacation."

I found this interview most helpful in getting a personal opinion on teaching. I valued the opportunity of asking questions of pertinent concern to me and my future. I feel it is experiences like these that will better prepare me for my vocation in elementary education.

In these three chapters we probed the experiences of new teachers. We saw them at work with students, enjoying the rewards of the relationship, grappling with tough challenges, committing, or not committing, themselves more deeply to teaching, and finally advising others who are preparing to teach.

We call the activity in which they are engaged "teaching." Now we are ready to ask: "What is teaching, really?" How would you answer?

Good Follow-up Reading and Viewing

BOOKS

Chandler, J. B., *Education and The Teacher*, chap. 7, "Who Should Teach," and chap. 8, "Preparation for Teaching." New York: Dodd, Mead & Co., 1961. Chapter seven includes an informative section on the personal attributes of the teacher. Chapter eight treats the inter-related roles of liberal education, subject matter fields, and professional education in teacher preparation.

Evans, Eva Knox, *So You're Going To Teach*. Danville, Ill.: The Interstate Printers and Publishers, 1951. A popular, yet sound, treatment of what the new teacher may expect. Written from a teacher's viewpoint. Contains apt cartoons.

Metropolitan School Study, *The Newly Appointed Teacher*. New York: Bureau of Publications, Teachers College, Columbia University, 1950. This well-written pamphlet looks at a new teacher and her problems. Valuable for the student who is looking ahead to teaching.

Redefer, F. L., and Dorothy Reeves, *Planning a Teaching Career*. New York: Harper & Brothers, 1960. A practical book written for those who plan to teach, as well as those who have taught. Full of helpful and specific information.

Richey, Robert W., *Planning for Teaching*, chap. 3. New York: McGraw-Hill Book Co., Inc., 1958. This chapter includes valuable self-rating scales for helping a prospective teacher judge his competency for teaching.

Smith, Frances C., *Find a Career in Education*. New York: G. P. Putnam's Sons, 1960. A discussion of professional opportunities in education and ways to prepare for them.

Thomas, Lawrence G., *et al.*, *Perspective on Teaching*, chap. 15, "How Do Potential Teachers Enter the Profession?" Englewood Cliffs, N.J.: Prentice-Hall, Inc., 1961. A concise, comprehensive description of what the prospective teacher should expect as he undertakes a teacher education program.

Wilson, Charles H., *The Teacher Is a Person*, pp. 51-59, 93-102. New York: Henry Holt & Co., Inc., 1956. These selections present a lively account of the first year of teaching.

Woodring, Paul, *New Directions in Teacher Education*. New York: The Fund for the Advancement of Education, 1957. The interim report of the work of the Fund for the Advancement of Education in the areas of teacher education and recruitment.

Wynn, Richard, *Careers in Education*, chap. 9, "Preparation for Teaching." New York: McGraw-Hill Book Co., Inc., 1960. A discussion of the needs of the student teacher and of essential areas of teacher education. A graphic presentation of teacher-preparation programs.

PERIODICALS

Adams, Don, "Wanted: Angry Young People in Education," *Peabody Journal of Education*, Vol. 37, No. 5, March, 1960, pp. 262-67. A good statement of the challenges facing young people who enter the profession of education during the 1960's.

Brembeck, Cole S., "Content and Process in Teacher Education," *Michigan State University Basic College Quarterly*, Vol. 4, Fall, 1958, pp. 14-19. A proposal for unifying into a sensible whole both content and process in the education of teachers.

Chase, Francis S., "How and By Whom Are Our Teachers To Be Taught," *The Educational Forum*, Vol. 23, May, 1959, pp. 389-98. An excellent statement of the subject matter and professional program needs of elementary, intermediate, and high school teachers.

Hardaway, C. W., "Factors Considered by School Superintendents in the Selection of Beginning Teachers," *Teachers College Journal*, Vol. 21, January, 1950, p. 80. This article catalogues the factors which superintendents of schools weigh most heavily in selecting beginning teachers.

Lambert, Sam M., "Beginning Teachers and Their Education," *Journal of Teacher Education,* Vol. 3, No. 4, December, 1956, p. 350. Twenty-six hundred first year classroom teachers in urban school districts report interesting facts about themselves and their positions.

Linden, Arthur V., "Across a Placement Desk," *Teachers College Record,* Vol. 55, October, 1953, pp. 37-44. The director of a large teachers' college placement office describes a variety of positions in education and appraises them, both from the viewpoint of the employer and of the position-seeker.

Nelson, Nels B., "Exploring Teaching," *NEA Journal,* Vol. 47, February, 1958, p. 139. A high school principal explains his school's plan for giving prospective teachers realistic experience as teaching assistants in an eight weeks' summer program.

U.S. Office of Education, *Teaching as a Career,* pamphlet 122, Washington, D.C., 1959. How should you choose a teaching field? How can your prepare for it? This pamphlet is a valuable source of helpful information.

FILMS

Elementary Teacher: Beginning Student Teaching

Discusses the training and functions of the teacher in a world of rapid change. Shows a student teacher as she acquaints herself with a classroom, a school and its program, and with the experiences of practice teaching. Uses flashbacks to emphasize the points being discussed by the teaching supervisor and the student teacher during an evaluation of the latter's progress. (Indiana University, black and white, 10 minutes.)

Not By Chance

Good teachers are not made by chance but are the result of professional training. Current practices in teacher education. (National Education Association, black and white, 28 minutes.)

Preparation of Teachers

The preparation of teachers in the U.S. as illustrated by the program at Ball State Teachers College in Indiana. (Govt.; United World Films, Inc., black and white, 20 minutes.)

Teacher

Importance of the teacher in building future citizens; types of training teachers receive; satisfactions of their work. (Encyclopaedia Britannica Films, Inc., black and white, 16 minutes.)

Who Will Teach Your Child?

How to attract the particularly gifted into teaching. Problems and rewards of good teaching; trials of poorly qualified inexperienced teachers; need for expert teachers. (McGraw-Hill Book Co., Inc., black and white, 23 minutes.)

PART 2

TEACHING: WHAT IS IT?

CHAPTER 4

EXPERIENCED TEACHERS SPEAK

"The teacher leads you to the threshold of your own mind."

KAHLIL GIBRAN

The Prophet, in Kahlil Gibran's little masterpiece with the same title,[1] speaks of occupations. Men from various walks of life come to seek the wise teacher's counsel. The builder steps forward to ask the Prophet about houses, the doctor about healing, the merchant about trading, and the lawyer about justice. Then a teacher, getting the attention of the Prophet, said, "Speak to us of teaching."

WHAT IS TEACHING?

Implied in the teacher's request is a question: What is teaching? Is it the act of giving knowledge to students, the teacher wants to know? "No," said the Prophet, because no one can reveal anything to you unless it "already lies half asleep in the dawning of your own knowledge." How about wisdom? Cannot the teacher give wisdom? "Not so," answers the Prophet, because the teacher "gives not of his wisdom, but rather of his faith and lovingness." Teaching is not a transfer from someone who *has* to someone who *has not*. "And why not?" asks the teacher. Because, concludes the Prophet, "The vision of one man lends not its wings to another man."

Then if the teacher cannot give his knowledge to the student, why not bring the student to his knowledge, "invite him to enter the house of his

---

1 Kahlil Gibran, *The Prophet*. Reprinted by permission of publisher. (New York: Alfred A. Knopf, Inc., 1923, 1951), pp. 65-65.

wisdom"? Not if he is wise, says the Prophet. Instead, the teacher "leads you to the threshold of your own mind." Teaching is the art of leading students to discover something which they already possess.

The Prophet punctures what he thinks are misconceptions about teaching. On the positive side he isn't as explicit. He implies that teaching is a fine art in which qualities already latent within the student are nourished and made to blossom. The teacher leads the student to his own fulfillment, using the stuff of which the student, not the teacher, is made. Teaching is not the act of imposing, hints the Prophet; it is more like coaxing forth. Its focus is on the student, rather than on the teacher. The good teacher encourages his student to get along without him, to grow away from him, to become his own whole self. For the Prophet, teaching is the art of drawing out something which is implicit within the learner.

> 1. What do you think? Is Gibran's Prophet right? If he is right, if the teacher cannot give his knowledge to his students, if one person's ideas cannot give their "wings" to the ideas of another, what is teaching, really?

Look At Another Point of View. Not everyone agrees with the Prophet. Other people hold that teaching is the art of putting something in the learner, something not previously there. That "something" which is put in might be facts, information, concepts, attitudes, or skills.

Cicero,[2] the polished Roman statesman of the first century B.C., believed in this approach to teaching. Amidst his busy political life he found time to write books on teaching and thought it was the responsibility of leading citizens to devote time to teaching the young. He liked to retreat to his villa in the hills outside Rome in the company of a group of young men. There, with his toga around him, he relaxed and taught.

Train the memory, he said to his young companions lounging about him. Fill the mind with the thoughts of great men. Memorize their speeches and writings. Recite them until you know them perfectly. The mind is a golden storehouse. Fill it with treasures. When you enter the arena of Roman life, you will draw on those treasures. So, Cicero sat and listened as his students recited, displaying their words from the storehouse of memory. Teaching, for Cicero, was the art of creating in students a full mind, by "putting in" the ideas of great men.

Here, then, are two contrasting definitions of teaching. The position represented by the Prophet says that learners have latent qualities

---

[2] Marcus Tullius Cicero, *De Oratore* (Cambridge, Massachusetts: Harvard University Press, 1942).

within them, like seeds awaiting germination. Teaching provides the congenial conditions—stimulation, encouragement, guidance—needed for development.

Not so, says the position taken by Cicero. The learner has capacity, yes, somewhat like a vessel capable of holding so much water. It is up to the teacher to put into the vessel worthy things deserving to be there.

Let us now put these two positions in the form of questions: *Is teaching the art of drawing out something implicit within the learner? Or, is teaching the art of putting in something not previously there?*

You recognize, of course, that these two questions represent polar, or black and white points of view. There's lots of room for different shades of gray between the black and white. Still, the controversy represented by these two questions is as old as any in educational history, and many practical implications flow from the two positions. Further, a teacher subscribing to the draw-out concept will tend to teach one way, while the teacher who believes in the put-in concept will tend to teach another way.

Check the two questions above against your own experience. Recall, if you will, a favorite teacher, one who influenced your life, perhaps caused you to consider teaching as a career. How would you describe his or her teaching?

Did this person draw out something which was already "half asleep" within you, as the Prophet put it? Did he cause you to do things for yourself which you may not have done otherwise? Did he coax from you ability which you were surprised to learn that you had? Did he prod you to launch out on your own in independent investigation?

Or did this teacher "give" you something which you did not previously possess, as suggested by the teaching of Cicero? Did he think it his job to introduce into your thinking facts, information, and concepts not already there?

Or did this "favorite" teacher actually do both of these, put in and draw out?

> 2. We said a moment ago that how a teacher answers the question "What is teaching?" helps to determine how he teaches. Taking a "favorite" teacher, (A) can you say which concept he favored? and (B) why you think so?

The Choice Of Answers Makes A Difference

We indicated that the controversy over these two points of view is an ancient one. In fact the derivation of the word "education" gives us a clue to its antiquity. Our word "education" derives either from the Latin word *educere* or *educare*. Latinists aren't sure which. But this argument illustrates our point. *Educere* means "to draw out." *Educare* means "to put in." The debate whether teaching involves drawing out something from the learner or putting something in began long ago.

We shall not trace the history of this long argument here but perhaps you would like to see how the point of view has made a difference in the way teachers behave and think.

We would not expect, of course, that one position or the other would result in identical teaching practices. As we said, there is plenty of room between these two poles for various shades of opinion. There is a great variety of practice within the general orbit of each position. In the examples which follow we can see this variety of expression. Still, at the center one can sense that the teacher has made his choice. He believes that in teaching he is essentially introducing into the experience of the learner a new dimension, or that he is coaxing forth and helping to develop latent possibilities already there. Which he chooses to do determines to a large extent how he teaches.

These Men Believed That Teaching Is The Art Of Developing Qualities Which Are Already Implicit Within The Learner

Socrates: "I am a sort of gadfly."

Socrates,[3] that thorn in the side of ancient Athens, held clear ideas about teaching. Teaching, for him, was the art of stinging young students to new thoughts and action. The elder Athenians found Socrates' teaching successful and deeply disturbing. A "corrupter of youth," they charged, and gave him the choice of hemlock or exile. As he sauntered along the streets of the ancient and beautiful city, the bright young men crowded around him until, finding the cool shade of a plane tree, they all sat down. There, leaning back against the trunk, Socrates created a thrilling classroom which is still the model for modern teachers. Without lectures, textbooks, or recitations (and here we see Socrates' conception of teaching) he taught as few have taught—by invigorating conversation on vital topics sparked by leading questions, designed to draw out his students. Getting answers, he asked more questions. He trapped his students with his questions and sat silent as they struggled to get out. Socrates was the adroit asker of questions. A teacher, for him, was like a human gadfly that pricks and stings to new thoughts and deeds.

Erasmus: "Children in the earliest stage must be beguiled and not driven to learning."

---

[3] Plato, *The Apology*. William Chase Green, ed., *The Dialogues of Plato*, Benjamin Jowett, trans. (New York: Boni and Liveright, 1935).

Erasmus,[4] that witty and incisive Dutchman of the Renaissance, loved to chide parents about their neglect of proper education for their children.

> Take the case of the father who grudges the pay of a decent tutor, whom he puts off with a lower wage than he gives his groom. Yet the same niggard will spend a fortune upon banquets and wine, upon play, jesters, and his mistress . . . At a single feast and dicing that follows he will lose two hundred pounds, but he complains of extravagance if his son's education costs him twenty. Frugality? Yes, by all means: but in this matter of all others frugality is no economy; it is another name for madness.

Erasmus believed that teaching was the art of stimulating the love of learning. "Children in the earliest stage," he wrote, "must be beguiled and not driven to learning." The teacher must have a "gentle and sympathetic manner," and a knowledge of "wise and attractive methods." If he has these, the student will find pleasure in his task.

> It is a hindrance to a boy's progress, which nothing will nullify, when the master succeeds in making his pupil hate learning before he is old enough to like it for his own sake. For a boy is often drawn to a subject first for his master's sake, and afterwards for its own. Learning, like many other things, wins our liking for the reason that it is offered to us by one we love. . . .
>
> It is the mark of a good teacher to stand toward his charge somewhat in relation to a parent: both teaching and learning are made easier thereby. He will also in a sense become a boy again that he may draw his pupil to himself . . . He will follow in his first instruction methods of the mother in the earliest training of the nursing. As she prattles baby language, stirs and softens baby food, stoops and guides the tottering steps—so will the master act in things of the mind. Slowly is the transition made to walking alone, or to eating solid food; the tender frame is thus carefully hardened. In exactly the same manner instruction is at first simple, taught by way of play, taught by degrees. The sense of effort is lost in the pleasure of such natural exercise: insensibly the mind becomes equal to harder tasks. Wholly wrong are those masters who expect their little pupils to act as though they were but diminutive adults, who forget the meaning of youth, who have no standard of what can be done or be understood except that of their own minds. Such a master will upbraid, exact, punish, as though he were dealing with

---

4 William Harrison Woodward, *Desiderius Erasmus, Concerning the Aim and Method of Education* (New York: Cambridge University Press, 1904), pp. 193-194, 204, 211-212.

students as old as himself, and he forgets that he was ever himself a child. Pliny warned such a one when he spoke thus to a master: "Remember that your pupil is but a youth still, and that you were once one yourself."

Teaching for Erasmus was wise and sympathetic counseling aimed at nurturing the love of learning. He believed that each child had the latent capacity to love learning. It was his job as teacher to draw it out and develop it.

Whitehead: "It is always possible to pump into the minds of a class a certain quantity of inert knowledge."

Alfred North Whitehead,[5] the British mathematician and philosopher who spent most of his professional life in America, thought and wrote a great deal about teaching. He quarrelled with Cicero's concept that good teaching fills the mind of the student with great ideas which may be drawn upon later as the need arises. "Let the student," he urged, "experience the joy of discovery *now*. Ideas which are not utilized are positively harmful." Whitehead conceded that:

> With good discipline, it is always possible to pump into the minds of a class a certain quantity of inert knowledge. You take a text book and make them learn it. So far, so good. The child then knows how to solve a quadratic equation. But what is the point of teaching a child to solve a quadratic equation? There is a traditional answer to this question. It runs thus: The mind is an instrument, you first sharpen it, and then use it; the acquisition of the power of solving a quadratic equation is part of the process of sharpening the mind. Now there is just enough truth in this answer to have made it live through the ages. But for all its half-truth, it embodies a radical error which bids fair to stifle the genius of the modern world . . . I have no hesitation in denouncing it as one of the most fatal, erroneous and dangerous conceptions ever introduced into the theory of education. The mind is never passive; it is a perpetual activity, delicate, receptive, responsive to the stimulus. You cannot postpone its life until you have sharpened it. Whatever interest attaches to your subject matter must be evoked here and now; whatever powers you are strengthening in the pupil, must be exercised here and now; whatever possibilities of mental life your teaching should impart, must be exhibited here and now. That is the golden rule of education, and a very difficult rule to follow.

5 Alfred North Whitehead, *The Aims of Education,* pp. 1-4, 8-9.

Whitehead began with the assumption that the student has a mind which "is a perpetual activity, delicate, receptive, responsive . . ." This mind, where properly stimulated, is capable of great discoveries. Discovering is a private matter. Someone else cannot discover for us. We do it ourselves. What, then, is the role of the teacher in assisting discovery? According to Whitehead it is to stimulate these active, delicate, and receptive minds to make new discoveries on their own. How? By strengthening and exercising the powers already within them.

These Men Believed That Teaching Is The Art Of Giving
The Learner New Qualities Not Previously There

Quintilian: "My ideal pupil will readily acquire the knowledge presented to him."

We have already observed that Cicero, the Roman statesman, believed that teaching should fill the mind of the learner with worthy ideas and should develop the capacity to retain and use them. More than a century later a fellow Roman, Quintilian,[6] was recognized as the great teacher of Rome. Petrarch, who lived thirteen hundred years after Quintilian, wrote him a "letter" and paid him the supreme tribute: "Thou art a great man, I grant, but thy greatest merit lies in thy ability to ground and to mold great men."

This first century Roman was modern in his approach to education. He believed that everyone could profit by an education. "There is no foundation in fact for the complaint," he wrote, "that to very few is given the power of understanding what is taught them but that the majority waste both time and labor through slowness of intellect; on the contrary, you will find many are clever at puzzling things out and quick at learning."

Quintilian advocated the use of psychology in teaching. In teaching the young do not make learning a burden, he said.

> For one thing especially must be guarded against, viz. lest one who cannot yet love studies come to hate them and even after the passing of childhood's years shrink from a bitter task, once undergone.
>
> Let this first instruction be in the form of play; let the pupil be asked questions and praised for his answers; let him never rejoice in ignorance of anything; sometimes when he will not learn, let another be taught of whom he will be jealous; let him compete sometimes with others and quite often think himself victorious; let

6 William Smail, *Quintilian on Education* (New York: Oxford University Press, Inc., 1938), pp. 11, 30, 73-74, 101.

him also be excited by rewards, which at that age are eagerly sought after.

Quintilian recognized the importance of individual differences in learners.

> It is usually and rightly esteemed an excellent thing in a teacher that he should be careful to mark diversity of gifts in those whose education he has undertaken, and to know in what direction nature inclines each one most. For in this respect there is an unbelievable variety, and types of mind are no less numerous than types of body. . . .
> Accordingly, most teachers have thought it expedient to train each pupil in such a way as to foster by sound instruction his peculiar gifts, and so to develop varied endowments most effectively in the direction of their natural bent. Thus, as an expert in wrestling, entering a gymnasium full of boys, tests them in all sorts of ways, both in body and in mind, and then decides for which type of contest each one is to be trained.

As a teacher, Quintilian was a "putter-in." He agreed with Cicero on the importance of a good memory. "A good memory," he wrote, "is the chief indication of ability in a pupil and its excellence lies in two things, ease of acquiring knowledge and accuracy in retaining it."

Quintilian's ideal pupil was one who will "readily acquire the knowledge presented to him and some things, too, he will elicit by questions; yet he will follow his master rather than seek to outrun him. Such precocity of intellect seldom, if ever, attains to full fruition."

Here we have the clue to Quintilian's answer to the question: "What is teaching?" It is the act of presenting knowledge to students. The good student can "readily acquire it." He may even ask questions to get more knowledge from the teacher. But he must not "outrun" the teacher. He must follow him. Why? So that the teacher can continue to give knowledge to the pupil. Should the pupil "outrun" the teacher, a new kind of teaching would be called for.

Matthew Arnold: "Call forth in every pupil a sense of pleasurable activity."

Matthew Arnold,[7] the respected British poet and essayist, earned his living by inspecting schools. For thirty years, from 1852 to 1882, he

---

[7] Matthew Arnold, *Reports on Elementary Schools,* 1852-82 (London: Wyman and Sons, Ltd., 1908), pp. 226-29.

travelled from school to school in his district, observing, assisting, and writing reports for the British Ministry of Education. These reports reveal Matthew Arnold's keen insights into educational matters.

He was a "putter-in," but he was concerned about some problems connected with this approach to learning. For example, knowledge is increasing all of the time. Should the teacher simply keep increasing the amount he puts in the mind of the student? Is this possible, since the children's general capacity remains about the same at a given age? Warned Matthew Arnold:

> Fresh matters of instruction are continually being added to our school programs; but it is well to remember that the recipient for this instruction, the child, remains as to age, capacity, and school time, what he was before, and that his age, capacity, and school time, must in the end govern our proceedings. Undoubtedly, there is danger at present of his being over-urged and over-worked, of his being taught too many things, and not the best things for him . . .

Matthew Arnold was concerned about the quality as well as the quantity of matters which were introduced into the child's mind. "Teachers know very well," he said, "that the strain upon a learner's mind arises not only from the quantity of what is put into it, but also from the quality and character; and the strain may be relieved not only by diminishing the quantity, but also by altering that quality and character."

He was equally interested in the way in which matters were introduced into the mind. He was opposed to introducing a number of "knowledges passively" in order "to store them up to be reproduced in an examination . . ." Rather, he wanted matters introduced in such a way that they gave the sense of pleasurable activity and creation. He states:

> Of course a great deal of the work in the elementary schools must necessarily be of a mechanical kind. But whatever introduces any sort of creative activity to relieve the passive reception of knowledge is valuable. The kindergarten exercises are useful for this reason, the management of tools is useful, drawing is useful, singing is useful . . . It is true, language, and geography, and history, and the elements of natural science are all capable of being taught in a less mechanical and more interesting manner than that in which they are commonly taught now; they may be so taught as to call forth pleasurable activity in the pupil. But those disciplines are especially valuable which call this activity forth most surely and directly.

At first glance it might seem as though Matthew Arnold were an exponent of the "draw-out" theory of teaching. He does speak of "calling forth pleasurable activity in the pupil." But let's ask: Why does he wish to call forth this pleasurable activity? His real purpose is to make what is put in more congenial with the student's interest. He was not really advocating drawing upon the student's own latent knowledge and experience. His real contribution as a "putter-in" was that he highlighted the importance of interest and creative effort in learning, and warned against simply storing up a number of "knowledges."

Phelps: "The teacher must be a Leader."

William Lyon Phelps [8] began his long and successful teaching career in a boy's school and later established himself at Yale University. Perhaps it was this first experience that led him to define teaching as leadership with a capital *L*.

> The teacher must be a Leader, a Master, in many cases a Lion-tamer, a manager of wild beasts . . . He is the Captain of the ship, and is as much alone in the school room as the captain is alone with his crew on the high seas. Those who have never taught have no idea of the loneliness and responsibility of a school teacher shut up in a big school room with a pack of wild boys and girls. The teacher can consult outside of hours with his superiors or colleagues; he can get advice and talk over his difficulties. But when he goes into the school room, shuts the door, takes the lonely seat behind the desk, and looks into the shining morning faces, then he is thrown back absolutely on himself. No power on earth can help him, and nothing can save the situation if he makes a blunder. Then he needs all his resources, all his courage, and infinite patience. I remember when I first taught school, hardly more than a boy myself, I was sent in evenings to preside over "study hour." This meant that I was to sit behind a desk in a big room filled with healthy boys, and see that no one spoke or made a noise for an hour. I could not interest them, for I too, could say nothing. They came jostling, tumbling, hilariously, in; I rang the bell which meant instant silence. That bell gave forth no uncertain sound; I put my whole personality into my finger as I pressed the electric button, and I tried to make it trill just the psychological length of time, neither too short nor too long. Yet, every time I rang that bell I wondered if they would really obey. They did, but I never recovered from my amazement of the miracle.

---

8 William Lyon Phelps, *Teaching in School and College* (New York: The Macmillan Company, 1918), pp. 12-14.

Here is still another interpretation of the put-in theory, or shall we say in the case of Phelps, the put-upon theory? William Lyon Phelps saw teaching as the forceful play of forceful personality upon the student. The words he uses to describe the teacher reveal his conception of his work—Leader, Master, Lion-tamer, manager of wild beasts, and Captain of the ship. The student is one who is acted upon by the teacher. He is to take orders, be obedient, and learn.

What Is Your Judgment Now? You have now listened to two sharply different answers to the question "What is teaching?" and you have observed how different people interpret the two points of view. What do you think?

Is teaching the art of developing something which is already implicit within the learner? For example, is it the art of:

a. awakening that which "already lies half asleep in the dawning of your own knowledge," as *The Prophet* says?
b. stinging students to new thoughts and deeds through adroit questions, as Socrates practiced?
c. stimulating the love of learning, as Erasmus counseled?
d. leading the student to experience the joy of discovery *now*, as Whitehead pointed out?

OR

Is teaching the art of adding something? For example, is teaching the art of:

a. filling the mind with great thoughts, as Cicero believed?
b. getting students to acquire knowledge with ease, and retain it with accuracy, as Quintilian advocated?
c. introducing knowledge in such a way as to call forth a sense of pleasurable activity, as Matthew Arnold wrote?
d. providing leadership with a capital *L,* as William Lyon Phelps thought?

3. We said earlier that a teacher subscribing to the draw-out concept will teach differently from one adhering to the put-in concept. How would you now describe the teaching which is suggested by the two ideas? Can you name five items which will tend to describe each way of teaching? In the next chapter we shall enter the classrooms of two teachers who practice these different concepts. There you will have an opportunity to see if your list fits these particular cases.

Test Your Choice Of Position

By this time you probably lean toward one of the two main points of view we have been describing. Perhaps you have pretty well decided what teaching is. Maybe you're now "on the fence."

Whatever point of view you choose you should understand it, know what it implies for the way you will teach, and be prepared to defend it as the best for you. Ultimately you must make your own decision. On such an important question as "What is teaching?", only you can answer.

One way to help get the right answer for you is to test the two points of view, ask questions about them. There are two fundamental questions which must be asked about each point of view. Let's look at them.

If, as Teacher, You Are Drawing Out Something Implicit Within the Learner:

What is it you are taking out? Here's a basic question. Obviously you are taking out something. What is that something? The advocates of this point of view can help us find answers. They recognized that the student has life beyond the classroom. From that life the student has learned a great deal. It consists of knowledge, attitudes, and skills, plus a vast reservoir of "half-learned" things. As Whitehead said, the student's mind is a "perpetual activity, delicate, receptive, responsive to the stimulus." Such a mind is constantly at work learning new things. The teacher taps this reservoir of learning and stimulates to further learning.

How did it get there in the first place? We've given the clue to the answer in the question above. It got there through the living, experiencing process. Then didn't somebody have to put it there in the first place? No, according to the adherents of this position. The mind, being active, reaches out and responds to all kinds of stimuli. In the act of reaching out and responding it grows and matures.

If, As Teacher, You Are Putting Something In The Mind Of the Learner:

What do you propose to put there? Cicero answered the question by saying, "The ideas of great men." Is this an adequate answer? Which men are great? Who should decide? What criterion shall we use to determine whose ideas shall be taught? The basic question is: What shall we teach? We are going to examine this question in chapter six.

How do you propose to put it there? In other words, what methods shall we use? Cicero and Quintilian believed in the exercise of memory as one of the best ways to learn. Matthew Arnold stressed the need to associate learning with pleasure and creative activity. William Lyon Phelps believed in firmness and discipline as prerequisites to learning. The basic question: How shall we teach? We'll return to this important question, too, in chapter six.

In this chapter we have dealt with a vital question: What is teaching? It is a big question, perhaps never fully answered, even by the best of teachers. Indeed, in a way, to teach is ever to enlarge one's conception of what teaching is. For this reason teaching can never be thought of as something small and menial. It is a large act, and it grows continually larger for those who pursue it with understanding.

This question will be implicit in every chapter in this book, and I hope that each new chapter will add something to your own answer. Now is a good time for you to formulate your own definition of teaching, keeping ever on the alert for ideas which enlarge it. This particular chapter has presented two points of view on teaching and illustrated these in the work of a few great teachers. We have also stated two questions which need to be asked about each point of view. The purpose has been to point out two alternatives in teaching and the issues connected to each.

4. Question three asked you to describe the teaching suggested by the two concepts discussed in this chapter. Now make a list of the strengths and weaknesses which you discover in each concept.

Seek To Enlarge Your Conception of Teaching

There are many resources at hand. In college or university we are constant participants in the give and take of teaching and learning. Public schools are nearby and numerous. Most public schools welcome observers, especially if advance arrangements are made. Perhaps we have close friends or relatives who are teachers. The exciting business of teaching and learning permeates much of the life that goes on in the home, church, office and plant where the student of teaching can observe, study, and participate.

You will do well to make use of these laboratories. Observe your own classes. Can you identify certain viewpoints regarding teaching at work? Interview your fellow students and instructors regarding their understanding of the nature of teaching. What difference do you observe in the teaching and learning from one class to another? Can you account for these differences?

Seek out opportunities to work with children and young people in teaching and learning situations. Such opportunities are plentiful in voluntary social agencies, summer camps, churches, playgrounds, scout organizations, and similar activities. "I got my first real understanding of teaching when I read stories in the children's wards of the hospital," reported one student. Another asked, "Are all boy scouts that wiggly?"

Such experiences as these can help you develop your own answer to the vital question: What is teaching?

In this chapter we have talked of teaching in terms of ideas about it, rather than of practice. In the next chapter we shall visit the classrooms of two teachers whose practices are very different. We want to find out what their practices suggest about their beliefs concerning teaching.

Good Follow-up Reading and Viewing

BOOKS

Barzun, Jacques, *The House of Intellect*. New York: Harper & Brothers, 1959. An interesting account of teachers in contemporary America.

Chandler, J. B., *Education and the Teacher*, chap. 9, "The Work of the Teacher." New York: Dodd, Mead & Co., 1961. A discussion of the various roles of the teacher: confidant, motivator, guide to learning, disciplinarian, *in loco parentis*, adviser, example, and judge.

Deuel, Leo, ed., *The Teacher's Treasure Chest*. Englewood Cliffs, N.J.: Prentice-Hall, Inc., 1956. Presents many viewpoints on various teaching practices. Literature from many sources about teaching.

Grambs, Jean D., "Roles of the Teacher," in *The Teacher's Role in American Society*, ed. Lindley J. Stiles. New York: Harper & Brothers, 1957. This chapter identifies the various roles expected of teachers by students, parents, community, and school. Among the questions treated are: How does the teacher's role develop? What does the teacher do? What is the social function of teaching?

Haskew, Laurence D., *This is Teaching*, chap. 3, "These are the Learners." Chicago: Scott, Foresman & Company, 1956. Different views of learners: clay, receptacle, or plant. Good discussion of how to study and understand learners. Strong implications for the work of the teacher and the nature of teaching.

Highet, Gilbert, *The Art of Teaching*, chap. 2, "The Teacher." New York: Alfred A. Knopf, Inc., 1950. A classic statement on the life and work of a teacher.

Redl, Fritz, and William W. Wattenburg, *Mental Hygiene in Teaching*. New York: Harcourt, Brace & World, Inc., 1951. Chapter ten describes a variety of functions which teachers perform in their daily work. Provides a definition of teaching from the viewpoint of the work carried on.

Smiley, Marjorie B., and John S. Diekhoff, *Prologue To Teaching*, Part 3, "The Purposes of Education." New York: Oxford University Press, 1959. Searching readings, both historical and contemporary, which examine the purposes of education. Includes readings dealing with the purposes of teaching languages, social studies, mathematics, and science. Teaching is defined in terms of the aims of teachers.

Thomas, Lawrence G., *et al.*, *Perspective on Teaching*, chap. 7, "What Do 'Teaching' and 'Learning' Mean?" Englewood Cliffs, N.J.: Prentice-Hall, Inc., 1961. A compendium of both traditional and modern answers to the question: "What is good teaching?"

PERIODICALS

Angus, Sylvia, "Are We Educating?", *The School Review,* Vol. 69, No. 2, Summer, 1961, pp. 151-56. The author contends that high school students are ill taught. The reason: "children have spent years drilling stupid, unrelated facts into their minds in the name of education."

Fenton, Edwin, "Working With High Schools: A Professor's Testimony," *The School Review,* Vol. 69, No. 2, Summer, 1961, pp. 157-68. A college professor of history rediscovers high schools, and in the process rediscovers teaching.

Hennings, Alice B., "I Like Teaching, But—," *The School Executive,* Vol. 73, June, 1954, pp. 58-60. An English teacher compares her job with one she held in an office as statistical typist.

Holt, Howard B., "Artist and Artisan in the Teaching Profession," *The Educational Forum,* Vol. 25, 1961, pp. 233-35. Proposes two hallmarks that identify the artist teacher as opposed to the artisan teacher.

Lynham, Adria B., "Teachers Are People," *NEA Journal,* Vol. 47, October, 1958, pp. 503-04. A catalogue of personal and social qualities needed for success in teaching.

Powell, C. F. A., "The Ideal Teacher," *NEA Journal,* Vol. 45, January, 1956, p. 31. What qualities do students like best in teachers? The writer asked 2,042 elementary, intermediate, and secondary students to list the traits and practices of the "perfect teacher."

Rummell, Frances V., "What Are Good Teachers Like?", *School Life,* Vol. 30, June, 1948, pp. 4-9 and July, 1948, pp. 7-11. Presents case studies of "distinguished examples of the best professional talent in the nation's classrooms today." Interesting accounts of the life and work of outstanding teachers.

Stemple, F. W., "Qualities of the 'Master Teacher,'" *The Educational Forum,* Vol. 25, January, 1961, pp. 227-31. An illuminating discussion of the qualities of Jesus as a teacher.

FILMS

Elementary School Children
(Part I) Each Child Is Different.

Differences in five fifth-grade children as they appear during the first day of school. Stresses the importance to good teaching of knowing such individual differences and their causes. (Kerkow; McGraw-Hill Book Co., Inc., black and white, 20 minutes.)

Elementary School Children
(Part II) Discovering Individual Differences.

A fifth-grade teacher studies the differences in background, abilities, and needs of the children in her room through observation, accumulative records, a behavior journal, discussion with other teachers, interviews with parents, and staff conference. (Kerkow; McGraw-Hill Book Co., Inc., black and white, 25 minutes.)

Guiding the Growth of Children

Seven cases demonstrate the importance of being interested in, and understanding, children in order to teach them well. (McGraw-Hill Book Co., Inc., black and white, 17 minutes.)

The School

Portrays an elementary school day, including the PTA meeting in the evening. (United World, black and white, 21 minutes.)

School in Centerville

Teaching conditions in a multi-teacher rural school. Planning procedures which relate curriculum to children's needs. Ways of working together for desirable learning experiences. Importance of recognizing individual differences in interests, aptitudes, and abilities. (National Education Association, black and white, 20 minutes.)

CHAPTER 5

TWO CLASSROOMS: TWO ANSWERS

"School for most of them was a necessary evil, alleviated only
by recess."

MARY ELLEN CHASE

"The sensible way is to get what is taught into the direct
experience of the pupils."

HENRY JOHNSON

The two cases presented in this chapter offer interesting comparisons and contrasts. In the first situation Mary Ellen Chase tells about her teaching experience as a college student in a small Maine coastal community. In the second, Henry Johnson tells us of his experiences with elementary school children in demonstration schools. Different points of view on teaching are apparent. As you read the cases, you can profitably raise certain questions:

1. What points of view on teaching are held by the two teachers? How do you think each would answer the question: What is teaching?

2. How does the teaching differ?

3. How does the learning differ?

4. Would you say that one approach is more effective than the other? If so, why?

5. What significance do these experiences have for you as a student of teaching?

MARY ELLEN CHASE GOES TO BUCKS HARBOR

In her autobiography, *A Goodly Fellowship*,[1] Mary Ellen Chase tells of her first teaching experience:

---

[1] Mary Ellen Chase, *A Goodly Fellowship*. (New York: The Macmillan Company, 1939), pp. 34-41, 44-45.

"The place was Bucks Harbor, Maine, a native community of fishermen, small tradesmen, farmers, and sailors. Most of the twenty-odd families were large and interlaced by marriage, as were most coast families in small settlements . . . There was one general store, which sheltered the post office, one small church, Methodist, I think, by nature, with no settled pastor. There are a hundred counterparts of just such a village on a hundred small harbors along the Maine coast.

The people of such a village were the products of their environment . . . Most of them were practically untouched by any outside influences since, after the manner of the Maine coast native, they looked upon their few summer visitors only with curiosity and a faint suspicion. The only persons who had been afield, or perhaps better, far afloat, were the men and boys who were deckhands on small steamers or who were engaged in fishing or in the coastwide schooner trade; and they were mostly around their own air-tight stoves in winter . . .

The school teacher of such a village was the object of interest, terse comment, and not infrequently, at least at the start, suspicion, particularly if she came from "away." Her appearance, manners, morals, friendliness or lack of it, were far more important elements in her success of failure than was any mental equipment which she might or might not possess. Maine coast natives, then even more than now, have a tendency to assume the worst until they have been convinced that their assumption is wrong; and to the people of Bucks Harbor a girl from college had just that much more to live down than she might have had as a product of the Castine Normal School or of no describable school at all.

6. How does your own community look upon new teachers? Do you think the size of the community makes a difference in attitudes toward new teachers?

This is the setting in which Mary Ellen Chase taught. We know something about the community, its people, and their attitudes. We are now ready to learn how Miss Chase met this situation. We enter the school.

My first morning in my first school was dedicated both to the theory and the practice of the survival of the fittest . . .

The spring was a late one, and certain boys of sixteen or older, who otherwise might have been at sea, were at school for a season, ostensibly to learn, actually to discover of what stuff the new teacher was made. Had my father himself been constructed of less inflexible stuff, could I have been sure of receiving understanding and sympathy at home instead of disappointment and contempt, I should then and there have run for cover, leaving the Bucks Harbor school to whatever fate awaited it.

But the fear of returning home in defeat was far more terrible than the fear of staying where I was; and I began my teaching experience with an unseemly display of passions which I had never known I possessed—anger and disgust, scorn and fury. I was a veritable Maenad in frenzy as I stormed up and down my narrow aisles. The pathetic pretense of courage, aided by the mad flourishing of the razor strap, brought forth to my amazement as though by magic the expression of respectful fear upon the faces of young giants who could have accomplished my terrified exit either by physical strength or by a like display of temper, and who had come to school with the express purpose of doing so. But no one moved to further insurrection, and although, when the reign of terror to which both forces had contributed had subsided, my quaking knees could hardly support me at my desk, I had no more trouble from discipline through eleven long weeks.

I have since wondered how a teacher, trained in modern and more pacific ways of governing a school, would have made herself mistress of such a situation, one moreover, whose parents possessed hearts and doors more readily open than did mine. Perhaps it is as well for the principles and the practice of the new education that district schools are fast disappearing from the American landscape. Perhaps the race is growing gentler! Surely even in the smallest of communities today there are other interests than the advent of a new teacher.

A young teacher told me recently that for other than patriotic reasons she should always look upon the American flag with respect and veneration. She said that in her first year of teaching when all other sources of interest failed and she felt herself becoming engulfed in the imminent dangers of inattention and recalcitrance, she was given to calling suddenly for a salute to the flag. She depended, she said, upon this break in affairs either to quell rising mutiny or at least to relegate it to a fresh and more easily handled start. We had no American flag at Bucks Harbor, and the now common words of salute had not yet reached our confines even if, at that date, they had been composed. But, instead of the flag, I shall always look with respect and veneration upon a razor strap, seeing in this ugly object not only the symbol of my emancipation from terror and disgrace, but as well the initial inspiration and vision which resulted two years later in my choice of a profession.

7. Recall how the one hundred practice teachers described in section one were "tested" by their students. How would you describe the difference between their students and Mary Ellen Chase's? Was the difference one of degree or kind?

The school at Bucks Harbor demanded of me more mental and physical agility than mere knowledge. I had forty-nine children of all ages from five to sixteen. When I had once sorted them out in accordance with age and progress, I found myself with twenty-nine classes a day to teach. The hours from nine until four, with fifteen minutes each morning and afternoon for recess, contained all told in minutes but three hundred and thirty. This resulted even by my poor arithmetic in a maximum of eleven minutes for each class, or to be more accurate, in ten, since the classes must move in order from their seats to the bench before my desk.

Since some combination of classes must be made if any child was to learn anything at all, I conceived the notion of hearing five reading lessons in quick succession while those who were not reading were doing problems in arithmetic at the blackboards. Although the corporal frame is subject to the boundaries of space, I soon learned that the mind can be in two or even three places at one time. One portion of my mind was riveted on the behavior of the children presumably at study in their seats; another portion fearfully scanned the blackboards in the hope that no assistance would be summoned; a third listened to and corrected the reading of those on the bench before me. By this method arithmetic and reading were out of the way by the ten-thirty recess, leaving decent room for four classes in geography from ten-forty-five until noon. I ruthlessly combined the afternoon grammar classes, since all alike needed the same fundamentals, and by two o'clock we had a clear straight-away for history, which we all liked best, and for spelling which closed the day for everyone but me.

Needless to say, we had no frills and extras in our school. We even had no music since the good day of outside music teacher, even for the rural schools, had not yet come, and since I myself could not carry a tune. Had I been able to do so, however, we had no song or hymn books and no time. Even the Lord's Prayer and the Bible reading had to be hurried so impending were arithmetic and reading. When we were once organized, we clicked on like a well-regulated machine from nine until four.

8. Now we know how Miss Chase organized her instruction. Does the way she did it tell you anything about her answer to the question: What is teaching?

I am sure that such an iron-clad program was bad for my children; no school at any time should be systematized to that extent. But I am equally sure that it was the best thing that could have happened to me. I had always been a dreamy child, given to states of absent-mindedness and particularly irritated by attention to detail. I had seemingly been born with no sense of time, and the rigorous order and discipline of home and school, although I had per force submitted to it, had not wrought the transformation hoped for by my parents. Two years of relative freedom at college had afforded blissful opportunities for the indulgence of all my worst mental habits; and the school at Bucks Harbor could not have presented itself at a more opportune moment. There was now no time for dreams of either past or the future. It was dangerous to lose one's head for the fraction of a second. On and on the minutes raced with questions to be quickly put or as quickly answered. There was no time even for self-pity, let alone self-indulgence. For eleven weeks the stark necessity of the Bucks Harbor school held me in a never-loosened vise. When they were over, I was a different person.

9. How do you evaluate your own college life as preparation for teaching? Does it have some of the same drawbacks Miss Chase describes?

The school-house was on a high ledge above the harbor. From its door one got a wide and lovely sweep of sea and islands, but I do not remember having much time to look at it. I stayed at my desk until supper time in the superintendence of dunces and in the correction of papers; and when I had once locked the school-house door, I had no extra life within me to be uplifted even by Penobscot Bay . . .

I grew to love my charges, and I think they liked me. School to most of them was a necessary evil, alleviated only by recess and by the stories I told or read to them for two hours on Friday afternoons as a reward for good behavior. Few of them saw in it any present pleasure or any step toward the future. Like all country children they were fond of animals and flowers, and like all coast children they were shrewd in the ways of wind and weather. They could manage boats under any circumstances, though again, like most coast children, few of them could swim. Swimming, indeed, seemed but an indulgence, a pastime enjoyed by summer visitors, before whom they were always shy and sometimes rude.

10. We now know some of the interests and abilities of Bucks Harbor children. Did Miss Chase make any attempt to "draw out" these and use them to teach? Do you see possibilities for doing so?

I am sure I taught them very little. It was I who was educated in Bucks Harbor. But I like to remember how their sharp faces glowed on Friday afternoons over *Treasure Island* and even over *The Story of a Short Life* and *The Little Lame Prince*. Their homes were relatively bookless, and such stories as these were new fields to them. Occasionally I see certain of them now, here and there as lesser officers on summer yachts or at the county fair as stout mothers with broods of far more sophisticated sons and daughters. Three of them are teachers who, I trust, have never emulated my desperate and stumbling efforts either at discipline or at instruction.

With the story of Bucks Harbor fresh in mind, how would you react to these additional questions?

11. At this early stage in her teaching career, how do you think Miss Chase would have answered the question: What is teaching?

12. Did her viewpoint on teaching fit the situation she confronted at Bucks Harbor?

13. The children of Bucks Harbor thought school was a necessary evil. Did the teaching help to change this attitude?

14. Where was the focus in the classroom—on the teacher, on the subjects, or on the students?

15. Would you have done some things differently had you been teaching in Bucks Harbor?

HENRY JOHNSON TEACHES ABOUT AN ISLAND

Henry Johnson,[2] like Mary Ellen Chase, began his teaching career in a rural community, Lake Johanna, Minnesota. There he confronted some of the same problems. In his lively autobiography *The Other Side of Main Street,* he remarks:

At school I had thirty-four pupils and thirty-four classes, ranging from the kindergarten up into the high school. I sat up nights working out schemes for combining classes and to some extent succeeded. But my class of one, aged twenty-one in chemistry, geometry, and general history, and some other classes of one, defied any combination I could devise.

At school the days sped smoothly by. The most interesting and interested pupils whom I have ever had always have been those immediately in front of me. At Lake Johanna I could make no comparisons but I felt sure that no pupils could be more interesting or interested. We were a group of friends working and playing together and for me, at least, the closing day came too soon. On the afternoon of that day, parents crowded the rooms and the county superintendent came to inspect us. A spelling match and an arithmetical exhibition showed the superintendent that we had made progress. Then we passed to our programs of songs, declamations, and essays, and ended with very pretty speeches to each other.

[2] Henry Johnson, *The Other Side of Main Street* (New York: Columbia University Press, 1943), pp. 48, 51, 88, 89, 215-20.

In his first teaching experience, and the others which followed, Henry Johnson involved the students in their own learning, making them active participants rather than indifferent sponges soaking up what he taught. He tried to get what was taught into the direct experience of the pupils.

> At the beginning I simply studied the lessons with the classes and tried to teach them how to study. After that, the initiative was left largely to the classes. I might say to a class, "You have only four lessons to prepare and I have thirteen. I haven't looked at the lesson in history for today. What did you make of it?" While different members were talking it over with each other, I would skim the lesson and then enter the discussion as sort of a bystander. The classes decided how much they could do for the next day, suggested things that they would like to know more about, and read each others papers . . .
>
> We were far from being text book slaves. Often we would pursue for an entire period a topic barely mentioned in the textbook. Sometimes we cast the textbook aside and did our own organizing. Sometimes I did all the talking. Most of the time we learned together and one of the things that I learned was a cordial respect for the ability and industry of my students.

Now we are ready to turn to three specific teaching experiences related by Mr. Johnson, the first of which provides the title for this section. Here are the questions worth keeping in mind as we study these three examples of teaching:

16. How would you describe Mr. Johnson's point of view on teaching? How do you think he would answer the question: What is teaching?

17. Where is the focus? On the teacher? the student? the subjects?

18. What appears to be the aim of the teaching? What is it the teacher seeks to do?

19. Do you think that more or less learning took place in these situations, than those described by Miss Chase?

> For many years it was my practice to illustrate principles laid down in my methods courses by demonstration lessons. I have thus taught at every level from the first grade to the university and have emerged with a conviction that almost anything can be taught in a sensible way. The sensible way is to get what is taught into the direct experience of the pupils. The experience of young children is of course limited, but much more can be brought within that experience than is suggested by any psychology with which I am acquainted or by any primary teacher whose work I have observed.

This view has often been challenged. Teachers in the Horace Mann School of Teachers College once objected to an outline of the history of Manhattan Island which I had prepared for a first grade on the ground that children did not even know what an island was. "How many of you," I asked the children, "know what an island is?" The teachers were vindicated. Not a single child knew. That was an ideal situation for me. The classroom looked out on 120th Street where the children played at recess periods. I told the children to think of walking along their play street as far as they could go and asked them what they would find "over there," pointing toward the west. "North River" they exclaimed in chorus. I pointed in the opposite direction. "East River," rang the answer. I pointed down Broadway. "The ocean," responded the class. I pointed up Broadway. Silence. "There's water up there, too," I said. More silence, silence so prolonged that it plainly became oppressive to the observers. I simply waited and prayed, waited until a little boy remarked dreamily, "Why, there's water all around us." That was what I wanted. "Have you ever been anywhere else where there was water all around you?" Hands waved all over the room. "Squirrel Island," said one. "Bear Island," said another. The children did not know what an island was, but they named many islands. Again I waited and prayed, waited until a little girl with pleased surprise exclaimed, "Why, we're on an island right here." That was what I wanted. "This island," I said, "has a name, too. Do you know what is is?" Nobody knew. "How many of you live on this island?" Most of them did. So I had the pleasure of telling them the name of their island. Manhattan seemed to them a queer name and started questions which led at once to the history of Manhattan Island.

20. Here is a classic example of the teacher acting as drawer-out. Earlier in chapter four, we asked two questions about this approach to teaching: (a) what is being drawn out? and (b) how did it get there in the first place? How would you answer these two questions in relation to this example?

In Charleston I planned for a first grade an exercise which the regular teacher declared "too subtle for the children of six." It was an exercise on Columbus of whom the children had already heard. A description of Columbus was read, with pauses for the children to look about the room for each feature mentioned in the description. Columbus had high cheekbones. "Do you see anybody here who has high cheekbones?" Columbus had an aquiline nose. A rapid sketch on the blackboard showed what an aquiline nose was like. "Do you see anybody here who has an aquiline nose?" And so on to the end of the description. When the reading was completed, the children were told to close their eyes and try to see Columbus.

Then one of the numerous alleged pictures of Columbus was shown and the children were asked: "Is this your Columbus?" A unanimous "no" came from the class with very good reasons. A third picture was accepted by one boy as his Columbus, but was rejected for very good reasons by the rest of the class. A fourth picture proved to be the Columbus of all the other children. To show that anyone could "do it" I had entrusted the exercise to a practicing student rated as dull and uninteresting and was myself sitting at the back of the room. After everybody except the one boy had accepted the fourth picture, a little girl in the front row turned toward me and said: "I'd like to know what Mr. Johnson thinks," and when I answered that I thought the fourth picture most like the description, the class, with the exception of the one boy who had found in the third picture his Columbus, stood up and applauded with a great clapping of hands."

21. Mr. Johnson reveals his choice of picture only *after* considerable discussion on the part of the children *and* after his opinion is asked for by a student. Do you think it would have made any difference had Mr. Johnson revealed his opinion first, before the students talked about it?

22. Albert North Whitehead said that teachers should lead students to "experience the joy of discovery now." Does Henry Johnson meet his requirement in this instance?

With a fifth grade in Charleston I raised the question of how we know about a thing that has happened. The class thought of three ways. We may know about a thing that has happened because (1) We were there. (2) Someone has told us. (3) We have read about it.

On their own initiative the children began to argue the relative merits of these three ways of knowing about a thing and fell into rather excited disagreement. Several of them stoutly maintained that the best way to know about a thing is to have somebody tell you. It so happened that a circus parade was about to pass the building. We could already hear the blare of the brass band. "In a few minutes," I said, "the circus parade will be right in front of our windows. There will be some elephants. Do you want to go to the windows and look at the elephants or would you rather stay in your seats and have me tell you about the elephants?" "We'd much rather have you tell us about them," quickly answered an advocate of that way of knowing about a thing. But, with some pressure from me, the class voted to see the elephants. The next day some of the children, in spite of having seen the parade, held to their conviction that the best way of knowing about a thing was to have someone tell you. Expecting this, I had written a short story and, after a few minutes of further argument, I invited John to step out into the hall with me. There I said: "John, I'm going to read to you a short story that I want you to tell William. Before you begin the story, tell William to listen carefully because he is to tell it to Irma. Tell him also to tell Irma to listen very carefully because she is to tell the story to Ruth. As soon as you have told William the story, return to your seat. Now listen very carefully." John listened very carefully and was sure that he could tell the whole story. Leaving John in the hall, I sent William out to find him, and as soon as John returned I asked Irma to find William. In this way instructions passed along with the story from pupil to pupil until the transmission embraced the entire class. Then I called upon the pupil who had been the last to receive it to tell the story. So little of the original remained that loud laughter broke from more than half of the class. Continuing in this reverse order, an increasing number of correct details appeared but laughter continued among those who were still to report. When John's turn came, he supplied more details than any of his predecessors but when I read what I had read to John, the whole class laughed. "Many stories that we read in history books," I said, "were told from person to person for hundreds of years before they were written down. Such stories are called oral tradition. What do you think of oral tradition as a way of knowing about what has happened?" The children's comments seemed to me very intelligent and I was not surprised when they turned critical eyes upon the other two ways of knowing what has happened. The good old game of gossip had thus furnished through direct experience an introduction to what the historian calls historical criticism.

A few days after this lesson a voice hailed me from across the street on my way to school and Irma came running to my side. "Oh, Mr. Johnson," she exclaimed, "we've been having such a good time with that game you taught us." "Game?" I said, "what game?" "In our history lesson," answered Irma. "We've been playing it at recess and after school," she continued, "and Ruth and I are friends again." "I didn't know," I said, "about any trouble between you and Ruth." "Oh, yes," Irma went on, "I was told that she had said mean things about me and for weeks I didn't speak to her, but after that game, that history lesson, I mean, I made up my mind to ask her if she ever said any such thing, and she never did, and now we're friends again." The lesson in historical criticism had not made Irma hypercritical. She had accepted Ruth's unsupported word. In further conversation with Irma as we walked on to school, it appeared that she liked true stories, better than "just stories." As an example of a true story, she cited George Washington and the cherry tree and I had not the heart to cast any discredit upon that classic. But I was glad that Irma and Ruth were friends again. To that extent the lesson in historical criticism had certainly "functioned."

VIEWPOINTS AFFECT PRACTICE

We now have these two approaches to teaching before us, as represented by Mary Ellen Chase and Henry Johnson. Miss Chase stepped into a tough teaching situation and handled it by organizing the students around the subjects taught. For relief and reward for good behavior she read stories which opened new vistas to her students. She kept a firm grip by kind regimentation. We get the feeling that she imparted a certain amount of subject matter to her not always willing students. The focus is not sharply upon the student's interests and motivations. The teaching and subject matter stand somewhat outside the life of the school. Miss Chase believed that there were certain things children should know, and she was there to teach them.

Henry Johnson approached teaching in a different way. He began with students, their knowledge, and their interests. He encouraged them to find answers for themselves, under his gentle prodding. He taught for the present. Knowledge was meant to be useful in the life of the child. While Miss Chase organized the students around the subjects, Mr. Johnson organized subjects around students.

Here are contrasting views of teaching in action. Within each classroom and behind each method there are always some living issues. For example: What shall we teach? How shall we teach? How do we learn? What is the proper focus for teaching?

Teachers need to formulate answers to these questions. To help us we shall participate, in the next chapter, in a discussion with two men who present sharply different points of view on the questions.

Good Follow-up Reading and Viewing

BOOKS

Brower, George J., "Why I Enjoy Working With Teachers," in D. Louise Sharp, ed., *Why Teach?* New York: Henry Holt & Co., Inc., 1957. A discussion of the qualities needed for success in teaching.

Chase, Mary Ellen, *A Goodly Fellowship.* New York: The Macmillan Co., 1939. This autobiography, from which the excerpt in this chapter is taken, is the story of a life spent in teaching, beginning in Bucks Harbor, and concluding at Smith College. As the author puts it: "Teaching has been, and is, the good life to me."

Haskew, Laurence D., *This is Teaching,* chap. 2, "To School." Chicago: Scott,

Foresman & Company, 1956. Portraits of six teachers and their classrooms, including a discussion of what the learners were like, what they are doing, why they were doing it, what they were learning, and what the teacher was doing.

Hilton, James, *Goodbye, Mr. Chips*. Boston: Little, Brown & Co., 1934. The story of a dedicated young man who earnestly pursues his profession of educating boys. He reveals his conception of teaching with sincerity and simplicity.

Jenkins, Gladys Gardner, Helen Shacter, and William W. Bauer, *These Are Your Children*, pp. 140-155. Chicago: Scott, Foresman & Company, 1949. An insightful discussion of the teacher's work and relationships with children, replete with helpful suggestions regarding classroom management.

Johnson, Henry, *The Other Side of Main Street*. New York: Columbia University Press, 1943. This biography, from which the excerpt in this chapter is taken, is the story of a full and fruitful life in education, covering many years and situations.

Rasey, Marie I., *It Takes Time*. New York: Harper & Brothers, 1953. The changes which have taken place in educational philosophy and practice present themselves concretely in episodes which extend from the author's first days in school to the later days of her teaching as a university professor.

Ross, Leonard Q., *The Return of Hyman Kaplan*. New York: Harper & Brothers, 1959. The narrator tells a rollicking tale of his experiences teaching in a night school for adults, focusing especially on one student, Hyman Kaplan.

Wynn, Richard, *Careers in Education*, chap. 5, "The Work of the Teacher." New York: McGraw-Hill Book Co., Inc., 1960. Informative glimpses into the work of elementary, high school, special education, and private school teachers, as told by the teachers themselves.

PERIODICALS

Benjamin, Harold R. W., "The Saber-tooth Tiger Returns," *Bulletin of the National Association of Secondary School Principals*, Vol. 42, April, 1958, 358-66. This engaging piece of satire mocks school curricula which do not consider the needs and interests of the learners.

Eckel, Howard, "How Can We Get Quality Teaching?", *The School Executive*, Vol. 77, June, 1958, pp. 19-21. What is the deeper quality of teaching which permeates the classroom and deeply influences all learners? This article discusses the personal qualities needed to bring out the best in the learners.

Mazzei, R., "Desirable Traits of Successful Teachers," *Journal of Teacher Education*, Vol. 2, December, 1951, pp. 291-94. What are the desirable traits of a successful teacher? This is an attempt to find the answer at the junior-high-school level, with 115 students providing their reactions.

Murphy, Anna Mary, "Madge Brown, Rural Teacher," and Matthews, Elizabeth M., "Edna Griffin, Big-City Teacher," *NEA Journal*, Vol. 49, 1960, pp. 50-53. Contrasting studies of teachers who work in very different situations.

Stiles, Lindley J., "Creative Teaching for Excellence in Education," *School and Society*, Vol. 87, No. 2158, September 26, 1959, p. 356. A concise and valuable statement of the requirements for creative teaching. The creative teacher "must stimulate independence in learning while subtly guiding the direction, rate, and quality of attainment."

FILMS

Learning Is Searching
A third grade studies man's early tools; how they were discovered and used. Process of search as a means of learning. (New York University, black and white, 30 minutes.)

Planning for Personal and Professional Growth
Case histories of four teachers illustrate importance of planning for growth. Why teaching is dull and frustrating for some—rich and rewarding for others. (McGraw-Hill Book Co., Inc., black and white, 19 minutes.)

Skippy and the Three R's
A first grade boy is taught reading, writing, and arithmetic by a teacher who utilizes the boy's interests and helps him realize his own need for learning. (National Education Association; Agra Films, Inc., black and white, 29 minutes.)

Three R's Plus
The curriculum, materials, and techniques of the elementary school. The valuable features which have been added during the last few years. Common questions of laymen answered. (McGraw-Hill Book Co., Inc., black and white, 27 minutes.)

Wilson Dam School
Progressive procedures in a typical day for children from early through upper elementary grades. The philosophy of drill when needed; learning by doing through shared experiences; and pupil-teacher planning of activities. (Tennessee Valley Authority, black and white, 20 minutes.)

PART **3**

LIVING ISSUES WITHIN CLASSROOMS

Chapter 6: Four Questions For The Teacher

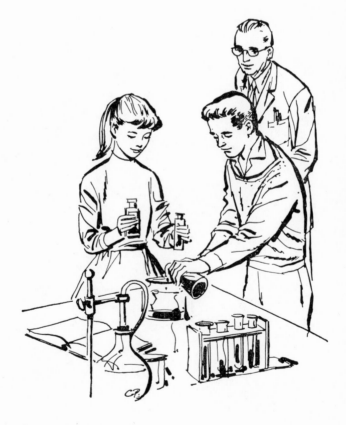

FOUR QUESTIONS FOR THE TEACHER

"The child becomes the sun around which the appliances of education revolve; he is the center about which they are organized."

JOHN DEWEY

"Primary is the thing to be learned. John is like every other boy in needing to be taught. He does not need to exist, for he exists already."

MARK VAN DOREN

We learned in chapter four that there are deep differences, indeed conflicts, in beliefs about teaching. In chapter five Mary Ellen Chase and Henry Johnson demonstrated how these differences can express themselves in the classroom. Now we are ready to examine some living issues which permeate all teaching and learning. There are many such issues. Here we select for examination only a few, but these few are apparent wherever teaching and learning take place. They are important. We shall return to them frequently throughout this book.

We call upon two men to help us sharpen these issues. John Dewey and Mark Van Doren are respected advocates of different beliefs about teaching and learning. You will see their contrasting positions shining through the teaching of Mary Ellen Chase and Henry Johnson. Indeed, if you look, you will find their arguments at work in the teaching and learning taking place all about you.

HERE ARE THE MEN

When John Dewey opened the doors of his experimental school in Chicago near the turn of the century, he swung open an age of revolution and excitement in education. Traditional education, he said, placed too much emphasis on matters outside the child. The child, whose life is rich in all kinds of experiences outside the school, must leave those experiences at the doorstep when he enters. Similarly, the experiences he has inside the school are unrelated to life outside and the child drops them at his desk when the bell rings. The good school is like a good home, only extended and organized. Here the child learns to use the tools for exploring the world around him. This world, the world in which the child lives, not a later one, is the important one. This is the world he should explore.

Through many volumes over many years, John Dewey spelled out the educational philosophy supporting his views. His great impact on American education is accepted, though many of his views are not.

Mark Van Doren, respected scholar, teacher and Pulitzer prize winner, states a different case. Good teaching, he says, has always treated children with respect and kindliness, made play of learning, made use of experiences surrounding the child. There is nothing new in this. But we fail the child, he claims, when we individualize him so much that we forget that he is like other human beings. Being alike, all children must acquire a common learning. Further, children must know more than the present. Fill their minds with treasures of the past, and they will profit from them in the future. To give children less is to cheat them.

In this chapter we shall listen as Dewey [1] and Van Doren [2] state their own views on four questions which are vital to classroom teachers. After each question you will be given an opportunity to formulate your own ideas and answers.

A word about the statements of the two men is in order. Each is a direct quotation from their writings and is generally representative of their positions. But short quotations cannot give us the full thinking of men who have written as extensively about education as have Dewey and Van Doren. They give us only the flavor of their thinking. These short statements will, I hope, stimulate you to learn more about the thinking of their authors.

Most of all, this short discussion is designed to help you sharpen your own answers to some fundamental questions in education. You may think you understand fully what it is Dewey and Van Doren are saying. But you need more than intellectual understanding. You need to build

1 John Dewey, *The School and Society* (Chicago: University of Chicago Press, 1943), copyright © 1915, 1943, Estate of John Dewey. Reprinted by permission.
2 Mark Van Doren, *Liberal Education* (Boston: Beacon Press, Inc., 1959). Copyright © 1943, 1959 by Mark Van Doren. Reprinted by permission of Nannine Joseph for Mark Van Doren.

ideas of your own and begin to see how you can use these ideas in teaching.

Here are the four issues which form the basis for our discussion: (1) How do we learn? (2) What shall we teach? (3) How shall we teach? (4) What is the proper focus for teaching? Let's look at each one.

How Do We Learn?

It makes a difference how a teacher answers the question: How do we learn? The answer will help determine how we teach.

On this question Dewey and Van Doren are closer together than on any of the other three questions.

For Dewey, learning and living are almost synonymous. The child learns naturally while experiencing the world around him. He learns some of his most complicated and difficult tasks without being taught in a formal way. He learns to talk, for example, by living among people who talk.

Learning, then, is activity centered. Children learn by being actively engaged in the life about them—working with tools, creating, and building. Dewey's charge against the traditional school is that it is a "listening" school where children are expected to be "sponges" soaking up the information given them.

Learning for Van Doren is somewhat the same. He agrees with the value of the "useful" arts in learning. Reading, writing, and arithmetic are best learned in the setting of play, he says, for "remember that children are never so serious as when they are making things up."

Dewey: "The tools with which the child may construct, create and actively inquire . . . have been for the most part lacking."

Some few years ago I was looking about the school supply stores in the city, trying to find desks and chairs which seemed thoroughly suitable from all points of view—artistic, hygienic, and educational —to the needs of the children. We had a great deal of difficulty in finding what we needed, and finally one dealer, more intelligent than the rest, made this remark: "I am afraid we have not what you want. You want something at which the children may work; these are all for listening!" That tells the story of the traditional education. Just as the biologist can take a bone or two and reconstruct the whole animal, so, if we put before the mind's eye the ordinary schoolroom, with its rows of ugly desks placed in geometrical order, crowded together so that there shall be as little moving room as possible, desks almost all of the same size, with just enough space to hold books, pencils, and paper, and add a table, some chairs, the bare walls, and possibly a few pictures, we can reconstruct the only educational activity that can possibly go on in such a place. It is all made "for listening"—because simply studying lessons out of a book is only another kind of listening; it marks the dependency of one mind upon another. The attitude of listening means, comparatively speaking, passivity, absorption; that there are certain ready-made materials which are there, which have been prepared by the school superintendent, the board, the teacher, and of which the child is to take in as much as possible in the least possible time.

There is very little place in the traditional school room for the child to work. The workshop, the laboratory, the materials, the tools with which the child may construct, create, and actively inquire, and even the requisite space, have been for the most part lacking. The things that have to do with these processes have not even a definitely recognized place in education. They are what the educational authorities who write editorials in the daily papers generally term "fads" and "frills." A lady told me yesterday that she had been visiting different schools trying to find one where activity on the part of the children preceded the giving of information on the part of the teacher, or where the children had some motive for demanding the information. She visited, she said, twenty-four different schools before she found her first instance.

Van Doren: "Reading, writing, and arithmetic are best learned in the setting of art—of use and play."

The child is properly interested in the useful arts, and is happy if he can practice them as a kind of poetry. If he is permitted to discover their principles as he works, he will already have made contact with general ideas; and it will be still better if the principles he discovers are important. This will be the case if the skills he is encouraged to seek are classic skills, somewhat as the games of children are classic—old, and dignified with ritual. Poetry as such will then be no foreigner to his imagination, and he will know when it is most real, he will have begun to be a critic; especially if all that he does is done in an order "calculated to stimulate his imagination and emotions, and directed as to become disciplines." Reading, writing, and arithmetic are best learned in the setting of art—of use and play. Their theoretical part can be made thus to yield its meaning directly, without the intervention of misleading terms. If the word "play" worries anyone, he should remember that children are never so serious as when they are making things up.

The foregoing paragraph might appear to be a description of

what today is called progressive education. Within limits it is, for progressive education has hold of a good tradition; it is not physically brutal, and it makes no monstrous claims on the child's reason. Also, it assumes that the child is to be happy while he learns. So far there is nothing in it newer than Plato, just as there is nothing in it with which a sensible and humane adult could disagree.

1. Recall, if you will, your own elementary school days. How much "listening" was involved in the learning? How much "activity"? Do you recall that you learned any better under one method than the other?

2. Now recall your high school days. Was there more or less "listening" than in the elementary school? More or less "activity"? Do you think that Dewey's and Van Doren's suggestions might be more appropriate for younger than for older students?

3. Now turn to your college learning experiences. Select for comparison a "listening" class and an "activity" class, for example, a "lecture" class and a "discussion" or "laboratory" class. Do you seem to learn better in one situation than another? Is there a difference in the kind of learning? If so, how would you describe that difference?

4. How do you think you learn?

What Shall We Teach?

Few questions can stir livelier discussion among educators and citizens. Few questions are more crucial. The content of our teaching reveals what we consider to be important in education.

What *shall* we teach? For example, should we concentrate on the world around us, its people and physical wonders? Or should we teach that "immense antiquity," as Van Doren puts it, which can help explain the world around us?

Dewey was concerned about the school's isolation from the life around it. What the student learned in school, he said, has little to do with the world outside which the student touches, sees, and experiences. This world is the proper subject matter for his learning. Knowing *this* world he will be in a better position to explore its past and probe its future.

Van Doren viewed the question differently. Dewey is too concerned with the present, he said. Behind the present is the past. Further, the child does not exist for the present. He is on his way toward the future. Why make so much of the present? Instead, give him ideas which, like seeds, are "destined to germinate in later years."

Dewey: "He is unable to apply in daily life what he is learning in school."

From the standpoint of the child, the great waste in the school comes from his inability to utilize the experiences he gets outside the school in any complete and free way within the school itself; while on the other hand, he is unable to apply in daily life what he is learning at school. That is the isolation of the school—its isolation from life. When the child gets into the school room he has to put out of his mind a large part of the ideas, interest, and activities that predominate in his home and neighborhood. So the school, being unable to utilize this every day experience, sets painfully to work, on another track and by a variety of means, to arouse in the child an interest in school studies. While I was visiting in the city of Moline a few years ago, the superintendent told me that they found many children every year who were surprised to learn that the Mississippi River in the textbook had anything to do with the stream of water flowing past their house. The geography being simply a matter of the schoolroom, it is more or less of an awakening to many children to find that the whole thing is nothing but a more formal and definite statement of the facts which they see, feel, and touch every day. When we think that we all live on the earth, that we live in an atmosphere, that our lives are touched at every point by the influences of the soil, flora, and fauna, by considerations of light and heat, and then think of what the school study of geography has been, we have a typical idea of the gap existing between the everyday experiences of the child and the isolated material supplied in such large measure in the school. This is but an instance, and one upon which most of us may reflect long before we take the present artificiality of the school as other than a matter of course or necessity.

Van Doren: "The context of life is not confined to the contemporary."

Too many progressive educators worship this world. It may be bad enough to worship the world, but this world alone is less than the child deserves to be given. And the truth is that there is no such thing. There is a temporal depth behind every living form, an immense antiquity in which most of its meaning resides. The child loves knowing that his environment has more than spatial dimension. The context of his life is not confined to the contemporary, and even though this is never to be the explicit burden of the teaching he gets—for he is no antiquarian—it can remain like an aroma of authority over everything he hears. The perhaps mythical child who is ordered to do what he pleases knows that if nothing else his family has conditioned his choice. He might know that his family has been conditioned by thousands of generations before it, and that there is such a thing as common wisdom the source of which even scholars do not pretend to trace. When Gargantua commanded that the words "Do what thou wilt" be posted over the doorway at the abbey of Thélème, he understood that those who would read them were already possessed, happily or not, with principles of order. They are in us whether or not we like it. And education is the thing that tells us whether they are good. It should not suppress the probability that they are as hoary as the human race . . .

Memory is the mother of imagination, reason, and skill. "We estimate a man by how much he remembers," says Emerson. "We like signs of richness in an individual, and most of all we like a great memory. Memory performs the impossible for man; holds together past and present, gives continuity and dignity to human life. This is the companion, this the tutor, the poet, the library, with which you travel. Any piece of knowledge I acquire today has a value at this moment exactly proportioned to my skill to deal with it. Tomorrow, when I know more, I recall that piece of knowledge and use it better." It might seem that Emerson had said everything on the subject, but he added: "The reason of the short memory is shallow thought." If he had taken one more breath and said, "The reason for shallow thought is a short memory," he would have exhausted his topic.

There should be no school in which the young mind fails to receive, like seeds destined to germinate in later years, a full sowing of sentences great men have spoken—poems or parts of poems, and passages of prose—along with pieces of powerful music, glimpses of powerful painting, classical formulas in mathematics, chemistry, and physics, and the patterns of certain instruments without which science is helpless. We take it for granted that the multiplication tables must be learned, but those other things are no less necessary to the mind. Passages of verse or prose come back to us in middle age with interest which there are no tables to compute; if they were put there to stay, they may modify every thought and action when thought and action count. A medical diagnostician of our day attributes many of his insights to the lines of poetry his father once made him learn; their influence is indirect, but all the more potent for that reason. And this influence is more than something he uses in his trade. The good in such cases is general. So likewise with those items of memory which are more important still; early images of noble men—Socrates, for single example. There is no later substitute for these . . .

Here are two fundamentally different views on the question: What should we teach? Dewey believed that the everyday experiences of the everyday world provided a rich resource for learning. Further, since this is the world which children see, feel and touch every day, they are naturally interested and want to learn more about it. Understanding this world, he reasoned, they are more likely to want to explore matters which they *cannot* see, feel and touch.

Van Doren believes that Dewey's approach leads to "worship of this world" and that "this world alone is less than the child deserves to be given." Further, he says, "There is no such thing as this world . . . there is a temporal depth behind every living form." Therefore young minds should receive "a full sowing of sentences great men have spoken," for these sentences "come back to us in middle age with interest which there are no tables to compute."

> 5. Recall the content of a subject which you took in high school. How would have Dewey and Van Doren evaluated this content, using the standards set forth above? Would they have differed in their opinion of it? If so, how?
>
> 6. Take a subject matter area in which you would like to teach. Think of content first which would permit you to develop the course along the lines suggested by Van Doren. Now do the same for Dewey. How does the content differ? In which do you feel students would find the greater interest?

How Shall We Teach?

In this book we have observed a variety of methods of teaching. The one hundred student teachers demonstrated many different methods. The eight great teachers, who gave us their points of view on teaching, revealed their teaching methods. Mary Ellen Chase and Henry Johnson described their methods in some detail.

When Dewey turned to teaching methods he thought of an ideal home, where the child learns through the "social converse and constitution of the family." The ideal home is more than teacher and pupil, parent and child. It is a total teaching environment where there is give-and-take participation in work and play. The ideal school does "systematically" what most households do "only in a comparatively meager and haphazard manner."

Van Doren is concerned that this view of teaching leaves a child too much "to his own devices." Freedom in a child needs "discipline" to bring it out.

Dewey: "Learning? Certainly, but living primarily."

> If we take an example from an ideal home, where the parent is intelligent enough to recognize what is best for the child, and is able to supply what is needed, we find the child learning through the social converse and constitution of the family. There are certain points of interest and value to him in the conversation carried on: statements are made, inquiries arise, topics are discussed, and the

child continually learns. He states his experiences, his misconceptions are corrected. Again the child participates in the household occupations, and thereby gets habits of industry, order, and regard for the rights and ideas of others, and the fundamental habit of subordinating his activities to the general interest of the household. Participation in these household tasks becomes an opportunity for gaining knowledge. The ideal home would naturally have a workshop where the child could work out his constructive instincts. It would have a miniature laboratory in which his inquiries could be directed. The life of the child would extend out of doors to the garden, surrounding fields, and forests. He would have his excursions, his walks and talks, in which the larger world out of doors would open to him.

Now, if we organize and generalize all of this, we have the ideal school. There is no mystery about it, no wonderful discovery of pedagogy or educational theory. It is simply a question of doing systematically and in a large, intelligent, and competent way what for various reasons can be done in most households only in a comparatively meager and haphazard manner. In the first place, the ideal home has to be enlarged. The child must be brought into contact with more grown people and with more children in order that there may be the freest and richest social life. Moreover, the occupations and relationships of the home environment are not specially selected for the growth of the child; the main object is something else, and what the child can get out of them is incidental. Hence, the need of a school. In this school the life of the child becomes the all-controlling aim. All the media necessary to further the growth of the child center there. Learning? Certainly, but living primarily, and learning through and in relation to this living. When we take the life of the child centered and organized in this way, we do not find that he is first of all a listening being; quite the contrary. . . .

Van Doren: "The teacher who withholds his authority . . . is like a friend who will never give advice."

Freedom in a child is like freedom in any human being; discipline is wanted to bring it out. There is no beaten track of instinct down which the child goes without learning how to run. He hesitates, is undetermined and is suggestible. There are suggestions which he cannot and will not take, and this is one sign of his freedom; but there are others for which he will be grateful, and these will grow into another sign of his freedom. The teacher who withholds his authority when it is desired is like the friend who will never give advice; he is no true teacher. If he says in excuse that tyranny destroys individuals, he has forgotten that persons starve without guidance, and love those who lead them well. An error in direction could scarcely be worse than refusal to direct. Most progressive education is libeled when it is accused of refusing to lead—to perform that is, "the duty of the adult to the freedom of the youth." When it does so refuse, there seems to be no reason why it should be known as education at all. The child does not want to be cheap, but left to his own devices he may miss what is most dear. He should and will forgive no teacher who thus abandons him.

Dewey, for the record, did not suggest that the child be "left to his own devices." In a home, a child *may* be left to his own devices. But in Dewey's "ideal" home the child's "misconceptions are corrected," and he "gets habits of industry, order, and regard for the rights and ideas of others . . ."

What, then, is the real difference between Dewey's and Van Doren's views on the question: How shall we teach? It is this (and the matter will become more apparent in the next question): Dewey uses the child's *total* environment to teach; Van Doren depends primarily upon the teacher. In Van Doren's classroom the dominant relationship is that which exists between teacher and student. In Dewey's classroom there are many dominant relationships and the teacher uses them all to teach. At first glance it might seem as if Dewey's teacher has refused to lead. Not so. But he is leading in a different way, more like a parent in the informal environment of a home, than like, for example, a director of a band. The methods are different.

7. In question six it was suggested that you think of content in a course area, first from Dewey's and then Van Doren's point of view. When we use content, we move into the area of teaching methods. How would you use this content in the classroom first from Dewey's standpoint, then Van Doren's? How will your teaching methods differ?

8. Which method do you think will best hold the interest of your students?

What Is The Proper Focus For Teaching?

Should teaching focus on the child or on the thing to be learned? For Dewey the child is the "sun" about which teaching revolves. His interests, capacities, and needs should govern teaching. Further, when children act, he says, they individualize themselves. This calls for a flexible curriculum suited to individual needs.

For Van Doren the child exists already. He needs most of all to be taught. The thing to be learned should be the focus for teaching. This conception calls for a "fixed" program suitable for all children.

Dewey: "The change which is coming into our education is the shifting of the center of gravity."

Another thing that is suggested by [traditional] schoolrooms, with their set desks, is that everything is arranged for handling as large numbers of children as possible; for dealing with children *en masse*, as an aggregate of units; involving, again, that they be treated passively. The moment children act they individualize themselves; they cease to be a mass and become the intensely distinctive beings that we are acquainted with out of school, in the home, the family, on the playground, and in the neighborhood.

On the same basis is explicable the uniformity of method and curriculum. If everything is on a "listening" basis, you can have uniformity of material and method. The ear, and the book which reflects the ear, constitute the medium which is alike for all. There is next to no opportunity for adjustment to varying capacities and demands. There is a certain amount—a fixed quantity—of ready-made results and accomplishments to be acquired by all children alike in a given time. It is in response to this demand that the curriculum has been developed from the elementary school up through the college. There is just so much desirable knowledge, and there are just so many needed technical accomplishments in the world. Then comes the mathematical problem of dividing this by the six, twelve, or sixteen years of school life. Now give the children every year just the proportionate fraction of the total, and by the time they have finished they will have mastered the whole. By covering so much ground during this hour or day or week or year, everything comes out with perfect evenness at the end—provided the children have not forgotten what they have previously learned. The outcome for all this is Matthew Arnold's report of the statement, proudly made to him by an educational authority in France, that so many thousands of children were studying at a given hour, say eleven o'clock, just such a lesson in geography; and in one of our own western cities this proud boast used to be repeated to successive visitors by its superintendent.

I may have exaggerated somewhat in order to make plain the typical points of the old education: its passivity of attitude, its mechanical massing of children, its uniformity of curriculum and method. It may be summed up by stating that the center of gravity is outside the child. It is in the teacher, the textbook, anywhere and everywhere you please except in the immediate instincts and activities of the child himself. On that basis there is not much to be said about the *life* of the child. A good deal might be said about the studying of the child, but the school is not the place where the child *lives*. Now the change which is coming into our education is the shifting of the center of gravity. It is a change, a revolution, not unlike that introduced by Copernicus when the astronomical center shifted from the earth to the sun. In this case, the child becomes the sun about which the appliances of education revolve; he is the center about which they are organized.

Van Doren: "It is the mind that is to be educated."

Progressive education misses being perfect elementary education when it ignores . . . the deep resemblances between human beings, calling for a fixed program of learning which no child may evade. . . .

"By dint of insisting that in order to teach John mathematics it is more important to know John than to know mathematics—which is true enough in one sense—the teacher will so perfectly succeed in knowing John that John will never succeed in knowing mathematics." This sentence of Maritain's is more than witty, it points to the primacy of the thing to be learned; and it assumes that John is like any other boy in needing to be taught. He does not need to exist, for he exists already; but his very existence presupposes a readiness to know what the mind can know at this stage. It is his mind that is to be educated and it must be assumed that his mind is human. It may have special powers and graces, and one hopes it has. They will make themselves known, however, only when the regular business has been done. The teacher's business is regular. It is the only way in the long run to ripen these individual differences which some progressive educators prefer to pick and leave in the raw. . . .

Elementary education can do nothing better for a child than store his memory with things deserving to be there. He will be grateful for them when he grows up, even if he kicks now. They should be good things; indeed, they should be the best things, and all children should possess them. Some of the problems which society is said to face in the future might already be on their way to a solution, if all persons were certain to have common sentiments, and the sentiments were sound. Educational research in the fields of janitor service and reaction-counting might switch to the question of what children ought to remember. Education can afford to hold conferences about this for a hundred years; about this, and about the content of teaching on every higher level; for education will be saved only when it is agreed that men must know the same things—which does not mean that they will believe the same things. It means rather that they will be protected, in the only way education can bring this about, against mass judgments at the eleventh hour.

Here we observe Dewey and Van Doren in their sharpest disagreement. Dewey wants the learner to be deeply involved in his own learning, the very subject of the learning. Van Doren takes his existence for granted and makes him the object, the target, the recipient of learning. Dewey's learner is acting and "undergoing." Van Doren's learner is being acted upon.

The two men draw different conclusions about the meaning of individual differences. For Dewey individual differences suggest a "flexible" curriculum, adjusted "to varying capacities and demands." Van Doren hopes that each mind *will* have "special powers and graces." But persons need "common sentiments," and "all children" should possess them. The focus should be on the total group and common needs, rather than on the individual.

> 9. Can you recall two teachers who represent the points of view of Dewey and Van Doren regarding the focus of teaching? Did the different points of view result in different teaching methods? Did the different approaches make any difference in the kind or amount of learning which took place?

We have now examined four questions which are important in the conduct of any classroom. Can you now formulate your own tentative answers to these questions? For example,

How do we learn? We learn by . . . What shall we teach? We should teach . . . How shall we teach? The methods we employ . . . What is the proper focus for teaching? The proper focus for teaching is. . . .

Your preparation for teaching is the process of refining and enlarging your answers to questions like these. The important thing is that you start now to formulate your own answers after carefully thinking about the kinds of alternate answers which Dewey and Van Doren have presented in this chapter. Obviously, they are not the only answers. It is a mark of your own good judgment if, in this chapter, you have thought of answers other than those presented, or detected flaws in the answers presented.

We are ready now to pursue further the matter of learning. In these first six chapters our attention has focused sharply on teaching, with reflective questions about learning. In the next two chapters we focus on learning. Chapter seven deals with the learning around us. Chapter eight examines the learning in tomorrow's schools.

Good Follow-up Reading and Viewing

BOOKS

Association for Supervision and Curriculum Development, *What Shall The High Schools Teach?* Washington, D.C.: National Education Association, 1956. This yearbook identifies some of the problems and issues involved in determining what shall be taught and describes ways of handling these problems.

Broudy, Harry S., *Building a Philosophy of Education,* chaps. 6, 7, 8. Englewood Cliffs, N.J.: Prentice-Hall, Inc., 1954. An interesting presentation of what should be taught and how it should be taught.

Caswell, Hollis L., ed., *The American High School.* New York: Harper & Brothers, 1946. Chapter one discusses eight issues which confront educators today.

Chandler, J. B., *Education and The Teacher,* chap. 5, "Aims of Education." New York: Dodd, Mead & Co., 1961. Presents a number of key statements of educational aims which have promoted heated discussion in recent years.

Dewey, John, *Experience and Education.* New York: The Macmillan Co., 1938. The selection in this chapter is taken from this book in which Dewey presents his analysis of the modern versus traditional concepts of education.

Grobman, Hulda, and Vynce A. Hines, "Teacher as Conservator of The Past Versus Leader for Change," in *The Teacher's Role in American Society,* ed. Lindley J. Stiles, pp. 103-18. New York: Harper & Brothers, 1957. Discusses the alternative bases for selecting curricular content, and presents a recommended curriculum.

Haskew, Laurence D., *This Is Teaching,* chap. 7, "Ends Sought by Teaching." Chicago: Scott, Foresman & Company, 1956. Analyzes different goals of teaching and suggests criteria for choosing among them.

Henderson, Stella V., *Introduction to Philosophy of Education,* chap. 16. Chicago: University of Chicago Press, 1947. An examination of key questions regarding curriculum content and teaching methods from the point of view of an idealist philosophy.

Mayer, Frederick, *The Goals of Education.* Washington, D.C.: Public Affairs Press, 1959. This book looks at educational aims in terms of their relation to the life and culture surrounding the school.

McCloskey, Gordon, *et al., Introduction to Teaching In America,* chap. 23, "Educational Issues Before Teachers and Other Citizens." New York: Harcourt, Brace & World, Inc., 1954. Eleven basic questions in American education today, including matters related to standards, content and curriculum, relation of education to everyday life, pupil interest, methods, and aims.

Montaigne, Michel de, "Of Pedantry," *The Essays of Michel de Montaigne,* trans. George B. Ives. Cambridge, Mass.: Harvard University Press, 1925. Montaigne lashes out at teaching that fills only the memory, and leaves "the understanding and the conscience empty." We learn only from "immediate knowledge, not through that of the past, as little as through that of the future."

Phenix, Philip H., ed., *Philosophies of Education.* New York: John Wiley & Sons, Inc., 1961. This paperback volume presents various points of view about the purpose of education, written by their outstanding proponents. Thoroughly readable, with examples, questions and answers.

Rockefeller Brothers Fund, *The Pursuit of Excellence: Education and the*

Future of America, Special Studies Project Report 5. New York: Doubleday & Company, Inc., 1958. Focuses on the issues and challenges confronting American education.

Russell, Bertrand, *Education and The Good Life,* pp. 23-31. New York: Liveright Publishing Corp., 1926. The British philosopher asserts that the real issue in education is: Should education aim at knowledge that has practical value or should it give pupils knowledge for its own sake? "It is useful to know that there are twelve inches in a foot, but . . ."

Scott, Winfield, and Clyde Hill, *The Great Debate.* Englewood Cliffs, N.J.: Prentice-Hall, Inc., 1959. A collection of writings from books, newspapers, and magazines written by the critics and the defenders of education. Brings into sharp focus current issues in American education.

Thomas, Lawrence G., *et al., Perspective on Teaching,* chap. 3, "How is the Curriculum Determined?" Englewood Cliffs, N.J.: Prentice-Hall, Inc., 1961. A discussion of the influences which help to determine what is taught.

Woodring, Paul, *Let's Talk Sense About Our Schools.* New York: McGraw-Hill Book Co., Inc., 1953. The author proposes a reconciliation between the extremes of all-out progressivism or traditionalism. An objective analysis of the influence of John Dewey on our schools.

PERIODICALS

Adler, Mortimer J., and Schilpp, Paul A. "Are There Absolute and Universal Principles on Which Education Should Be Founded?" *Educational Trends,* Vol. 9, July-August, 1941, pp. 11-40. An absolutist says "Yes," a relativist, "No."

Bestor, Arthur, and Bigelow, Karl W., "How Should America's Teachers Be Educated?" *Teachers College Record,* Vol. 56, October, 1954, pp. 16-24. This pro-and-con discussion of teacher education sharpens the issues on the questions: What should the schools do?, and, how should they do it?

Carr, William G., "The Purposes of Education," *NEA Journal,* Vol. 47, May, 1958, pp. 303-04. The author believes that in the United States the schools lean toward a position that adjusts the educational program to the learner. "By a judicious balance between protective authority and delegation of responsibility, they seek to build in children a sense of security and a desire to achieve self-direction."

Davidson, Henry A., "Should Johnny Compete or Co-operate?" *NEA Journal,* Vol. 49, October, 1960, pp. 30-32. A psychiatrist, parent, and educator state their views about the proper role of the learner in school.

Gatchel, Richard H., "Evolution of Concepts of Indoctrination in American Education," *The Educational Forum,* Vol. 23, March, 1959, pp. 303-14. An interesting study of the development and evolution of the concept of indoctrination in American education.

Grinnel, John E., "Our Most Dangerous Neglect," *Phi Delta Kappan,* Vol. 41, February, 1960, pp. 213-16. The author makes a plea that the schools do more than have youth "study the lives of great and good men." They must take active leadership in helping children and youth to handle pressing social problems.

Hand, Harold C., "The Case For a Common Learnings Program," *Science Education,* Vol. 32, February, 1948, pp. 5-11. Asserts that the needs of society and the needs of children should be combined to form a program of common learnings.

Kerlinger, Fred N., "Progressivism and Traditionalism, Basic Educational Attitudes," *The School Review*, Vol. 46, Spring, 1958, pp. 80-92. Reviews two studies which give partial answers to these questions: Are there people whose attitudes toward education are basically progressive? Are there people whose attitudes toward education are basically traditional? Do progressivism and traditionalism really exist? What is their nature?

Lancelot, W. H., "The Academic Scholars' Feud With The Educators," *The Educational Forum*, Vol. 25, January, 1961, pp. 161-65. An examination of the actual differences between subject matter and professional education specialists and a suggestion that the different viewpoints be reconciled.

Lerner, Max, "Americanization: Goals and Values," *NEA Journal*, Vol. 47, October, 1958, pp. 458-59. This widely known author contends that education's task is to shape young people "primarily as valued creators in a democracy, as young people who can develop their own kind of personality, their own kind of thinking in a society where our principal weapon is freedom."

"Let's Balance The Program," *NEA Journal*, Vol. 47, February, 1958, pp. 79-90. A series of three articles devoted to a fresh consideration of America's educational needs in a satellite-haunted world. The role of science, mathematics, and the humanities.

McCaul, Robert L., and Dunkel, Harold B., "Dewey Centennial Issue," *The School Review*, Vol. 67, Summer, 1959. This noteworthy issue is devoted to Dewey, his life, times, and influence. A good capsule overview.

Patrick, T. L., "A College President Speaks on Teacher Training," *The Educational Forum*, Vol. 25, January, 1961, pp. 199-202. Some excellent answers to fundamental questions raised in this chapter.

Pierce, Paul R., "Agreements on Curriculum," *Phi Delta Kappan*, Vol. 41, March, 1960, pp. 265-69. The author thinks there is over-emphasis on disagreements in education and presents evidence to show that curriculum authorities, especially, agree on certain basic principles.

Susky, John E., "How Would Dewey Answer Critics of 'Deweyism'?" *Phi Delta Kappan*, Vol. 40, October, 1958, pp. 24-27. The author uses Dewey references and quotations to answer critics who assert that Dewey's philosophy is responsible for an exclusive emphasis on methodology which neglects subject matter.

Taylor, Harold, "The Understood Child," *Saturday Review*, May 20, 1961, pp. 47-49, 66. This article asks whether the child-centered school helps the child grow to maturity, or creates new problems for him?"

FILMS

Curriculum Based on Child Development

Describes various techniques and procedures which can be used effectively in gearing a curriculum to the developmental level of the children. Shows what kinds of teaching materials and techniques can be used and what characteristics of the children they reflect. (McGraw-Hill Book Co., Inc., black and white, 12 minutes.)

Design of American Public Education

Compares the "assembly line" program of education with a democratic system's curriculum adapted to community and individual needs. Typical state, county, and local situations. Relation of organization to nature of the educational program. (McGraw-Hill Book Co., Inc., black and white, 16 minutes.)

Importance of Goals

A boy's natural curiosity thwarted in school; he becomes bored. By contrast, he readily learns to gain recognition, to overcome jealousy, and to keep his small newspaper business flourishing because there are definite goals involved. Teacher finally realizes what has been missing in the classroom. (McGraw-Hill Book Co., Inc., black and white, 20 minutes.)

Promoting Pupil Adjustment

Shows how important it is for the secondary school teacher to stress the social and emotional as well as the intellectual growth of his pupils. Points out that effective classroom learning is closely associated with the teacher's awareness of individual differences. (McGraw-Hill Book Co., Inc., black and white, 20 minutes.)

School—The Child's Community

Ways in which school can encourage children to accept responsibilities and share in the making of decisions that concern them. Student participation in the "community" activities of an elementary school. (Wayne University, black and white, 17 minutes.)

PART **4**

LEARNING: REMARKABLE PRODUCT OF TEACHING

Chapter 7: The Learning Around Us
Chapter 8: Learning in Tomorrow's Schools

THE LEARNING AROUND US

That's my name!

A LITTLE BOY

The little boy who lives at our house marched home from school recently, eyes flashing. Coming straight to the study, he announced: "Look Daddy, if you'll give me a piece of paper and a pencil, I'll show you a wonderful surprise!" Pulling himself up into a chair beside the desk, he gripped his pencil hard and bent over his urgent work.

Slowly he carved out four large block letters. He finished the final letter, laid down the pencil, and picked up the paper. With a burst of shameless pride he asserted: "I'll bet you don't know what that says." Detecting a moment's hesitation, he rushed on: "That's my name!" And so it was.

A month earlier his interest in making letters was only beginning. Now he could print his name. A month later he had increased his repertoire of letters and words considerably. He was learning.

WHAT IS LEARNING?

During these two months, a significant change had taken place in the little boy. We call this change learning. Learning is shown by changes in behavior resulting from life experiences. The little boy had experienced a whole series of new events. The result: learning which enabled him to print his name. Learning may be called the act of acquiring new behavior.

Learning Is A Common Experience Of Life

We sometimes mistakenly think of learning as something which goes on exclusively in classrooms, or results from reading books. Learning is far more pervasive. Living itself is a learning process. In fact, it's hard to keep people from learning. The teacher who complains that "Johnny simply won't learn" perhaps should say that he won't learn "the things I want him to learn." For Johnny is probably learning many things, among them a dislike for what the teacher wants him to learn.

People, children and adults, demonstrate each day their ability to change behavior through learning. Both teachers and parents observe these changes almost daily in children and youth. They are a constant source of inspiration and bafflement.

We know a great deal about learning. Research tells us much about what it is, the conditions which encourage or impede it, and the principles which seem to govern it. There is much, however, which we don't know about learning. Each teacher through study and skilled observation can add to our understanding of the remarkable process called learning.

WHAT MAKES LEARNING POSSIBLE?

Let's look closer at the learning demonstrated by the little fellow printing his name. What were the major factors at play in this scene? First, there is a *boy*. Like most normal children he is full of human potential for learning. His active body pulsates with life. He possesses the physical equipment necessary to learn. Second, there is an *environment*. It consists of all those influences which surround him at home, at school, and in the community. He has helped to create some of this environment, but for the most part it was ready-made when he arrived. If he keeps up his present impetuous pace, the chances are he will alter it some. Third, there is *interaction* between the boy and his environment. Neither the boy nor the environment will hold still. They are very much alive, acting upon one another, reacting, tugging, and pulling. The encounter between the two will leave its mark on each of them, sometimes in tears, sometimes in laughter.

In these three—the *boy,* the *environment,* and the *interaction* between the two—we have the three major factors which generate learning and make it possible. Let's look at the three more closely.

The Boy Is Full Of Learning Potential

Let the boy represent any child full of human learning potential. Count his physical assets for learning. Learning is an active process and the boy is active. He goes to life; he does not wait for it to come to him. He reaches for what he cannot touch, runs to what he cannot understand, tastes what he cannot otherwise figure out. He stands rather than sits, runs rather than walks, yells rather than talks. He eats with gusto, sleeps with abandon, lives the hours in between with daring. He enjoys living.

His life consists of new experiences, and each new experience is capable of producing new learning. Why? Largely because his physical endowments have made him capable of experiencing and learning. His keen senses are gateways to the world around him. Through them he gets vivid impressions of his environment. Through sight the three dimensional world comes pouring in upon him. His ears are the sound track, recording all the exciting sounds within reach. Through smell he discriminates between sensations pleasant and unpleasant. By taste he flavors his world. By touch he examines it. Through all these senses he learns about his world, interprets it, accepts or rejects it, adds to his ever-increasing understanding of it.

What if he had none of these senses? Without his physical endowments for learning, he would be isolated, cut off from the stimulation to learn. He would not learn. Or, if any of his physical equipment is impaired through accident or poor health, his learning ability will surely be impaired. Good health is essential to good learning.

> 1. Not all ill health or physical disability affects the ability to learn. It depends, of course, upon the nature of the illness or impairment. Have you ever lived or worked with a person whose ill health or physical disability was such that it affected his learning? Can you describe how the learning was influenced?

The Environment Determines What And How We Learn

A healthy body equips the boy to learn. What he learns and how he learns depends in large measure upon his environment. The environment determines what he shall see, hear, smell, touch, and taste. If this environment is alive, full of exciting learning experiences, he will probably learn rapidly and well. If his environment is dull, repetitious, and without challenge, he will probably learn slowly and poorly.

Return for a moment to the little boy and his printed name. Can we identify factors in his environment which helped him in his achievement? In a way such an attempt is risky. Such factors are hard to identify. Some factors which an adult may name may not be important at all in the life of the child. And there is a pretty good chance that an adult may overlook completely certain factors which were very important in enabling the child to achieve a particular learning. With this limitation in mind, we can examine a few of the environmental influences which helped the boy to learn to print his name.

The home is the young child's center of living. From the beginning, words used in the home are important. The most important people in his life use them. With words he is loved, disciplined, taught. When he uses his first nonsense syllables he is cuddled and rewarded. His meaningless prattle grows into meaningful words with which he discovers he can control his environment. He asks for things and makes his feelings known.

Then one day he discovers that words are also contained in children's books. They are associated with interesting pictures and stories. He continually begs for "just one more story." He starts to notice individual words. "What does that word say . . . *that* word?" Then comes the big discovery. His name is also a word. *His* name, the most important word of all. He looks at it in print, completely absorbed.

He begins to recognize the individual letters in his name. Then he sees those letters in the word of the story. He interrupts the reading to point to a letter. "That's in my name," he shouts, proud of his new learning.

He recognizes other letters besides those in his name. His knowledge of letters is spreading to include the whole alphabet.

During this time he fills many sheets of paper with carefully drawn letters. Short words from stories are copied. These he proudly displays; they are properly admired. He requests that his handiwork be hung on the wall above his bed for all to see.

While these events have been going on at home, equally significant events have been happening at school. There the little boy joins 25 other youngsters, all learning to use words and letters. There the teacher, representing the important adult in his life, writes letters and words on the chalkboard, flashes them on cards, uses them in sentences, and reads them in stories. The school has reinforced the importance of using words and letters.

It also increased the satisfaction for doing so. The boy likes the "fun" of going to the blackboard to pick out a letter the teacher has asked him to find, or to make the first letter of his name. He enjoys the stimulation of the peer group.

One thing is significant in this brief analysis. At no particular point is the child specifically "taught" to print his name. Then how did he learn? The answer has deep implications for all who teach. Review the main features of the environment. Words and letters were of vital importance. They were important continuously in the life of the child. They were connected with his deepest motivations: bodily wants, parental and teacher approval, exciting stories, status within the peer group, his name. He was always free to experiment with them on his own, to try his own hand at writing and copying. Page after page was filled; pencil after pencil was worn to a nub. We said earlier that it was almost impossible to keep people from learning. In this environment it would have been almost impossible to keep the boy from learning. Had he not learned to print his name, one would suspect some special defect. ☀ The point is this: Learning is a normal process resulting from life experiences. We will learn those things which pervade our environment. Teaching becomes a problem in creating those environmental conditions which encourage the kind of learning which is desired. ☀

> 2. Select a skill which you know, for example, driving a car, typewriting, swimming, or riding a bicycle. What role did the environment play in your learning? Did it impede or encourage? What factors in the environment caused you to learn?

Interaction With The Environment Helps Determine The Rate And Quality Of Learning

The boy learned to print his name because he was able to interact with his environment. The rate and the quality of learning depend upon this inter-stimulation. It is almost impossible to imagine a child completely cut off from his environment. Still, opportunities to interact with surroundings certainly differ among children. Some children are permitted to participate freely with their surroundings; they are permitted to dabble, work, and experience. Such freedom encourages learning. For other children the environment is full of "off limits" and "taboo" signs. Some of these are needed, of course, for the sake of the child's health and safety. Beyond these limits, however, too many restrictions may stifle his natural desire to explore his world.

"Off limits" and "taboo" signs can be erected for a child in many ways. Authoritarian parents will ask that a child accept their word instead of firsthand exploration on the part of the child. The child may be permitted to explore freely, but he may be punished if the results of his exploration are bad, for example, if his clothes are torn or if the dish is broken. A few such incidents will certainly discourage further learning through exploration.

What is the ideal interaction for learning? It encourages full participation of the child with his environment in those areas which fall within his general range of development. It permits give and take, trial and error, exploration. The environment is available to the child, subject to the normal precautions to protect his health, safety, and the rights of others.

> 3. In question two you selected a skill which you know and examined the environment in which you learned it. Now look more closely at the *interaction* that took

place between yourself and the environment as you were learning the skill. How did the interaction effect your learning?

4. Recall for a moment the put-in and draw-out concepts of teaching about which we spoke in chapter four. Which of these concepts, in your opinion, is more apt to lend itself in practice to a free interaction between the learner and his environment? Can you explain why?

THESE FACTORS STIMULATE LEARNING

We have just examined those factors which make learning possible. Other factors stimulate and facilitate learning. These also are apparent in the case of the little boy and his name. We can use his experience to illustrate.

The factors which we shall discuss here are five in number: (1) *Readiness,* (2) *Motivation,* (3) *Satisfaction,* (4) *Activity,* and (5) *Security.*

Readiness Tells Us When A Child Can Learn

There came a time when the little boy was ready to print his name. When he was ready, he learned to do so. Would pushing him to print his name at an earlier time have hastened his accomplishment? It is doubtful. Perhaps a week or so, possibly a month, could have been gained. It may have been gained at the expense of his attitude toward learning, with damaging effect later.

There is time for learning. The time comes when the sum of all the factors which influence it combine to produce the desired result. The little boy was apparently ready physically. His muscular coordination had developed to the point which permitted him to hold and move the pencil. His sight was capable of monitoring those movements, of making a correction when needed. Mentally and emotionally he was prepared.

When are we ready to learn? Each stage of development has its own appropriate tasks. The child who begins to color cannot keep the crayon inside the lines. Later when his muscular coordination is improved, he has no difficulty doing so. Roller skating is difficult, if not impossible, for the young child to learn; it is easy when he grows older.

Readiness influences the child's interests. The child who shys away from other children at three years of age is eager to play with them at six. The little boy who likes girls at five years of age has changed his opinion at ten, and will reverse himself again at fifteen.

Readiness applies to school learning. Learning to read is a good example. Experienced teachers expect that children of the same age will learn to read at different times and with different degrees of skill. They become "ready" to read at different times. The same may be said for learning arithmetic or other school subjects.

The implication for teachers is clear. The teacher must know the signs of readiness for a given learning and must plan the instructional program to fit the individual readiness of children.

> 5. Let's assume that you are teaching in a typical graded school system. You have thirty to forty students of approximately the same chronological age. But in terms of readiness to learn what you are teaching you discover they are many different ages. What are some of the things you might consider doing in order to meet this situation? Ask an experienced teacher how he handles this problem.

Motivation Creates A Desire To Learn

Readiness alone is not enough. There must be desire to learn. Motivation is the driving force which causes us to want to learn. We feel the need to learn. We are motivated.

The little boy wanted very much to write his name. Others around him were writing their names, even his name. His efforts were praised and he achieved status by his new accomplishment.

Motivation derives from many sources. Mostly it springs from our wants. If the new learning promises to satisfy some of our wants, we improve our chances of learning. We learn those things which we want to learn; when learning satisfies the wants, we may be said to be motivated.

> 6. Do you do better scholastically in certain subjects than others? Is it possible to explain this in terms of motivation, or the lack of it? Can you explain why you are more motivated to learn certain subjects than others?

Satisfaction Encourages Learning

Learning is encouraged when the results are satisfying to the learner. If the results are distasteful, learning will take place slowly or not at all. Or, things learned will be quickly unlearned.

Writing his own name is a satisfying experience in many ways for a child. It is creative. It is immediately rewarding, can be seen, held up, admired. He gets a thrill in holding the pencil firmly, guiding it according to his own will, watching the name unravel.

Immediate satisfaction is important in learning. The promise of delayed satisfaction is not a strong stimulant to learning, though teachers and parents use it repeatedly. "Eat your vegetables in order to grow big and strong," has questionable appeal. "Learn algebra now because you will need it later," has probably caused few students to learn algebra.

Learning, to be effective, should carry within it its own and immediate satisfactions.

> 7. Take a subject area in which you would like to teach. Can you make a list of five ways in which the subject can be taught in order to yield immediate satisfactions to the learners in your class?

Activity Promotes Learning

We said that learning is an active process. The little boy found pleasure in the activity of learning to write his name. He was anything but passive about it. He was not a sponge, soaking up the knowledge necessary to write his name. He learned to print his name through action which was appropriate to learning. He actually experienced the learning as it took place. In a sense he earned through work the right to his new skill. He bent over sheet after sheet of paper in trial and error experimentation. He spent hours copying letters from books and magazines. He poured over many of his favorite stories looking for familiar letters. In acquiring new skill he was constantly on the offensive, ever in motion, attacking the unknown.

Traditional education frequently ignored the activity aspect of learning. It made sponges of learners, with the teacher providing the material to be soaked up. Children were supposed to sit quietly, be attentive, read lessons, recite. Personal exploration in order to learn was missing.

Now we know that "learning" and "experiencing" are closely related. To ask the learner to learn while being inactive is asking the difficult, if not impossible. Learning is a very personal affair. It must be achieved by the individual through his own efforts. In a very real sense it cannot be "given" to him. He cannot be "taught," except as he is given opportunity to teach himself. He is his own best teacher and, in a sense, his only teacher.

What does this mean for those of us who call ourselves teachers? It means that we cannot really teach at all, in the usual sense. We must provide the right materials, in the right environment, under the right leadership to permit the learners to teach themselves. This is a big, big, order, a much bigger order than confronted the traditional teacher in the traditional classroom. Here the teacher could prepare a lesson plan to cover the entire class, teach the plan through lecture, drill, and recitation. The student's job was to soak up what was given and give it back to the teacher on request. The activity on the learner's part was limited to this.

The modern teacher needs to be more resourceful, but the job is more rewarding. His job is to put each pupil into a position of self-learning and exploring. He surrounds him with the tools of learning, creates a classroom climate conducive to it, and directs the activities. But it is always the pupil who carries out the activities and in the process learns by teaching himself.

8. Turn again to a subject you would like to teach. Can you name five activities which you could develop which would help the learner's "teach themselves"?

Security Is A Pre-condition For Learning

Learning is encouraged if the learner feels secure in his environment. Experienced teachers can readily identify those children who have insecure home lives. The classroom, too, can be an insecure place for a child. Perhaps he is not accepted by the other children. He may not feel secure in the affections of the teacher. His attempts at learning may be frustrated by repeated failure. He lacks confidence. Such insecurity has a measurable effect on how well he learns.

Feelings of security, on the other hand, foster learning. They free the learner of emotional blocks which impede learning. They permit him to concentrate on the matter at hand.

One source of security is acceptance. If the child feels that he is accepted by those persons who are significant in his life, his learning potential will be greater. His peers, his teacher, his parents are all "important others." How they view his learning efforts is important to him. It shapes his own attitude toward learning.

The little boy discussed earlier sensed that printing his name was a valued achievement both at home and at school. His efforts along the way to the big achievement were supported by the important people in his life. He was encouraged in many ways. Paper and pencils were provided for his explorations in print. Questions about the shape of letters were willingly answered. His work was admired and corrections suggested. All this implied that what he was doing was important, and it was freely endorsed by the important adults in his life. Moreover, what he was doing suggested that *he* was important to the adults in his life. He had good reason to feel secure and to learn.

9. Consider again the put-in and draw-out approaches to teaching. Do you think one approach is more apt to encourage feelings of psychological security in the learner than the other?

We have examined an example of learning, which we define as a change in behavior resulting from life experiences. The little boy's seemingly simple act of learning to print his name is really a complex act, involving many elements.

Basic elements in a learning situation are the *person* and his human potential for learning, the *environment* in which he lives, and the *interaction* which takes place between the two. These three, put together, make learning possible. The human potential for learning is high when the physical and emotional resources are sound. The environment is good for learning when it is alive with learning challenges. The interaction is favorable toward learning when the environment is freely available to the learner, and when it invites exploration.

Other elements encourage and stimulate learning: Readiness means that the learner is prepared to accomplish the task set before him. All of the factors necessary to learn are focused in readiness. Motivation is the drive to learn. When learning can fulfill wants, motivation results. Closely associated with motivation is satisfaction as a stimulant to learning. Learning which involves pleasurable activity as it is carried on will be more effective than learning which does not give such satisfaction. Activity enriches learning experiences. Learning is an active, rather than passive, process. Feelings of well-being and security release the learner to acquire new behavior free of impediments.

We are now ready, in the next chapter, to bring together what we know about learning. We ask: What makes for good *school* learning? In order to get an answer we shall take a field trip, a different kind of field trip. We shall visit a school system which never was! Indeed, it has no schools at all. But it does have an effective system of teaching and learning. If this sounds puzzling, the answer is that we shall visit Utopia.

Good Follow-up Reading and Viewing

BOOKS

Barker, Roger T., and Herbert F. Wright, *One Boy's Day*, pp. 67-113. New York: Harper & Brothers, 1951. A record of one day in the life of a seven year old boy.

Bettelheim, Bruno, *Love Is Not Enough*. Glencoe, Ill.: The Free Press of Glencoe, Illinois, 1950. Case studies of emotionally disturbed children with an active aversion for learning. The studies illuminate the problem of working with more "normal" children who may not like studying.

Burton, William H., *The Guidance of Learning Activities*. New York: Appleton-Century-Crofts, Inc., 1944. An informative discussion of learning, what it is, and how it takes place.

Cantor, Nathaniel, *The Teaching-Learning Process*. New York: Dryden, 1953. A college class of prospective teachers raises questions with their professor about the teaching-learning process. Result: a lively presentation of a modern view.

Corey, Stephen M., *Psychological Foundations of General Education*, Part I, National Society for the Study of Education Yearbook. Chicago: University of

Chicago Press, 1952. A sound discussion of the principles of learning.

Cronbach, Lee J., *Educational Psychology*, chap. 3, "An Introduction to the Learning Process." New York: Harcourt, Brace & World, Inc., 1954. Since learning involves a change in behavior, the author begins by noting seven elements of behavior and proceeds to discuss what we mean by learning and how we tend to oversimplify learning theories. Excellent classroom portrait of learning.

Dewey, John, *The Child and the Curriculum*. Chicago: University of Chicago Press, 1902. This early book of Dewey's is considered a classic in the treatment of learning and education.

Frandsen, Arden, *How Children Learn*, chap. 8, "Motivation and Learning." New York: McGraw-Hill Book Co., Inc., 1957. A good discussion of motivation and some excellent illustrations of classroom motivation.

Gates, Arthur, *et al.*, *Educational Psychology*. New York: The Macmillan Co., 1942. Chapter nine develops a definition of learning and discusses the learning process.

————, *Educational Psychology*, chap. 10, "The General Nature of Learning II." New York: The Macmillan Co., 1948. Describes the learning process as the effort to surmount obstacles and attain goals. The concepts of "trial and error," "insight," and "differentiation" are defined and discussed.

McCloskey, Gordon, *et al.*, *Introduction to Teaching in America*, chap. 8, "What is Learning?" New York: Harcourt, Brace & World, Inc., 1954. An excellent discussion of modern concepts of learning.

Thomas, Lawrence G., *et al.*, *Perspective on Teaching*, chap. 8, "Why Children Don't Learn What They Are Taught." Englewood Cliffs, N.J.: Prentice-Hall, Inc., 1961. Learning is viewed through the teaching act, with four aspects of the act described.

Trow, William Clark, *The Learning Process*. Washington, D.C.: National Education Association, 1954. This thirty-three page pamphlet is a part of the "What Research Says" series and presents a capsule account of readiness, goal attainment, reward and punishment, and repetition.

PERIODICALS

"About Motivation," *NEA Elementary Instructional Service Leaflet,* The Association, Washington, D.C. A useful eight-page leaflet illustrating how teachers can discover and use that motivation which comes from within and has a self sustaining quality of its own.

Burton, William H., "Basic Principles in a Good Teaching-Learning Situation," *Phi Delta Kappan,* Vol. 39, March, 1958, pp. 242-48. A long-time leader in the guidance of learning activities sets forth a concise set of principles soundly based on research. Included topics: general purposes of learning, general principles of learning and relearning, the group process, security, motivation, readiness, and principles of teaching.

"Creativity," *NEA Journal,* Vol. 50, March, 1961, pp. 17-27. A series of four valuable articles on creativity, dealing with research findings, creativity in the elementary classroom and a summer arts center.

Dowell, Pattie Simmons, "Learning Workshop," *NEA Journal,* Vol. 49, March, 1960, pp. 56-57. Illustrates how the elementary classroom can be made into an attractive learning workshop.

Morgan, Gerthon H., "How To Facilitate Learning," *NEA Journal*, Vol. 49, October, 1960, pp. 54-55. The author draws on concepts which explain growth, development, and behavior, and suggests some facts which can help the teacher to facilitate learning.

Thomas, Murry R., "Invitation to Learning," *NEA Journal*, Vol. 48, March, 1959, pp. 61-63. An interesting discussion of readiness, motivation, and individual differences.

Vincent, Nicholas M. P., and Helen L. Merrill, "Effective Classroom Motivation," *Peabody Journal of Education*, Vol. 38, July, 1960, pp. 10-13. The authors describe motivational factors and suggest that if students are motivated to work and study they will have little desire or time to create disturbances.

Wright, Herbert F., "How The Psychology of Motivation is Related to Curriculum Development," *Journal of Educational Psychology*, Vol. 39, 1958, pp. 149-56. The author explores the concept of "pupil needs" in education and explains how they may be used in teaching.

FILMS

Effective Learning in the Elementary School

A fifth grade teacher relates some of her experiences in making learning more effective; how she uses unit-study projects and student-teacher planning to increase motivation for learning basic skills. (McGraw-Hill Book Co., Inc., black and white, 20 minutes.)

Making Learning More Meaningful

Teaching through the use of concrete experiences. Examples from third grade arithmetic class. Motivation and learning based on child interests. (McGraw-Hill Book Co., Inc., black and white, 11 minutes.)

Motivating the Class

Importance of motivation in good teaching. A young math teacher loses the attention of his students through failure to arouse their interest, then succeeds through learning situations of immediate concern to them. Individual differences; competition; purposeful activity. (McGraw-Hill Book Co., Inc., black and white, 19 minutes.)

Motivation Through Unit Teaching

Motivation as key to learning and achievement; how basic needs of pupils for security, success, recognition, and knowledge are used to achieve understanding, skills, attitudes, interests, and social skills through unit teaching. (Iowa State Teachers College, black and white, 25 minutes.)

LEARNING IN TOMORROW'S SCHOOLS

The most Utopian thing in Utopia is that there are no schools
at all.

JOHN DEWEY

The New York Times [1] once asked John Dewey to write an article
describing education in Utopia. For the article Dewey cast himself in
the role of an inquisitive visitor in the land of the Utopians. He observed their educational system and asked questions about it. Dewey's
account of his mythical visit to Utopia forms the case for discussion in
this chapter.

Utopia is an ideal place which does not really exist. It is the kind of
place man would create for himself were he not limited by the hard
realities of this world. Still, Utopias are valuable. They remind us of
what can be, and they encourage us to make this world better. For this
reason we are going to visit the educational Utopia about which John
Dewey wrote.

Utopia will never be attained; perhaps it should not be. Indeed, it
would not be Utopia if it were attainable. But in comparing educational
Utopia and educational reality we achieve a clearer understanding of
reality, and we are in a better position to improve upon it.

We said Utopias were not attainable. This isn't quite true. Man has
a way of attaining them which, once attained, cease to be Utopias. Man
must then create new Utopias, farther yet beyond his reach. This comment has relevance in the case of Dewey's article. As you will discern,
(in the space of approximately one generation) we have made great

---

[1] *The New York Times,* April 23, 1933.

strides toward achieving the Utopia which Dewey described. One's imagination cannot resist the exciting speculation about educational changes that are likely to take place in the coming generation.

The basic questions which Dewey's Utopia raise are these: What is an ideal place in which to learn? What is it really like? How close are we coming to making our schools ideal places in which to learn?

Many factors in a school influence the learning which goes on there. Several of these important factors are (1) the physical environment; (2) the teacher; (3) the way learning is carried on; and (4) the objectives of the learning.

Let's cast these influences in the form of questions: What is the best physical environment for school learning? What qualities should teachers possess? How should learning be carried on? What should be the learning objectives?

In this chapter we shall observe how the Utopians answered these questions in relation to their own learning enterprise. But we want to do more than that. We want to develop answers for ourselves and our own classrooms. Our procedure will be to observe the Utopian practice in relation to each question and then examine its implications for our own school learning.

WHAT IS THE BEST PHYSICAL ENVIRONMENT FOR SCHOOL LEARNING?

If you were to design a school in order to promote the best possible learning, how would you design it? Would you make it one big building with long corridors and classrooms on each side? Would you make a campus-type school with clusters of rooms scattered about with open places between? Do you think the design of a school makes any difference in the learning which takes place there?

What would your classrooms be like? What kind of furniture would you have? How would you arrange your classroom? How about the lighting? Color scheme?

All these factors influence learning. Let's see how the Utopians whom Dewey visited handled them.

> The most Utopian thing in Utopia is that there are no schools at all. Education is carried on without anything of the nature of schools, or, if this idea is so extreme that we cannot conceive of it as education at all, then we may say nothing of the sort at present we know as schools. Children, however, are gathered together in association with older and more mature people who direct their activity.

The assembly places all have large grounds, gardens, orchards, greenhouses, and none of the buildings in which children and older people gather will hold much more than 200 people, this having been found to be about the limits of close, intimate personal acquaintance on the part of the people who associate together.

And inside these buildings, which are all of them of the nature of our present open-air schools in their physical structure, there are none of the things we usually associate with our present schools. Of course, there are no mechanical rows of screwed-down desks. There is rather something like a well-furnished home of today, only with a much greater variety of equipment and no messy accumulations of all sorts of miscellaneous furniture; there are more open spaces than our homes have today.

Then there are the workshops, with their apparatus for carrying on activities with all kinds of material—wood, iron, textiles. There are historic museums and scientific laboratories, and books everywhere as well as a central library.

1. Why do you think the Utopians had no schools at all, at least no schools as we think of them?

2. Do you think children will learn among gardens, greenhouses, workshops, laboratories, and libraries—all furnished like a home, except with more equipment? Will they learn better than in traditional schools?

From Dewey's description we gather that there are no formal classes, no lessons in the usual sense, no rigid assignments. There apparently are no school bells which signal the end of one activity and beginning of another. Interests govern the schedule rather than arbitrary time limits.

Then actually what is there in this Utopian learning setting? Mostly, the physical setting provides the opportunity to learn through personal exploration and *activity*. The Utopians believed that learning is stimulated when children can teach themselves through observation and experimentation in gardens, greenhouses, workshops, laboratories and libraries. Doing, under supervision, is the important element in learning for the Utopians. They believed that the environment should be *available* to children. Children should not be confined to desks. The "school" should be a work place where the children *interact* freely with their surroundings.

Would a child feel *secure* in these surroundings? The environment does not threaten or punish. The emphasis is upon opportunity to explore interests and develop them. The environment is that of a home, rather than an impersonal institution.

Are the Utopians recognizing the problems of *readiness?* Probably so. There is a great range of learning activities available to children. Most children would find an activity suited to their present development. The children are not forced into a lock step curriculum in which each child does the same thing as all the other children.

Do you think children would be *motivated* to learn in this environment? Do the available activities touch the immediate wants and interests of children? We know that children are less interested in abstractions than concrete things which they can actually experience. If a child did not already possess motivation to learn, I think we can say he might develop some here as he ranged across the large number of available activities.

Would learning in this environment bring immediate *satisfaction* for the learners? The chances are pretty good that learners would enjoy their learning. We know that children are absorbed by things concrete and real. They love to handle and touch, to take apart and create. They like best the direct experience.

Before leaving the topic of physical environment in Utopia, let us compare it with real schools. How do they differ? Utopian schools are magnificently furnished, with gardens, greenhouses, museums, scientific laboratories, and workshops. Only a select few of our schools can afford all of these. Yet, a revolution is taking place in school building design, and many schools have some of these features and are finding them all conducive to learning. With their bright colors, light and airy spaces, functional furniture, and exciting instructional materials, the schools have borrowed heavily from those in Utopia.

Perhaps the main thing we can learn from the Utopians is this: Physical environment has great influence upon learning. The school and the classroom, which provide the qualities which Utopians had achieved, extend a cordial invitation to learning.

> 3. Recall a new school you have observed recently. (If you haven't seen a new school recently, perhaps you can visit one). Talk to the teachers and administrators about their school building as a place to learn. How do you evaluate this physical environment for learning? Prepare a report on your observations for the class.
>
> 4. Check the references at the end of this chapter on school building design. Then prepare a report on what you think the school building of 1980 will be like.

WHAT QUALITIES SHOULD TEACHERS POSSESS?

We observed in Chapter 7 how important adults are in a child's learning. They influence *all* the factors of learning. They are an important part of the environment. They govern the interaction of the child and his environment. They motivate or fail to motivate, give satisfaction or withhold it, encourage or discourage activity, give security or insecurity. Who teaches helps to determine who learns and what is learned.

Who, then, should teach? What standards should be used for selection? What qualities would you look for? Here are the qualities which Dewey reports the Utopians sought:

> The adults who are most actively concerned with the young have, of course, to meet a certain requirement, and the first thing that struck me as a visitor to Utopia was that they must all be married persons, and, except in the exceptional cases, must have had children of their own. Unmarried, younger persons occupy places of assistance and serve a kind of initiatory apprenticeship. Moreover, older children, since there are no arbitrary divisions into classes, take part in directing the activities of those still younger.

> The activity of these older children may be used to illustrate the method by which those whom we would call teachers are selected. It is almost a method of self-selection. For instance, the children aged say from about 13 to 18 who are especially fond of younger children are given the opportunity to consort with them. They work with the younger children under observation, and then it soon becomes evident who among them have the taste, interest, and the kind of skill which is needed for effective dealing with the young.

> As their interest in the young develops, their own further education centers more and more about the study of processes of growth and development, and so there is a very similar process of natural selection by which parents are taken out of the narrower contact with their own children in the homes and brought forward in the educational nurture of larger numbers of children.

As you observed, there are really three levels of teachers in Utopia, depending upon experience. Married persons with children of their own are the senior teachers. Younger, unmarried persons serve as interns. Older children take an active part in directing the activities of still younger children. All three groups have two qualifications in common. First, they enjoy working with children and young people. They want to teach. They have really selected themselves for teaching. Second, all three groups began their teacher education by actually working with children.

> 5. This question will give you an opportunity to learn more about the teacher education program in your college or university. Compare Utopian teacher education with your own program of preparation. In what respects is it like and unlike your own?

The Utopian concept of learning to teach is more advanced than our own. Preparing to teach, said the Utopians, is not a program of college study alone. It is much broader. It involves many years of life experiences beyond the campus. One does not "take" a teacher education course, in their view. Rather, one "lives" it, starting with an early interest in working with younger children, moving into assisting positions, and finally, after marriage and children, assuming full charge of the education of larger groups of children.

Formal teacher education is closely articulated with actual teaching experience in Utopia. It isn't something apart. Utopia's "teachers" continue to study child growth and development as their experience with children widens. Study and experience are continuously combined.

What Can Prospective Teachers Learn From The Utopians?

What does the Utopian plan for selecting and training teachers have to offer us? Several items are noteworthy.

First, the teacher education program in Utopia makes use of those factors which make learning possible. The prospective teacher is in an *environment* filled with teaching and learning. Both children and adults in Utopian education are learners. The environment invites *interaction*. There is much opportunity to participate in the educational process.

Factors which encourage learning are present and available to the prospective teachers. They are *motivated* by teaching activities which they want to do, and have, through experience, selected themselves to do. Such activity produces *satisfaction* for the prospective teacher. The learning experience is enriched by *activity*. The prospective teacher is not a mere observer, but an active participant in the learning process.

Would a prospective teacher in Utopia feel a sense of *security* in his learning? Certain elements in the situation would help him in this regard. Insecurity frequently springs from inexperience. Utopian teachers begin modestly as children working with other, younger children. They move on to more and more responsible activities, until, finally years later, they assume full charge of large groups of children. This is a confidence-building time.

During this period there are other persons more experienced in teaching to whom one may turn for counsel when problems arise. Teaching is regarded as a complex and difficult art which no one ever really completely masters. Good teachers are good learners, seeking new ideas and help wherever they may be found. The teacher in training can feel secure in his learning role, for he knows he is not expected to have every answer. He is always the good student, learning to be the good teacher.

6. In question five we asked you to compare your program of teacher education

with that in Utopia. Now read the references on teacher education at the end of
the chapter. Prepare to discuss this question: What is the best way to prepare for
teaching?

Let's look now at the proposal that only married persons with children
be granted full teacher status. Here Utopians are obviously too Utopian.
If we imposed this restriction, many American classrooms would be
without teachers. But should such a restriction be imposed, even if
teachers were available? Many of us know excellent teachers who are
single, or if married, without children. And frequently they are excellent
in part because they are single, or childless. Having no families of their
own they "adopt" their students and give large amounts of time to en-
riching their teaching.

We should not, however, miss the Utopian point. Only those who have
really earned the right to teach should teach. Utopians believed that one
of the best ways to achieve this right was through the maturing experience of marriage and child rearing. These experiences, they thought,
give one the insight into child growth and development demanded for
superior teaching.

Another important Utopian concept is that learning to teach involves
more than academic training. Utopian teachers "grew" into their positions by experiencing many aspects of teaching as they studied the art.
Such opportunity surrounds the modern student preparing to teach.
Frequently, these opportunities go unrecognized and unused. Every college classroom is a teaching-learning laboratory where prospective
teachers can study learning first-hand. Elementary and secondary schools
can be visited. Numerous opportunities exist in the community to work
with children and young people. The opportunities for observation and
participation are not exclusive with Utopia; they are real. They should
be used.

HOW SHOULD LEARNING BE CARRIED ON?

How we carry on learning is of crucial importance. It makes a difference how teachers work with students. It makes a difference what students
see and hear and experience.

Let's observe how the Utopians conducted the learning enterprise.

> The work of these educational groups is carried on much as
> painters were trained in, say Italy, when painting was at its height.
> The adult leaders, through their previous experience, and by the
> manner of selection, combine special knowledge of children with
> special gifts in certain directions.

They associate themselves with the young in carrying on some line of action. Just as in these older societies younger people were apprentices who observed the elders and took a part along with them in doing at first some of the simpler things and then, as they got more experience, engaged directly in the more complex forms of activity, so in these directed activities in these centers the older people are first engaged in carrying on some work in which they themselves are competent, whether painting or music, or scientific inquiry, observation of nature, or industrial cooperation in some line. Then the younger children watching them, listening to them, begin taking their part in the simpler forms of the action—a minor part, until as they develop they accept more and more the responsibility for cooperation.

Here Is A Real-life Example Of Learning Through Apprenticeship

It happens that I am writing this chapter in an Asian country where the young learn many skills in a manner described by the Utopians. This country is not yet industrialized. It is made up primarily of small farmers, herdsmen, artisans, shopkeepers and servants. Formal schooling is not available to the masses. In this situation little boys tend to step quite naturally into their father's or family's occupation, while the little girls assume the retiring domestic role of the mother. They learn the things they need to know by first observing their elders and then taking part "along with them in doing at first some of the simpler things and then, as they got more experience, engaging directly in the more complex forms of activity."

Take as an example, the shepherd boy who is a familiar sight along every road and country lane. One's first reaction is: "How young to be tending a flock of sheep!" Yet, observe him, and one sees that he knows well what he is about. He shepherds his sheep with great skill along the paths to and from the pasture land. Where fences are unknown he can keep his flock within boundaries, even though greener pastures beckon his sheep beyond. He knows how to protect the sheep from menacing dogs and he can use his stick with great effectiveness. He can recognize poisonous weeds and steer his sheep away from them. At ten years of age he is a good shepherd.

This boy grew up in his vocation and was probably never aware that he was learning it. When he was very small his father or older brother took him along while they tended the flock. To protect him from the hot sun he was put down in the shade of a bush. From there he watched and listened. As he grew older he ran after the sheep, assisting his father in rounding up the strays. In the spring, at lambing time, he watched his father work with the ewes. He was shown how to teach a new lamb to suckle. At shearing time he was there, assisting first, then later catching, throwing, and holding the sheep for the shearer.

From his earliest years he knew the value of the flock to his family. From the wool he saw his mother and sisters card yarn from which family clothes were made. The flock provided meat for the table. The wool and sheep which were sold brought the family its meager cash income.

Here, then, is a learning situation in which the young first observe their elders carry on significant tasks in which they are skilled. Gradually, naturally, they start to take part. Finally, their own skill is developed and they are capable of training others.

Learning Through Apprenticeship Has Great Merit

First, learning takes place in a completely natural kind of way. There are no "lessons," no "classes," no trumped up "rewards and punishments." It takes place as a part of normal living.

Second, the learner sees the connection between one aspect of the task and the whole task. The shepherd boy can easily see what caring for a new lamb means to his family's welfare, because he has observed the life cycle of a sheep and its relationship to what he wears and eats. He does not need to be told that learning to care for sheep is important. This is one of the accepted values by which his whole family survives.

Third, the teacher is "associated" with the young in carrying out some line of action. In a sense, the father of the shepherd boy is a co-worker, superior only in knowledge and skill. His role of teacher and worker is one. He is both doer and teacher. The two roles blend so harmoniously that it would be difficult, if not impossible, to separate them. Teaching and learning attain their finest fruit in this happy blend.

Fourth, this kind of teaching incorporates within itself the factors which stimulate learning. The shepherd boy takes on new tasks as he becomes ready to do so. There is no lock-step curriculum that dictates arbitrarily what he should be capable of doing at a certain stage. As he demonstrates his *readiness,* he simply assumes new responsibilities. His motivation comes from his environment in which flock tending is the accepted way of life. His *satisfaction* comes from assuming an adult role early in life. His learning is filled with the kind of *activity* that delights a boy's heart. And he can feel a strong sense of *security* in taking his accepted place in the family.

It is no surprise that this boy at ten years of age has already learned his life's work. Can American teachers teach with the same effectiveness? Or, can American children learn in school with the same effectiveness?

Is Apprenticeship Teaching And Learning Possible In Our Schools?

The differences between the world of the shepherd boy and our world are vast, and they profoundly affect how we teach and how we learn. Look at some of the differences.

First, how many American boys and girls have an intimate knowledge of their father's work? Except in rural areas, few have the opportunity to see their fathers at work, or to gain an intimate understanding of their work. The chances are that the father works far away from home in an environment unknown to the child. The same may be said of the opportunity of young children generally to observe other adults at work.

Second, the parent's work is such that it is impossible for the child to apprentice in it. The chances are the work is specialized, technical, and beyond the reach of children. It would be cruel to subject a child to it. The shepherd boy's work was within his grasp.

Third, our industrial and technical society does not make provision for educating children within the production process. We have delegated education to schools and professional teachers. In this act, we, in a sense, removed school learning from real life.

Fourth, modern specialized work permits even the mature worker to see only a piece of the entire operation. The satisfaction which comes in seeing something created and completed is missing. It is incompatible with mass production upon which our economy depends.

How shall we evaluate the Utopian methods of teaching and learning? Taken literally they do not fit our world. Utopians apprenticed their children directly into the productive and creative life of their adult society. We have created schools for helping to prepare our young for adulthood.

What Values Do Utopian Methods Have For Us?

Actually, there are many values in the Utopian methods of teaching and learning. The learning qualities are sound. These we can adapt to our teaching in a school setting. Let's examine some of the Utopian concepts to see how they apply to the conduct of learning in the classroom.

First, the Utopians believe that learning takes place best when the teacher is "associated" with the young in the learning enterprise. Teaching and learning for them is a joint adventure. In Utopia the teacher does not "tell" the young what they should know. They "associate" with them in order to help them discover what they should know. This kind of teaching is within grasp of every teacher. It requires a "cooperative venture" attitude toward students and learning. It doesn't mean that the teacher gives up his prerogatives as teacher. It does mean that he adopts a "we" rather than a "you" attitude.

Recall Henry Johnson's narrative in chapter five of his teaching Manhattan children about "their island." Here his attitude was one of "Come, let us discover the answer together." And he skillfully led them toward the answer.

Second, Utopian teachers associate with the young on *significant* lines of action. The teachers are themselves the persons who are carrying on the productive and creative work of Utopia. In this the Utopian teachers have a natural advantage which we shall probably never completely recapture. At that historic point at which we delegated teaching to professional teachers and established schools, we broke with Utopian education. But this does not mean that significant learning activities are not available. Our communities are alive with significant learning opportunities, and the good teacher is skillful in making them available to students. The teacher who accomplishes this is engaging in productive and creative business of the highest order.

Third, Utopian teachers, by being "associated" with students on "significant" matters, carry on a "line of action." "Action" is the key word. Utopian students learn through "doing" under the skilled direction of the master.

Activity teaching is within grasp of most educators. Yet, classes frequently bog down into boring inactivity. Good teachers see opportunities to use activity learning in any subject. The author recalls visiting a ninth grade social studies class which was engaged in a unit on the Civil War. History, at first glance, would not seem to lend itself to "some line of action." Not true in this classroom. The teacher had discovered the various interests of the students which might have application in the study of the Civil War. Two projects are vividly recalled. Several boys had special woodworking interests and were skillful with tools. These boys made a replica of Fort Sumter after studying its location and details. They gave a graphic report on the fall of Sumter, demonstrating as they went along.

Another group of students played in the band and had special interests and abilities in music. They made a study of Civil War music and delighted the entire class with a concert. Here were "lines of action," dealing with a significant study encouraged and guided by a teacher who felt "associated" with his students.

How should learning be carried on? Our teaching methods must be geared to how we learn. We learn, as the Utopians discovered, by observing, listening, and experiencing matters which are significant to us. We learn best from those with whom we are associated in a joint venture of discovery. Learning takes place best in the course of carrying on activity which is considered important by both the learner and the teacher.

7. What can the Utopian conduct of learning mean for your own conduct of a classroom? Can you name five specific things which this discussion has suggested to you?

We are now ready to examine how the Utopians answered the final vital question on the objectives of learning.

WHAT SHOULD BE THE LEARNING OBJECTIVES?

Learning should have purpose. It seeks to do something, to keep something as it is, or to change something. What should its purpose be? Should learning have any goals beyond helping children and young people to grow up into responsible human beings? Should learning equip one simply to acquire knowledge and store it away for later use? Or should it create attitudes necessary for effective living?

The Utopians had strong feelings about these questions. Listen, as Dewey concludes the narrative of his visit to Utopia.

Naturally, I inquired what were the purposes, or, as we say now, the objectives of the activities carried on in these centers. At first nothing puzzled me more than the fact that my inquiry after objectives was not at all understood, for the whole concept of the school, of teachers and pupils and lessons, had so completely disappeared that when I asked after the special objectives of the activity of these centers, my Utopian friends thought I was asking why children should live at all, and therefore they did not take my questions seriously.

After I made them understand what I meant, my question was dismissed with the remark that since children were alive and growing, "Of course, we as the Utopians, try to make their lives worthwhile to them; of course we try to see that they really do grow, that they really develop." But as for having any objective beyond the process of a developing life, the idea still seemed quite silly. The notion that there was some special end which the young should try to attain was completely foreign to their thoughts.

By observation, however, I was led to the conclusion that what we would regard as the fundamental purposes were thoroughly ingrained in the working of the activities themselves. In our language, it might be said to be the discovery of the aptitudes, the tastes, the abilities and the weaknesses of each boy and girl, and then to develop their positive capacities into attitudes and to arrange and reinforce the positive powers so as not to cover up the weak points but to offset them.

I inquired, having a background of our schools in mind, how with their methods they ever made sure that the children and youth really learned anything, how they mastered the subject matter, geography, and arithmetic and history, and how they ever were sure that they really learned to read and write and figure. Here, too, at first I came upon a blank wall. For they asked, in return to my questions, whether in the period from which I came for a visit to Utopia it was possible for a boy or girl who was normal physiologically to grow up without learning the things which he or she needed to learn—because it was evident to them that it was not possible for anyone except a congenital idiot to be born and to grow up without learning.

When they discovered, however, that I was serious, they asked whether it was true that in our day we had to have schools and teachers and examinations to make sure that babies learned to walk and to talk.

It was during these conversations that I learned to appreciate how completely the whole concept of acquiring and storing away things had been displaced by the concept of creating attitudes, by shaping desires, and developing the needs that are significant in the process of living.

The Utopians believed that the pattern which exists in economic society in our time affected the general habits of thought; that because personal acquisition and private possession were such dominant ideals in all fields, even if unconsciously so, they had taken possession of the minds of educators to the extent that the idea of personal acquisition and possession controlled the whole educational system.

They pointed out not merely to the use in our schools of the competitive methods of appeal to rivalry and the use of rewards and punishments of set examinations and the system of promotion, but they also said that these things were merely incidental expressions of the acquisitive system of society and the kind of measure and test of achievement and success which had to prevail in an acquisitive type of society.

So it was that we had come to regard all study as simply a method of acquiring something, even if only useless or remote facts, and thought of learning and scholarship as the private possession of the resulting acquisition. And the social change which had taken place with the abolition of an acquisitive economic society had, in their judgement, made possible the transformation of the center of emphasis from learning (in our sense) to the creation of attitudes.

They said that the great educational liberation comes about when the concept of external attainments was thrown away and when they started to find out what each individual person had in him from the very beginning, and they then devoted themselves to finding out the conditions of the environment and kinds of activity in which the positive capacities of each young person could operate most effectually.

8. Try to project yourself into a classroom of your own. You are the teacher, and it's up to you to determine the objectives. Do you find any of the Utopian objectives useful?

Dewey tells us that the Utopians were puzzled when he asked them why they carried on the particular activities in their learning centers. The idea of objectives and purposes was foreign to them. They began with the assumption that children represent "developing life" and there was no need for objectives beyond this. Later Dewey discovered that the purposes of learning were so thoroughly *ingrained* in the activities carried on in Utopia, that external objectives had long been forgotten.

Let's illustrate the point this way. What if we had asked the father of the shepherd boy the questions which Dewey asked Utopians? Suppose we had asked: "What is your purpose in having your young son run after the sheep?" He, too, would have been puzzled, and would have found it difficult to answer. The activities connected with sheep-herding were so much a part of their way of life that objectives beyond these were not considered. This was the way the boy would naturally grow up and develop. Briefly stated, the activities of learning and the purposes of learning were one. They could not be separated.

9. Can you name learning activities in which you have engaged where the purpose for the learning and the activity through which you learned were almost identical?

How can you make sure that children really do learn? Dewey asked. Here, too, the Utopians were puzzled. Everyone learns what he needs to learn. No normal child can grow up without learning. Do you have to give examinations to make sure that babies learn to walk and talk? they ask.

What, then, we might ask, does a child *need* to learn? Did the shepherd boy *need* to learn how to tend sheep? Did the little boy *need* to learn how to print his name? Does a child *need* to learn to talk? The answer lies in the learning environment, subject to the physical capacities of the learner. The shepherd boy's entire environment focused upon his learning to tend sheep. It was completely natural for him to learn to do so. The little boy, we pointed out, was certainly destined to learn to print his name, subject as he was to all of the environmental influences encouraging him. To learn to speak is a cultural necessity for a child. The hundreds of influences of his "talking" environment make it almost impossible for him *not* to talk.

> 10. Can you list five things a teacher can do to encourage the *need* to learn English, or another subject of your choice?

Is it the purpose of learning to acquire and store away things? No, said the Utopians; real learning takes place when we throw away external attainments and begin to develop the positive capacities of the young. This is the real objective of learning. It is not to acquire high marks, honors, and rewards. It is to discover what each person has "in him," and then create learning activities within an environment which develop his positive capacities.

The Utopians do us this service: they hit us forcefully with the importance of environment in learning. And, they stir us to think about the kind of environment we need to create in our own schools and classrooms. The basic question: How can a teacher create the kind of school environment which will cause learners to *need* to learn that which is taught? Many factors, of course, are outside the teacher's control. Many are within his control. How can he muster *these* in the cause of learning?

SKETCH A REAL SCHOOL

To round-out this discussion let's sketch a school in which we use the best ideas we know. Let it represent an ideal place for learning, a school of tomorrow. Many of our schools today incorporate some of these ideas. Many, too, fall short.

The school is set on ample grounds amid space enough for both work and play. The well-lighted and ventilated buildings are designed so that children feel more like they are at home than in an "institution." They do not get lost in the crowd.

The classrooms are more than sitting places. They are well stocked with materials, tools, and equipment with which the student can work. The library, laboratories, shops, as well as classrooms, are thought of as work areas.

The senior teachers have gained their positions through long training and work with children. Newer teachers are given opportunities to learn "on the job." Regular teachers are assisted by students who have indicated an interest in teaching (the Future Teacher idea). Teachers teach because they like to teach and enjoy working with children and youth.

Learning is conducted around activities which are real, rather than "trumped up." Students and teachers feel "associated" in the pursuit of these real activities. But the teacher is director and leader.

The teaching is tied closely to the life outside the school, and the work takes place both inside and outside the school.

The objective of the entire enterprise is to discover the full potential in each child and develop it to the highest possible extent. Subjects which are taught are used for this purpose. Geography, arithmetic, and history, as examples, are learned because the child is made to feel that they are important in his life. He *needs* to learn them. We give him ample opportunity to use them.

The whole environment has an air of stimulating excitement about it, because those who work there find satisfaction in learning.

11. Can you recall a former teacher who incorporated in his teaching some of the features described by Dewey? Describe this teacher and his methods in a short report. As an example, read the student report below.

THIS TEACHER MADE MUCH OF LITTLE

Frequently good teachers can create exciting learning in un-ideal surroundings. Good teaching does not have to wait for all conditions to be right. As an illustration read this student's report of his ninth grade science teacher.

Every One Of Us Was A Living Part Of That Science Class,
And Not Just a Spectator

Reported by
RICHARD ANSTINE

I remember one teacher who, I believe without a doubt, was the most unusual teacher I have ever known. He made a Utopia from practically nothing.

My family and I had just moved to a new community and I was preparing to enter the ninth grade. Like every new student, I had qualms about the new school. I had just come from a town that had a fairly new junior high school, and the one I was about to enter was rather old and drab looking. At the beginning of the first day of school I was getting along quite well, but rather disappointed in the school building itself. After the first one or two classes I felt that maybe getting adjusted might not be as difficult as I had previously thought—that is until I entered my third class, general science.

The school I had left the previous spring had a wonderful science laboratory equipped with all of the gadgets a junior high school student could possibly want. As I entered my new science laboratory and saw a square room with very little equipment, no color, and only two windows, I felt as though I had left civilization. Then the teacher entered the room with his suit coat off, shirt sleeves rolled up unevenly, hair uncombed, and his tie loosened with his shirt collar unbuttoned. This, I was sure, promised to be my most disappointing class.

After talking, very informally, about science for three days, he announced that there was no text book for the course, but directed our attention to the east wall where there were twenty or twenty-five science books that we were welcome to use anytime we felt the need. Then he passed out to each of us mimeographed papers, dealing with generators. At my previous school we would have had a real generator and not just a mimeographed picture of one.

But as time passed my attitude began to change for the better and I began to get interested, more interested than I had ever been at my previous school. Undoubtedly, this teacher, Martin Johnson, was the hardest working man on the faculty. Each and every day we entered class he had something new and different prepared for us to work with. It would have been so much easier for him to have taught from a text, but so much less interesting for us. Everyday we had problems to work on, sometimes individually and sometimes as a group.

Now I know the reason why the laboratory didn't have a large amount of equipment; those problems Mr. Johnson gave us took us to the actual situation whenever it was possible. I can remember taking my problems to the school's heating plant, the local dairy, the local garage, and the small stream that ran behind the football field. All of this was a part of our class and was done during the class period. Even our homework was of this order.

Every one of us was a living part of that science class and not just a spectator looking at it through a text book. As a final project for the year the whole class, as a group, built a radio transmitter from scrap parts and, believe it or not, it actually worked.

The most remarkable aspect of Mr. Johnson was all of his classes throughout the years, even with all of his variations, learned about the same things. There was never a class that slighted any of the subject matter. I've had many teachers I've enjoyed very much, but without a doubt Mr. Johnson created the most lasting impression.

In the next section we shall pursue a question raised in this chapter: How shall a teacher "associate" himself with the student? A teacher can work with a student in many ways. We shall look at three ways with appropriate examples.

Good Follow-up Reading and Viewing

BOOKS

Conant, James B., *The American High School Today*. New York: McGraw-Hill Book Co., Inc., 1959. The former president of Harvard surveys high schools today and offers thought-provoking recommendations for their improvement. He considers separately the small, large city, and suburban high schools.

————, *Education in the Junior High School Years*. Princeton, N.J.: Educational Listing Service, 1960. A distinguished educator makes fourteen recommendations for the American junior high school, including suggestions on subjects, skills, schedules, instruction, homework, and promotion.

Cressman, George R., and Harold W. Benda, *Public Education in America*, chap. 13, "Necessary and Desirable Physical Provisions for Education." New York: Appleton-Century-Crofts, Inc., 1961. A discussion of new developments in school building design, equipment, and supplies, and how these are related to learning.

Department of Elementary School Principals, *Elementary School Buildings . . . Design For Learning*. Washington, D.C.: National Education Association, 1959. Includes sections on "translating children's needs into terms of designs," "school buildings and the learning programs," "school plant planning," "planning in terms of the community," and others.

Goodlad, John I., and Robert H. Anderson, *The Nongraded Elementary School*. New York: Harcourt, Brace & World, Inc., 1959. The authors believe that the graded structure of elementary education has outlived its usefulness and should be abandoned.

Grambs, Jean D., "The Sociology of the 'Born Teacher,' " in Arthur Foff and Jean D. Grambs, eds., *Readings In Education*. New York: Harper & Brothers, 1956. The various roles of a teacher are described and analyzed in terms of their implications for students preparing to teach.

Henderson, Stella, *Introduction To Philosophy of Education*, chap. 16, "The Good School." Chicago: University of Chicago Press, 1947. A philosopher of education describes her conception of a good school, its teachers, teaching, curriculum, aims, philosophy, and physical plant.

Hicks, Granville, *Small Town*, pp. 244-252. New York: The Macmillan Co., 1947. The trustee of an elementary school believes that the modern school must do a great deal that other institutions, particularly the farm-home, did for their great-grandparents. What boys and girls currently learn outside of school is important, but it is not connected so directly with what they need to know.

Lieberman, Myron, *The Future of Public Education*. Chicago: University of Chicago Press, 1960. Has been called "one of the most penetrating analyses of the American educational system that has yet been given in the twentieth century." Public education, the author asserts, is less effective than it can or ought to be.

McCuskey, Dorothy, "How Do You Know A Good Teacher?" in Arthur Foff and Jean D. Grambs, eds., *Readings in Education*. New York: Harper & Brothers, 1956. A lively discussion of the significant characteristics of good teachers, their classrooms, the way they work with students, and their beliefs.

Morse, Arthur D., *Schools of Tomorrow—Today!* New York: Doubleday & Company, Inc., 1960. Describes dynamic experiments in today's schools, includ-

ing team teaching, classroom management, grouping, guidance, flexible sched-
uling, promotion, pupil reporting, teaching machines, and TV teaching.

Richey, Robert W., *Planning for Teaching*, chap. 6. New York: McGraw-Hill
Book Co., Inc., 1958. A description of what teachers are like, their backgrounds,
and social and occupational status.

Shane, Harold G., "The Future Challenges the Present," in *The American
Elementary School*. New York: Harper & Brothers, 1953. A succinct statement
of problems facing elementary education.

Skinner, B. F., *Walden Two*. New York: The Macmillan Co., 1948. An eminent psychologist creates a thought-provoking Utopia in which significant questions are argued. Of special interest to the prospective teacher is the way in
which education is carried on.

Trump, J. Lloyd, *Images of the Future*. Washington, D.C.: National Education Association, 1959. Suggests a number of ideas to further the quest for quality in education. The specific proposals are worthy of discussion by all who
are concerned about the future of education.

PERIODICALS

Ahrens, Maurice R., "Tomorrow's Elementary Teacher," *NEA Journal*, Vol.
47, January, 1958, pp. 21-22. The author suggests three possibilities for teacher
preparation in the future: the opportunity to apply learnings in actual experience with children, experience combined with each professional course, and
"blocks" of core courses.

Ashby, Lloyd W., "Sizing Up The Sixties," *The Nation's Schools*, Vol. 65,
January, 1960, pp. 49-51, 84, 86. A superintendent of schools makes some interesting predictions about educational changes in this decade.

Babcock, Chester D., "The Teacher, TV, and Teaching Machines," *NEA
Journal*, Vol. 49, No. 5, May, 1960, pp. 30-31. A discussion of the new media
and their significance in the teacher's future.

Barr, A. S., "Characteristics of Successful Teachers," *Phi Delta Kappan*, Vol.
39, March, 1958, pp. 282-83. A description of three different approaches to becoming an effective teacher.

Baynham, Dorsey, "A School of the Future in Operation," *Phi Delta Kappan*,
Vol. 42, pp. 350-54. A sketch of a modern high school, its students, teachers,
program, and architecture.

Campbell, Edward A., "New Spaces and Places for Learning," *The School
Review*, Vol. 68, Autumn, 1960, pp. 346-52. A coonsulting architect proposes
that schools of the future be built to accommodate more than children and
youth. The school should be a cultural-scholastic-recreation center for the whole
community.

Coombs, Philip H., "A Vice-President in Charge of Heresy," *Phi Delta Kappan*, Vol. 41, March, 1960, pp. 243-47. A well-known educator asserts that "our
past procedures have failed to keep either the curriculum or the teachers up
to date." The schools must institute "far reaching internal changes and improvements."

Gilchrist, Robert S., "Promising Practices in Education," *Phi Delta Kappan*,
Vol. 41, February, 1960, pp. 208-11 and March, 1960, pp. 269-74. Promising in-
novations in education.

Haskew, Laurence D., *et al.*, "Teacher Education," *NEA Journal*, Vol. 48,

April, 1959, pp. 15-31. This excellent series of articles by able educators explains America's design for teacher education. Subject matter and professional courses, certification, and common practices are treated.

Ivey, John E., Jr., and Godbold, Bryghte D., "MPATI: Breakthrough in Educational Television," *Phi Delta Kappan*, Vol. 42, February, 1961, pp. 192-96. Describes the Ford Foundation-supported Midwest Program of Airborne Television Instruction.

McAulay, J. D., "Elementary Education—Five Straws in the Wind," *Phi Delta Kappan*, Vol. 41, June, 1960, pp. 394-96. The author surveys a group of elementary schools to identify recent and promising changes.

Moore, Raymond S., "Work Education—The Missing Link?" *Phi Delta Kappan*, Vol. 41, December, 1959, pp. 102-04. The author believes that work is one of the "strongest links in the chain of educational experiences for our children."

Perkins, Larry, "Invitation to Learning," *NEA Journal*, Vol. 47, April, 1958, pp. 252-53. A school architect illustrates how many attractive and functional modern schools have a "come-hither" look.

Pisaro, Samuel E., and Emmerson, Gardner H., "No More Pencils, No More Books . . . ," *Phi Delta Kappan*, Vol. 42, May, 1961, pp. 363-64. A satire on what education will be like when schools are fully automated.

Ruark, Henry C., Jr., "Technology and Education," *Phi Delta Kappan*, Vol. 44, June, 1961, pp. 287-392. An enlightening summary of the whole range of recent developments in educational technology and their meaning for teachers and teaching.

Rudyer, N. B., and Thomas, Donald R., "Demography and Education," *Phi Delta Kappan*, Vol. 41, June, 1960, pp. 379-85. Two fascinating articles that explain how the population explosion will affect teachers and schools in the next twenty years.

Taylor, James L., "Learning Laboratories for Elementary School Children," *School Life*, Vol. 41, January-February, 1959, pp. 17-18. A specialist in school plant planning explains how traditional classrooms are gradually yielding to classrooms specifically designed to allow for differences among children.

"Today and Tomorrow in Elementary and Secondary Education," *NEA Journal*, Vol. 47, January, 1958, pp. 14-31. An exciting series of articles which give an overview of elementary and secondary education. Discusses the ungraded plans, the self-contained units, predicts what is ahead in elementary teacher education, blueprints the advantages in new school building designs, and reports on experiments in secondary-school staff utilization.

Trow, William C., *et al.*, "Psychology of Group Behavior: The Class as a Group," *Journal of Educational Psychology*, Vol. 41, 1950, pp. 322-38. The authors examine research on the group process and raise questions about school practice. Forces within the group, the authors claim, determine what the student learns. Suggests that teachers need to determine which forces will operate in the group and subject which they plan to teach.

Trump, J. Lloyd, "A Better High School Program," *NEA Journal*, Vol. 49, April, 1960, pp. 41-43. Six suggestions for improving our high schools.

FILMS

And No Bells Ring

Ideal school of the future. Emphasizes the teacher's freedom from routine procedures and concentrates on instruction requiring creative ability. (National Education Association, black and white, 60 minutes.)

Broader Concepts of Curriculum

Survey of a modern secondary school curriculum. How needs of youth may be served through a wide variety of learning experiences. (McGraw-Hill Book Co., Inc., black and white, 20 minutes.)

Field Trip

Proper planning, conduct, and follow-up of a field trip experience. High school pupils carrying out plans for a field trip through Dismal Swamp of Virginia. Illustrated characteristics of well-conducted community study. (Virginia State Department of Education, color, 11 minutes.)

Fight for Better Schools

Needs for better and greater school facilities in United States. Two-year campaign by citizens of Arlington, Va., for better schools. Work of National Citizens Committee in focusing national attention on educational needs. Progress in Arkansas, Delaware, Connecticut, Kentucky, and New York. (March of Time; McGraw-Hill Book Co., Inc., black and white, 21 minutes.)

How Good Are Our Schools?

An excellent documentary film produced by CBS and narrated by Ralph Bellamy. Highlights the findings of the 1959 Report of Dr. James B. Conant. (National Education Association, black and white, 28 minutes.)

Junor High School Story

An overview of a good junior high school program as illustrated by scenes from forty-nine California junior high schools. A wide variety of teaching, guidance, and social activities ranging from instruction in spelling to the student council in action. (Jr. H.S. Council, Inc., color, 28 minutes.)

"Pop" Rings the Bell

The part the well-equipped school plant will play in maturing leaders of tomorrow. Education as a good investment. (National School Service, black and white, 21 minutes.)

Teachers for Tomorrow

Teacher preparation in the School of Education, University of Wisconsin. Processes of general education, selection, professional course work, observation, participation, student teaching, and placement. Emphasizes critical need for elementary teachers. First-year graduates in typical teaching situations. (University of Wisconsin, black and white, 22 minutes.)

PART 5

THE TEACHER AT WORK WITH STUDENTS

CHAPTER 9

NONDIRECTED LEARNING

It is rarely your business to suggest what he should learn.

JEAN JACQUES ROUSSEAU

How should a teacher work with students? When Rousseau, the provocative Frenchman, was asked that question, he did not hesitate. Let the teacher be casual, he said. Don't tell the child what he should learn. It is his business to want to learn. The teacher's job is only to awaken his desire and put learning within his reach. The child must do the reaching.

In this book we have studied several ways of working with students. The Utopian teachers were not as casual in their leadership as Rousseau. Neither did they dominate. They "associated" actively with children, permitting the children to participate with them in their own line of work. They assumed that children, in this kind of relationship, would learn what they needed to know.

Mary Ellen Chase was a dominant leader in her classroom in Bucks Harbor. She told the children what they should learn and when.

Henry Johnson's leadership was a still different kind. He planned what should be learned and took an active part in classroom proceedings. But he involved students at an early stage and encouraged them to carry on.

Mark Van Doren expressed yet another judgement about teacher leadership. He believed in full adult responsibility in teaching. The child knows that he is not yet a man. For this reason there are certain learnings which he should not be permitted to evade. The child should have freedom, yes, but "discipline is wanted to bring it out." Teachers provide the discipline.

WHAT KIND OF LEADERSHIP BECOMES YOU?

Every teacher confronts the question: What kind of leadership is most becoming to me? Granting my own abilities and limitations, what kind of leadership can I give in order to bring out the best within my students?

It is a vital question and it is never fully answered. Leadership should be a growing quality. Good teachers are always becoming better leaders, growing with experience, maturing the kind of leadership for which they are individually best suited.

It is through our leadership that teaching is best expressed and it is through leadership that we best teach. Students are apt to remember best of all the particular flavor of the teacher's leadership. The details of the subject matter may have slipped from mind, but the impact of the teacher's leadership is remembered. This is probably another way of saying that a teacher teaches best through the force of his leadership. The child first studies the teacher, and then the subject. It is the teacher who helps to kindle or dampen the desire to learn, build or destroy confidence, arouse or suppress curiosity. These values must rank high in teaching. They are taught quietly, incidentally, almost without the teacher and student being aware. And for this reason, they are taught powerfully.

Most of us can recall former teachers who taught incidentally and powerfully through their leadership qualities. I recently received word of the death of a former high school teacher. He was such a teacher! Though I had not seen him for years, I felt a deep and sudden loss. This hulk of a man had great rounded shoulders, a massive face, wild and wiry hair. He was as stern as he was kind. In subject matter teaching he expressed his best leadership. Through his questions he would prod and gently shove his students to find answers for themselves. He expected much, and in expecting he usually got it. Under his direction students were surprised to learn what they could do. He coaxed forth the best in each of us.

In this and the next two chapters we are going to study examples of three kinds of learning which result from three different ways of working with students. We'll analyze these examples, ask questions about them, look at their strengths and weaknesses. They do not represent pure forms and leadership. There are no pure forms. Good teachers have rich reservoirs of leadership. Many kinds of leadership somehow meet in them and make a sensible whole.

Our purpose in studying three different ways of working with students is to discover the broad spectrum of learning and leadership in teaching, observe the implications of each, and select from the different types those things which may be useful.

The teacher may conduct learning in such a way that it is *Nondirected,* Directed, or Dominated. Let's take a brief look at each of these ways before we examine them in detail.

NONDIRECTED LEARNING PUTS LEARNING RESOURCES WITHIN REACH

When Jean Jacques Rousseau set forth his ideas on teaching, he did so in a novel manner. He selected a child of his imagination to educate, named him Emile, and explained step by step how he educated him. In a way, Rousseau was a poor man to give advice. He abandoned his own wife and child, took up a life of self indulgence, and told other people how to raise their children. But if the inconsistency in his life ever bothered him, we cannot detect it in the intriguing story of Emile. Had it bothered him, he would not have been Rousseau!

The very daring of his proposals must be reckoned with; indeed, it has been for many years. His ideas are expressed in modern teaching, and many educational leaders have been influenced by his work. He deserves our scrutiny.

Rousseau's relationship with Emile was casual and nondirective. He made learning resources available. Emile studied only those things which interested him. He studied when he wanted to, and in his own way. He set his own goals for learning, depending upon his present interests. Rousseau did not interfere or direct. "I am pretty sure Emile will learn to read and write before he is ten," he wrote, "just because I care very little whether he can do so before he is fifteen; but I would rather that he never learned to read at all, than that his art should be acquired at the price of all that makes reading useful. What is the use of reading to him if he always hates it?"

DIRECTED LEARNING IS PLANNED AND GUIDED

Students remembered Professor Louis Agassiz, the Harvard University naturalist, and several of them have written about the leadership which he gave to his students in the laboratory at Cambridge. Learning with Agassiz was an experience to be remembered.

He was a directive teacher. Several of his students have told the story of the fish, an incident which reveals the professor at his directive best. It is also one of the gems in the literature on teaching. We shall listen to Samuel H. Scudder, one of Agassiz's students, tell it in the next chapter.

Agassiz determined when the student was ready to study the fish. He provided the fish and gave the student an assignment. ("Look at it . . . by and by I will ask what you have seen.") When the student was wrong, Agassiz said so; when he was on the right track, Agassiz was warmly encouraging. Like Rousseau, he refused to give the student answers. The student had to find these for himself.

DOMINATED LEARNING CONTROLS THE LEARNING PROCESS

About the same time that Rousseau was lashing out at traditional education in France, a prominent English mother was dominating the education of her children. She had nineteen! This fact may explain her firm and disciplined approach.

Suzanna Wesley, the mother of John and Charles Wesley, controlled practically all the elements in the education of her children. As teacher, she planned exactly what her children should learn and when they should learn it. She dealt out punishments and rewards.

It was, however, in her beliefs about education that we best see her dominating leadership. Children, she believed, learn best when they are submissive to adult leadership. Indeed the prerequisite to learning is submissiveness. "In order to form the minds of children," she wrote, "the first thing to be done is to conquer their will."

When John Wesley became a man he asked his mother about her principles for educating the family. In answer she wrote her son a letter setting forth her views. We shall study this letter.

HOW SHOULD YOU STUDY THESE CASES?

Rousseau, Agassiz, and Wesley are not presented here as models of the way a teacher should work with a student. You should not expect to find their counterparts in classrooms. Nor are they models to be copied. Each case is set in a situation greatly different from that of a normal classroom. Rousseau is teaching a single boy outside a formal school. Agassiz is instructing Scudder in a science laboratory in what amounts to independent study. Susanna Wesley is teaching her own children in her own home.

This choice of situations far removed from normal classrooms is deliberate. We are not looking for practices which we can lift up, or borrow, and place in our own classrooms. Rather, we are in search of significant ideas about teacher-student relationships which are to be found in these examples of three different ways of working with students. These, when molded to our own particular situations, can be meaningful and useful. Significant ideas handled in this way, may have application to your own or anyone else's teaching. These cases, thus, are illustrative of kinds of relationships, rather than of classroom practices.

What we are searching for in these cases are answers to such questions as these: What view do these teachers hold of students? What view do they hold of themselves as teachers? What do they think the job of the student is? The teacher? How do they think learning takes place? What are they trying to accomplish through their teaching? What kind of influence are they having on their students? It is in our search for answers to questions such as these that we can find appropriate ways to work with students.

In each of these cases you will see implications for classroom teaching, even though the situations are vastly different. For example, Rousseau creates a situation in which Emile could teach himself about astronomy. The nondirective classroom teacher is skillful in creating learning situations in which students can make discoveries for themselves. Agassiz trained Scudder to carry on independent investigations. The classroom teacher is equally capable of training groups of students to do the same. Wesley, who believed in the dominance of the teacher, planned and controlled the whole learning process. So must the classroom teacher who believes in this way of working with students.

In the cases, then, look for the revealing ideas *behind* the practice of these three teachers, ideas which may suggest to you worthwhile ways of working with students in your own classroom.

ROUSSEAU MAKES HIS POINT

As we enter the story, Rousseau [1] is giving his reasons for the nondirective approach to Emile. He has just said that a child should do "nothing because he is told; nothing is good for him but what he recognizes as good."

> If children are not required to do anything as a matter of obedience, it follows that they will only learn what they perceive to be of real and present value, either for use or enjoyment; what other motive could they have for learning? The art of speaking to our absent friends, of hearing their words; the art of letting them know at first hand our feelings, our desires, and our longings is an art whose usefulness can be made plain at any age. How is it that this art, so useful and pleasant in itself, has become a terror to children? Because the child is compelled to acquire it against his will, and

---

[1] Jean Jacques Rousseau, *Emile,* trans. Barbara Foxley (New York: E. P. Dutton and Company, Inc., 1911), pp. 81-82, 141-44.

to use it for purposes beyond his comprehension. A child has no great wish to be perfect himself in the use of an instrument of torture, but make it a means to his pleasure, and soon you will not be able to keep him from it.

People make a great fuss about discovering the best way to teach children to read. They invent "bureaux" and cards; they turn the nursery into a printer's shop. Locke would have them taught to read by means of dice. What a fine idea! And the pity of it! There is a better way than any of those, and one which is generally over-looked—it consists in the desire to learn. Arouse this desire in your scholar and have done with your "bureaux" and your dice—any method will serve.

Present interest, that is the motive power, the only motive power that takes us far and safely. Sometimes Emile receives notes of invitation from his father or mother, his relatives or friends; he is invited to a dinner, a walk, a boating expedition, to see some public entertainment. These notes are short, clear, plain and well written. Some one must read them to him, and he cannot always find any-body when wanted; no more consideration is shown to him than he himself showed to you yesterday. Time passes, the chance is lost. The note is read to him at last, but it is too late. Oh! If only he had known how to read! He does his best, and at last he makes out half the note; it is something about going tomorrow to drink cream—where? With whom? He cannot tell—how hard he tried to make out the rest! I do not think Emile will need a "bureaux." Shall I proceed to the teaching of writing? No, I am ashamed to toy with these trifles in a treatise on education.

Here we have the crux of Rousseau's argument. Children learn only what is of real and present value. And what is of real and present value? Those things which can be used and enjoyed. Such matters spring from within a child's own interests, not an adult's. Adults, therefore, should not expect a child to learn anything because he is told or as a matter of obedience. The teacher should be nondirective in his relationship with a child. How do you react to the argument?

1. Rousseau waits to take up reading until Emile has missed a party because he cannot read the invitation. (a) Would you wait? (b) Would you "create" some situation in which you could teach reading? (c) Or, would you simply start to teach reading? Explain your choice.

2. Would you classify Rousseau as a "drawer out" or "putter in"?

3. Do you agree with Rousseau's condemnation of teaching aids? Is it possible that teaching aids themselves may stimulate a child's interests, and thereby help to make the learning both useful and pleasant? What do you think?

Now Rousseau develops further his method of nondirective teaching.

> Do not forget that it is rarely your business to suggest what he
> ought to learn; it is for him to want to learn to seek and find it.
> You should put it within his reach, you should skillfully awaken
> the desire and supply him with means for its satisfaction. So your
> questions should be few and well-chosen and as he will always have
> more questions to put to you than you to him, you will always have
> the advantage and will be able to ask all the oftener, "What is the
> use of that question?" Moreover, as it matters little what he learns
> provided he understands it and knows how to use it, as soon as you
> cannot give him a suitable explanation give him none at all. Do
> not hesitate to say, "I have no good answer to give you; I was wrong,
> let us drop the subject." If your teaching was really ill-chosen there
> is no harm in dropping it altogether; if it was not, with a little care
> you will soon find an opportunity of making its use apparent to
> him.

If it is not the teacher's job to tell the student what to learn, what is
his job? Here we have Rousseau's answer. The teacher should (a) put the
thing to be learned within the child's reach, (b) awaken his desire to
learn, and (c) supply him with the means of satisfying that desire.

4. Can you cite any former teachers of your own who used Rousseau's ideas?
How would you describe their methods?

5. Rousseau remarks that "it matters little what he (the student) learns, provided
he understands it, and knows how to use it." Do you agree? Explain your reaction.

Now Rousseau gives us an example of how *not* to use his method.

> I do not like verbal explanations. Young people pay little heed
> to them, nor do they remember them. Things! Things! I cannot
> repeat it too often. We lay too much stress upon words; we teachers
> babble, and our scholars follow our example.
> Suppose we are studying the course of the sun and the way to
> find our bearings, when all at once Emile interrupts me with the
> question, "What is the use of that?" What a fine lecture I might
> give, how many things I might take occasion to teach him in reply
> to his question, especially if there is anyone there. I might speak
> of the advantages of travel, the value of commerce, the special
> products of different lands and the peculiar customs of different
> nations, the use of the calendar, the way to reckon the seasons for
> agriculture, the art of navigation, how to steer our course at sea,
> how to find our way without knowing exactly where we are. Politics,

natural history, astronomy, even morals and international law are
involved in my explanation, so as to give my pupil some idea of all
these sciences and a great wish to learn them. When I have finished
I shall have shown myself a regular pedant, I shall have made a
great display of learning, and not one single idea has he understood.
He is longing to ask me again, "What is the use of taking one's
bearings?", but he dare not for fear of vexing me. He finds it pays
best to pretend to listen to what he is forced to hear. This is the
practical result of our fine systems of education.

But Emile is educated in a simpler fashion. We take so much
pains to teach him a difficult idea that he will have heard nothing
of all this. At the first word he does not understand, he will run
away, he will prance about the room, and leave me to speechify
by myself. Let us seek a more commonplace explanation; my
scientific learning is of no use to him.

Rousseau knows well what kind of teaching he is against. This is the
kind of teaching he wishes to change.

> 6. Rousseau says that this kind of approach teaches a student "to pretend to
> listen to what he is forced to hear." In your judgement do the students you know
> learn such pretense? If so, how do you account for it? Can you find the reasons
> within the kind of learning they are engaged in?
>
> 7. In your opinion what kind of teaching inspires *genuine* listening on the part of
> the student?
>
> 8. How much of your own education consists of "talk"? How much of "things"?
>
> 9. Think of your own teaching subject area. What are the "things" you can use
> in teaching?

Rousseau now gives us an example of his nondirective approach to
Emile.

We were observing the position of the forest to the north of
Montmorency when he interrupted me with the usual question,
"What is the use of that?" "You are right," I said, "let us take time
to think it over, and if we find it is no use we will drop it, for we
want only useful games." We find something else to do and
geography is put aside for the day.

Next morning I suggest a walk before breakfast; there is nothing
he would like better; children are always ready to run about, and
he is a good walker. We climb up to the forest; we want to wander
through its clearings and lose ourselves; we have no idea where
we are, and when we want to retrace our steps we cannot find the
way. Time passes, we are hot and hungry; hurrying vainly this way

and that we find nothing but woods, quarries, plains, and not a
landmark to guide us. Very hot, very tired, very hungry, we only
get further astray. At last we sit down to rest and to consider our
position. I assume that Emile has been educated like an ordinary
child. He does not think, he begins to cry; he has no idea we are
close to Montmorency, which is hidden from our view by a mere
thicket; but this thicket is a forest to him, a man of his size is
buried among the bushes. After a few minutes' silence I begin
anxiously—

Jean Jacques. My dear Emile, what shall we do to get out?

Emile. I am sure I do not know. I am tired, I am hungry, I am
thirsty. I cannot go any further.

Jean Jacques. Do you suppose I am better off? I would cry too if
I could make my breakfast of tears. Crying is no use, we must look
about us. Let us see your watch; what time is it?

Emile. It is noon and I am hungry!

Jean Jacques. Just so; it is noon and I am so hungry, too.

Emile. You must be very hungry indeed.

Jean Jacques. Unluckily my dinner won't come to find me. It is
twelve o'clock. This time yesterday we were observing the position
of the forest from Montmorency. If only we could see the position
of Montmorency from the forest—

Emile. But yesterday we could see the forest, and here we cannot
see the town.

Jean Jacques. This is just it. If we could only find it without
seeing it.

Emile. Oh! My dear friend!

Jean Jacques. Did not we say the forest was—

Emile. North of Montmorency.

Jean Jacques. Then Montmorency must lie—

Emile. South of the forest.

Jean Jacques. We know how to find the north at midday.

Emile. Yes, by the direction of the shadows.

Jean Jacques. But the south?

Emile. What shall we do?

Jean Jacques. The south is opposite the north.

Emile. That is true; we need only find the opposite of the
shadows. That is the south! That is the south! Montmorency must
be over there! Let us look for it there!

Jean Jacques. Perhaps you are right; let us follow this path
through the wood.

Emile. (clapping his hands.) Oh, I can see Montmorency! There
it is, quite plain, just in front of us! Come to luncheon, come to
dinner, make haste! Astronomy is some use after all.

Be sure that he thinks this if he does not say it; no matter which, provided I do not say it myself. He will certainly never forget this day's lesson as long as he lives, while if I had only led him to think of all this at home, my lecture would have been forgotten the next day. Teach by doing whenever you can, and only fall back upon words when doing is out of the question . . .

Let's look closer at Rousseau's leadership in this situation. First of all Rousseau resists the urge to "tell" Emile the answer to his question: "What is the use of that?", when they are observing the position of the forest north of Montmorency. Can he let the matter rest there? No. He must seek some way to make the study of the course of the sun useful to Emile. Emile must see for himself that such knowledge is useful. Rousseau, having resisted the direct approach, must now select another.

Second, he suggests an activity which Emile likes—a walk. His teaching will be in the context of play.

Third, Rousseau creates a problem situation. They get "lost." Note here that Rousseau is a part of the problem, along with Emile. As far as the student is concerned, they are both lost.

Fourth, Rousseau reinforces the problem. He might have said, "We're not really lost. We'll soon find our way out." He waits for Emile to get hungry.

Finally, he casually suggests the key idea. "If only we could see the position of Montmorency from the noon time shadow." The clincher is Emile's: "Astronomy is some use after all." This is nondirective teaching.

This sequence of events demonstrates a significant point about nondirective teaching: The teacher must be skilled in his art. Nondirective teaching is a carefully worked out approach to the teaching process. At first glance it might appear that Rousseau is taking a *laissez faire* attitude toward Emile, letting him go entirely his own way. Look further and you will see that Rousseau is "in charge" all the time, though he seems not to be. Therein lies the art of nondirective teaching.

Rousseau kept a keen eye on Emile for signs of readiness to learn about a given subject. He planned activities and structured problems in order to make use of Emile's growing interests. He used the art of suggestion to lead Emile to valid conclusions. These matters were carefully worked out. They just didn't happen.

Similarly, the classroom teacher who uses non-directive teaching plans carefully and carefully executes his plans. He prepares interesting materials of instruction, and presents his students with problem situations for them to solve. He uses suggestion to lead them along.

10. Visit several school classrooms and look for elements of non-directive teaching and learning. Before the visit make a list of the items you should look for. (The

references at the end of this chapter will help you make a good list.) Make a
report on your observations.

The Nondirective Teacher Believes That Students
Are Basically "Good"

Perhaps any kind of leadership is best revealed in the attitudes of the
leader. What attitudes does the non-directive teacher hold toward students?

Such a teacher believes that students are basically "good." They have
the power to select items for learning which will be profitable to them.
They are capable of a high degree of self-direction. There is a regard for
the concept of readiness. The child will learn what he is ready to learn.
To attempt to teach him anything else is unjustifiable adult imposition.

Children learn that which is enjoyable and useful to them. Utility is
the key word. If learning is not useful it should not be introduced into
a child's education. He may learn to listen politely, but he will not learn.
He may even come to hate learning.

On the whole, adults should tread lightly in the child's domain. The
child is capable of self-development with an adult's easy touch. He
should not be forcefully bent to conform to the adult will. He is a rather
autonomous state with some prerogatives of his own. The adult should
encourage this independence rather than stifle it. The child must be free
to learn and free to act upon what he has learned.

The Nondirective Teacher Behaves in a Certain Way

The non-directive teacher does not have a prescribed amount of work
which his students must cover in a given time. He believes that the
amount of work accomplished should be governed by the students themselves, their capacities, interests, and natural enthusiasm for the activity.
Instead of insisting that they stick to his own schedule of work, he will
look for other interests within the group and from these develop new
activities. As Rousseau remarked: "If your teaching was really ill-chosen
there is no harm in dropping it altogether; if it was not, with a little care
you will soon find an opportunity of making its use apparent."

The nondirective teacher looks constantly for opportunities to make
the use of learning "apparent." He watches his students to discover their
interests and inclinations. He suggests activities which tie into these
interests and inclinations. He looks for problem situations to which his
students can apply their talents. He resists giving answers. He feels he is
there to guide, suggest, and stimulate the desire to learn.

His manner is one of casual friendliness. He identifies himself with students and their problems. Recall that when Rousseau and Emile were "lost," Rousseau answers Emile's complaints with, "Do you suppose I am any better off? I should cry too if I could make breakfast of my tears."

The nondirective teacher has patience. Students, left on their own, will frequently take up projects with enthusiasm, work at them briefly, and drop them. Some students, indeed, may never show real interest in learning opportunities around them. They may even interfere with other students who do wish to work. Other students may be so accustomed to firm guidance that a teacher who refuses to give it will frustrate and annoy them. With all of these the teacher will exercise patience and tact. He must lead without seeming to lead.

Planning is done with the students. Much time is spent in discussing what projects the students wish to consider. As plans unfold, the teacher works with individuals and small groups in carrying out the plans. Students have freedom to move about, gather information, make observations as they wish. In their activities, the teacher is encouraging and helpful.

WHAT IS THE ROLE OF THE STUDENT IN NONDIRECTED LEARNING?

What is the role of the student under non-directive leadership? As we just indicated, students react differently to leadership, depending upon their previous experiences. Emile, being used to nondirective leadership, reacted violently against Rousseau's experiments with more directive leadership. "At the first word he does not understand," explains Rousseau, "he will run away, he will prance about the room, and leave me to speechify by myself."

Some children, in contrast to Emile, are used to directive or dominating leadership in adults. They may react just as positively as Emile if they are suddenly exposed to completely nondirective leadership. They will be lost, without a sense of direction or purpose. Adults have previously provided direction and purpose. Suddenly these are removed. Without resources of his own the child may go through a period of difficult adjustment. Later we shall observe how Suzanna Wesley's children reacted when they were suddenly freed from dominant leadership. The results were not pleasing to Mrs. Wesley.

What then is the role of the child? Is it to learn what the adult wants him to learn? Obviously not, since he cannot be sure what the adult wants him to learn. Is it to please the adult? Perhaps, but he has discovered that what pleases him seems to please the adult most. He soon learns that his role is to test the world around him, select those activities which interest him most, and develop them in his own way. In this endeavor he knows he is largely free. Adults are there, to be used when crises arise. But he has learned that it does no good to run to them continuously. They simply ask more questions ("My dear Emile, what shall we do to get out?") and give some moral support.

In his independent way he is growing up, assuming the responsibilities appropriate to his development, and, like Emile, is increasing his confidence in his ability to find his way out of problems when he is momentarily lost.

Life for him is not without its demands. Indeed they may be great. But he feels they are demands of his own making and he finds pleasure in them.

HOW IS NONDIRECTIVE LEARNING EVALUATED?

How does the non-directive teacher evaluate the work of students? How shall the report card be marked? Nondirective teaching calls for appropriate evaluation procedures. Students have been encouraged to be individuals. Can the same standard, then, be applied to all the students in the class? Obviously not. Each student may have carried on a different project, one which he personally selected and developed. How shall it be judged in relation to other projects? Such an effort would be difficult and possibly unfair.

The teacher must find a more reliable base for assigning grades. He must ask: What is it I'm attempting to develop in my students? He may answer: The ability to work independently; individual resourcefulness; the ability to select useful work; the ability to plan and carry through a learning activity; and the ability to evaluate the quality of work but make corrections as the work proceeds. These are goals suited to all students within the class, and may serve as a basis for evaluation.

How, then, shall an evaluation be made? The students of the non-directive teacher are constantly involved in their own learning. Can they be excluded from the consideration of what grades they shall receive? To do so would be inconsistent with nondirective teaching. The students are consulted and asked to rate themselves: How did you feel about your progress? Were you satisfied with your achievement? What would you say that you learned? If you were doing the project over, what would you do differently? What grade do you feel that you earned?

Some students will overrate themselves, others underrate themselves. Some will demonstrate the ability to measure themselves with candid accuracy. The nondirective teacher accepts these judgements as an important part of education, but he will help, through suggestions and questions, all students to view their work objectively. Finally, after full discussion, the teacher must accept the student's claim to a particular mark.

HOW SHALL WE JUDGE NONDIRECTIVE LEARNING?

First let's look at its faults. The activities and learning experiences carried on under poor nondirective leadership are apt to be "catch-as-catch-can," representing the whims of students rather than those genuine interests capable of sustained development.

The school has an obligation, which it should accept, to give children a series of orderly experiences which stimulate their growth and development. These activities should be important ones, not trivial ones. They should lead on to more and larger experiences. The child should always be aware that his own education is considered of crucial importance by parents and teachers. "Stumble on" activities are not good enough.

Unplanned learning experiences frequently confuse students and lead to aimless work habits. Students don't know where they are going because no clear-cut goals have been marked out. Students who have not learned to plan their work may be even more at a loss under unskilled nondirective leadership.

Much time is spent in planning. I recall a fifth grade teacher whose class decided to do a project on American Indians. So much time was spent in planning to study the Indians that the Indians never got studied. Had the teacher taken a more active part, done some pre-planning of her own, she may have accomplished more and still involved the students in a liberal way.

Good nondirective leadership has marked advantages. Students who share goals are usually more eager to achieve them. They are more apt to cooperate and plunge into the work with enthusiasm. Discipline problems may be fewer. Many students will accomplish more work under such leadership.

Learning to make decisions, plan and execute work of one's own choice, is a part of growing up. It leads to maturity. Learning such things may be more important in the long view than the specific subject matter dealt with in achieving these values.

The personal relationships between the nondirective teacher and the student are usually good. The teacher usually is liked by students. Student resistance is low and freedom of expression is high. Surrounding all, there is a feeling of joint enterprise, mutual adventure, and common satisfaction in work.

Good Follow-up Reading and Viewing

BOOKS

American Association of School Administrators, *Paths to Better Schools.* Washington, D.C.: National Education Association, 1945. Chapter five discusses ways of relating learning to the needs of children and learning by doing.

Barzun, Jacques, *Teacher in America,* chap. 2. Boston: Little, Brown & Co., 1945. A penetrating discussion of the teacher's relationship to his students.

Bush, Robert N., *The Teacher-Pupil Relationship,* chap. 2. Englewood Cliffs, N.J.: Prentice-Hall, Inc., 1954. Reports the results and analyses on teacher-pupil relationships. Chapter two has special significance for the prospective teacher: a detailed case study of a teacher and her pupils in an urban high school.

De Lima, Agnes, *The Little Red School House.* New York: The Macmillan Co., 1942. This book demonstrates how the principles and practices of the newer approach to education may be applied under the limitations of crowded city schools, with specific examples.

Frandsen, Arden N., *How Children Learn,* chap. 4, "Teacher-guidance of Learning Activities." New York: McGraw-Hill Book Co., Inc., 1957. Reviews research experiments on teacher-guidance in learning. Sheds light on the question: How much guidance should a teacher give in order to promote maximum learning?

Jersild, Arthur T., and Ruth J. Tasch, *Children's Interests and What They Suggest For Education.* New York: Bureau of Publications, Teachers College, Columbia University, 1949. This comprehensive work is concerned with the interests of children and how the teacher may channel these interests in the classroom.

Kinder, Frederick G., *Exploring Children's Interests.* New York: Science Research Associates, 1952. The author demonstrates how knowledge of children's interests can be used to make school work more meaningful.

Kluckhohn, Clyde, "Student-Teachers," in *The People in Your Life,* Margaret M. Hughes, ed. New York: Alfred A. Knopf, Inc., 1951. A noted anthropologist illuminates the student-teacher relationship and suggests that the teacher recognize that each student has different needs. "One has to deal with some kinds of students in one way, in a way that with them will be very successful," but equally unsuccessful with another sort of person.

Lindgren, Henry Clay, *Educational Psychology in the Classroom,* chap. 11, "Child Centered Approaches to the Learning Situation." New York: John Wiley & Sons, Inc., 1956. A discussion of the newer approaches to education and specific examples of how they can be implemented in the classroom.

McCloskey, Gordon, *et al., Introduction to Teaching in American Schools,* chaps. 9, 10, 11, 14. New York: Harcourt, Brace & World, Inc., 1954. Case descriptions of teachers at work with children in which various approaches are apparent.

Pratt, C., *I Learn From Children.* New York: Simon & Schuster, Inc., 1948. A teacher relates her experiences in breaking with traditional ways of working with children and developing programs to meet the needs of children.

Richey, Robert W., *Planning For Teaching,* chap. 6, "Learning to Guide the Growth of Pupils." New York: McGraw-Hill Book Co., Inc., 1958. The importance of teacher-pupil planning and building effective relationships with students. Includes a good check list to determine whether a teacher is "effective."

Russell, Bertrand, *Skeptical Essays*. London: Allen & Unwin Ltd., 1955. A thought-provoking essay on freedom and authority in education. Says the author: "Every child, left to itself, will sooner or later swallow pins."

Stratemeyer, Florence B., *et al.*, *Developing a Curriculum For Modern Living*. New York: Bureau of Publications, Teachers College, Columbia University, 1947. Chapter five identifies and analyzes the learning opportunities which confront children and youth in everyday situations and shows how teachers can use these to help students to develop an ability to solve problems and achieve worth-while purposes.

Thomas, Lawrence G., *et al.*, *Perspective on Teaching*, chap. 12, "How Do We Know Whether Children Are Making Progress?" Englewood Cliffs, N.J.: Prentice-Hall, Inc., 1961. A good survey of approaches to evaluation.

PERIODICALS

Bush, Robert Nelson, "A Study of Student-Teacher Relationships," *Journal of Educational Research*, Vol. 35, May, 1942, pp. 645-56. This research study describes the relationship existing between a number of teachers and their students and formulates an hypothesis concerning the characteristics of an effective student-teacher relationship.

Gross, Richard E., and Frederick J. McDonald, "The Problem-Solving Approach," *Phi Delta Kappan*, Vol. 39, March, 1958, pp. 259-65. A scholarly discussion of the meaning of problem-solving as a method of teaching, and a review of relevant research.

Heffermber, Helen, "Evaluation—More Than Testing," *NEA Journal*, Vol. 47, April, 1958, pp. 227-29. States that educators who have kept up with the progress that has been made in child study and the learning process are putting increased emphasis on understanding the child as compared with testing him.

Markey, Oscar B., M.D., and Gladys Herbkersman, "An Experiment in Student Responsibility," *The School Review*, Vol. 69, Summer, 1961, pp. 169-80. An interesting experiment in the teaching of English in which the teacher moves to the side lines, and the students assume a large share of the responsibility for teaching themselves.

Moulton, J. Paul, "Other-directed and Inner-directed Teachers Look at Education," *The School Review*, Vol. 45, Winter, 1957, pp. 442-56. A valuable study which attempts to determine how teachers with different personality orientations view the teacher's tasks.

Robinson, Donald W., "Democracy Is Not For Children," *Phi Delta Kappan*, Vol. 42, pp. 361-62. A teacher traces the pitfalls of "democracy" in the classroom.

Rockwell, Jack G., "Pupils Responsibility For Behavior," *Elementary School Journal*, Vol. 51, January, 1951, pp. 266-70. This article suggests ten teaching methods for helping pupils take responsibility for activities and conduct in the classroom.

Thelen, Herbert A., "The Experimental Method in Classroom Leadership," *Elementary School Journal*, Vol. 53, 1952, pp. 76-85. This article lists four functions of a leader who is helping a group to become self-directive. The author believes that leaders should not be passive. He outlines what they should do instead of laying out tasks to be performed.

FILMS

Guiding the Growth of Children

Demonstrations of a teacher's influence on student growth and development. Importance of guidance as a teacher's function. (McGraw-Hill Book Co., Inc., black and white, 18 minutes.)

Learning Through Cooperative Planning

Cooperative planning techniques in elementary school shown through school council, planning and participating in community's spring clean-up campaign, and school exhibit of accomplishments. Stresses essential steps in group of planning. (Columbia University, black and white, 18 minutes.)

Practicing Democracy in the Classroom

Examples of democratic methods in a Kalamazoo American history class. Shared responsibility in student-teacher planning. (Encyclopaedia Britannica Films Inc., black and white, 21 minutes.)

Teacher as Observer and Guide

Six school situations illustrate the following concepts: guiding pupils to better ways of solving their problems; developing artistic talent; promoting the growth of character and citizenship; and providing needed assistance for slow learners. (Columbia University, black and white, 22 minutes.)

Teacher and Pupils Planning and Working Together

Students are shown learning to work together. They organize themselves into functional groups to make and carry out plans for investigation and to present their findings and recommendations in a group report. (McGraw-Hill Book Co., Inc., black and white, 19 minutes.)

We Plan Together

Eleventh grade class cooperatively plans a core program. Adjustment of a new student; new techniques in rating individual progress and growth. (Columbia University, black and white, 20 minutes.)

CHAPTER 10

DIRECTED LEARNING

"Take this fish and look at it."

LOUIS AGASSIZ

When Rousseau taught Emile the importance of astronomy, he suggested a walk in the woods, contrived to get lost, and then asked: "My dear Emile, what shall we do to get out?"

When Louis Agassiz [1] began to teach Samuel Scudder ichthyology in his laboratory at Harvard, he pulled a fish from a jar of yellow alcohol, laid it before him and said: "Look at it . . . and by and by I will ask you what you have seen." He left, and Scudder was alone with the fish and assignment.

There are some similarities between the leadership provided by Rousseau and Agassiz. Both refused to give their students ready-made answers. Both Emile and Scudder were given a great deal of freedom to explore and find answers. The responsibility in each case was fixed on the student. Both students faced problem situations which they found disconcerting: Emile being lost, and Scudder facing an alcohol soaked fish, unable to see what the professor thought he should see.

But here the similarity ends. The real differences lay in the kind of leadership provided by the teachers. Emile's learning activities depended upon his immediate interests. He pursued them or dropped them, depending upon his motivation. He set his own standard of achievement, and if his progress were evaluated, he did the evaluating. In all this Rousseau was friend and guide, but not director.

[1] Samuel Scudder, "In The Laboratory With Louis Agassiz," *Every Saturday*, April 4, 1874, pp. 369-70.

Agassiz gave Scudder the fish, instructed him in the use and care of it, and told him to observe it. He would come back to check Scudder's progress. Agassiz made clear that there were definite things to be learned about the fish, that these things were important to know. It was up to Scudder to learn them. In this Agassiz would be the friendly director, pointing out mistakes, commending good efforts, and pointing the way.

THE DIRECTIVE TEACHER MAKES THESE ASSUMPTIONS
ABOUT TEACHING AND LEARNING

The difference between non-directed and directed learning is profound. The teacher who directs learning makes different assumptions about teaching. He believes that it is his responsibility to plan the learning activities of the young. Youth should be given the advantage which experience and maturity have given him. The teacher should spare students the trials and errors of undirected learning.

He considers it important to know all that he can about his subject, and he transmits his knowledge to students in the best possible manner. He does advance planning for teaching and makes important decisions, such as what should be taught, where, and how. He believes that he is a paid representative of society and that he is expected to assume these responsibilities and not delegate them to youth.

The directive teacher holds a different view on the role of interest in learning. Rousseau waited for Emile to develop interest. Agassiz believed that interest comes from work which reveals new discoveries. Interest grows with understanding, and understanding is achieved through application. The fish which was at first revolting to Scudder became an object full of mystery and fascination when he applied himself to it. It was not so at first. This interest grew under the friendly prodding of the instructor.

Agassiz did not have as much confidence in the inherent "goodness" of youth as did Rousseau. Rousseau believed that Emile had a "built in" sense or right direction which, if not distorted by meddling adults, would bring him out all right. Agassiz had a different view. He believed that Scudder had neither a "built in" sense of right, nor wrong direction. He was simply capable of learning, and how he came out would depend upon how well he learned. And how well he learned was a part of Agassiz's responsibility as teacher.

Now, let us turn to Scudder's own story of his experiences while working in Agassiz's laboratory. Here are some questions worth keeping in mind as we enter the laboratory.

1. How do you think Rousseau would evaluate Agassiz's teaching?

2. How do you think Agassiz would evaluate Rousseau's teaching?

3. If you were given a choice of having either Rousseau or Agassiz as a teacher, which would you choose? How do you explain your choice?

WE ENTER THE LABORATORY OF LOUIS AGASSIZ

It was more than fifteen years ago that I entered the laboratory of Professor Agassiz, and told him I had enrolled my name in the Scientific School as a student of natural history. He asked me a few questions about my object in coming, my antecedents generally, the mode in which I afterwards proposed to use the knowledge I might acquire, and, finally, whether I wished to study any special branch. To the latter I replied that, while I wished to be well grounded in all departments of zoology, I purposed to devote myself specially to insects.

"When do you wish to begin?" he asked.

"Now," I replied.

This seemed to please him and with an energetic "very well," he reached from a shelf a huge jar of specimens in yellow alcohol.

"Take this fish," said he, "and look at it; we call it a haemulon, by and by I will ask you what you have seen."

With that he left me, but in a moment returned with explicit instructions as to the care of the object entrusted to me.

"No man is fit to be a naturalist," said he, "who does not know how to take care of specimens."

I was to keep the fish before me in a tin tray, and occasionally moisten the surface with alcohol from the jar, always taking care to replace the stopper tightly. Those were not the days of ground-glass stoppers and elegantly shaped exhibition jars; all the old students will recall the huge neckless glass bottle with their leaky, wax-besmeared corks, half eaten by insects, and begrimed with cellar dust. Entomology was a cleaner science than ichthyology, but the example of the Professor, who had unhesitatingly plunged to the bottom of the jar to produce the fish, was infectious; and though this alcohol had a very ancient and fish-like smell, I really dared not show any aversion within these sacred precincts, and treated the alcohol as though it were pure water. Still, I was conscious of a passing feeling of disappointment, for gazing at a fish did not commend itself to an ardent entomologist. My friends at home, too, were annoyed, when they discovered that no amount of eau-de-Cologne would drown the perfume which haunted me like a shadow.

Let's pause a moment after this brief introduction to Professor Agassiz. What is your first impression of him? How would you describe him as a teacher? Let's look at some specifics.

The professor treated the fish with great care and instructed Scudder in giving it similar care. "No man is fit to be a naturalist," he said, "who does not know how to take care of specimens." In this act Agassiz made clear to Scudder his own estimate of the importance of the task he was undertaking. It was not just any fish; it was a particular kind of fish with special value. It was worthy of study. An expectation was already set up in the student's mind. Certain standards were there. It was expected that the student would live up to them.

4. Do you think that students tend to want to live up to the expectations of teachers? Does it make any difference if the teacher's expectation is high or low?

A tone was already established in the laboratory. The teacher was not making work for the student. There was no amount to be "covered," then forgotten. The teacher's earnest, infectious manner told Scudder that Agassiz believed deeply in what he taught, was enthusiastic about it, and hoped the student would share the enthusiasm.

Agassiz knows that Scudder does not have this enthusiasm at present. However, he believes that he can help Scudder develop that enthusiasm through his kindly, yet exacting, directions. He is not waiting on Scudder; he is leading.

5. Agassiz is both exacting and friendly. Do you feel these values conflict with one another in teaching?

Let us see how Scudder tackles his assignment.

In ten minutes I had seen all that could be seen in that fish, and started in search of the Professor—who had, however, left the Museum; and when I returned, after lingering over some of the odd animals stored in the upper apartment, my specimen was dry all over. I dashed the fluid over the fish as if to resuscitate the beast from a fainting-fit, and looked with anxiety for a return to the normal sloppy appearance. This little excitement over, nothing was to be done but to return to a steadfast gaze at my mute companion. Half an hour passed—an hour—another hour; the fish began to look loathsome. I turned it over and around; looked it in the face—ghastly; from behind, beneath, above, sideways, at a three-quarters' view—just as ghastly. I was in despair; at an early hour I concluded that lunch was necessary; so, with infinite relief, the fish was carefully replaced in the jar, and for an hour I was free.

On my return, I learned that Professor Agassiz had been at the Museum, but had gone, and would not return for several hours. My fellow students were too busy to be disturbed by continued conversation. Slowly, I drew forth that hideous fish, and with a feeling of desperation again looked at it. I might not use a magnifying-glass; instruments of all kinds were interdicted. My two hands, my two eyes, and the fish: it seemed a most limited field. I pushed my finger down its throat to feel how sharp the teeth were. I began to count the scales in the different rows, until I was convinced that that was nonsense. At last a happy thought struck me—I would draw the fish; and now with surprise I began to discover new features in the creature. Just then the Professor returned.

Note Scudder's behavior in this episode. After ten minutes of observing the fish he has seen all he can see; he goes in search of the professor. He has exhausted his own resources and needs support. The professor is not available, and he is thrown back upon himself and the fish, the latter growing more loathsome with every glance. He has another look at the fish; it is no use. After lunch he tries again. He wishes for outside assistance in the form of a magnifying glass. Forbidden. Again he is thrown back upon himself, his two hands, his two eyes, and the fish. It is a "limited" field. Having to teach himself is a new and unpleasant experience.

Finally, almost at the end of his wits, he gets a happy thought—draw the fish. That is the turning point. He begins to find satisfaction in something which he, not the professor, has decided. He has made his own decision and it is rewarding. He has started to teach himself at last.

6. Had Scudder been under Rousseau's guidance, do you think he would have persisted to the point of making his own decision to draw the fish?

7. How do you explain the fact that Scudder's interest picked up after he began to draw the fish?

8. What part does unhappiness play in learning? Before Scudder began to find any satisfaction in studying the fish, he experienced frustration and unhappiness. Did this serve to hasten or delay the time that he picked up the pencil and began to draw the fish?

In this incident we see a major assumption in directed learning. It is that interests grow as we are introduced to new and, possibly at first, uninteresting activities. Asks the teacher: Why should students have an interest in matters about which they are as yet uninformed? Interest comes with understanding. As teacher it is my business to introduce students to new and unexplored regions. They may not find much interest in them at first. But as they gain insight, they will gain interest. Having gained some interest they can proceed independently.

Note, too, the student relationships in Professor Agassiz's laboratory. Each student is carrying on an individual project. There is little socialization or joint learning among students. Each is working under the leadership of the directing professor. Scudder notices that each student is bent on his own project. He senses that he should not interrupt and so returns to his own work.

9. Do you think the students in the laboratory might have learned more had they worked in teams, as well as alone?

Professor Agassiz returns to the laboratory.

"That is right," said he; "a pencil is one of the best of eyes. I am glad to notice, too, that you keep your specimen wet, and your bottle corked."

With these encouraging words, he added: "Well, what is it like?"

He listened attentively to my brief rehearsal of the structure of parts whose names were still unknown to me: the fringed gill-arches and movable operculum; the pores of the head, flesh lips and lidless eyes; the lateral line, the spinous fins and forked tail; the compressed and arched body. When I had finished, he waited as if expecting more, and then, with an air of disappointment:

"You have not looked very carefully; why," he continued more earnestly, "you haven't even seen one of the most conspicuous features of the animal, which is as plainly before your eyes as the fish itself; look again, look again!" and he left me to my misery.

"I was piqued; I was mortified. Still more of that wretched fish! But now I set myself to my task with a will, and discovered one thing new after another, until I saw how just the professor's criticism had been. The afternoon passed quickly; and when, toward its close, the Professor inquired:

"Do you see it yet?"

"No," I replied, "I am certain I do not, but I see how little I saw before."

"That is next best," he said, earnestly, "but I won't hear you now. Put your fish away and go home; perhaps you will be ready with a better answer in the morning. I will examine you before you look at the fish."

This was disconcerting. Not only must I think of my fish all night, studying, without the object before me, what this unknown but most visible feature might be; but also, without reviewing my new discoveries, I must give an exact account of them the next day. I

had a bad memory; so I walked home by Charles River in a dis-
tracted state, with my two perplexities.

How would you describe Agassiz's behavior in this scene? He commends
Scudder for the use of the pencil in drawing, the good care of the specimen. Then straight to the business: "What is it like?" He is disappointed
with the answer and says so. The standards are still high, the expectation
great. He leaves Scudder to his misery, as he tries again. He still doesn't
see it, though he does see how little he "saw before." This draws a half
compliment: "That is next best," and the suggestion that Scudder quit
for the day. More anxiety.

Note the learning hurdles in Agassiz's laboratory. There is a series of
them. In fact learning itself is assumed to be the practice of surmounting
increasingly difficult hurdles. The professor commends the student for
one achievement and promptly sets before him another more difficult
hurdle.

Agassiz passes judgement: "You have not looked very carefully," he
tells his student. He believes that improved learning results from correction of errors. He does not gloss over, or tell the student, "Well, you
tried." He is fully honest. At first the student reacts negatively. He is
mortified. But he tries again and begins to see new and more productive
efforts. He is still not free of anxiety. Now he must take his problems
home and return with an answer.

10. How do you react to Agassiz's criticism of Scudder's work? Do you think it
is well handled?

Let's return to the scene in the laboratory the next morning.

The cordial greeting from the professor the next morning was
reassuring; here was a man who seemed to be quite as anxious as
I that I should see for myself what he saw.

"Do you perhaps mean," I asked, "that the fish has symmetrical
sides with paired organs?"

His throughly pleased "of course!" repaid the wakeful hours of
the previous night. After he had discoursed more happily and
enthusiastically—as he always did—upon the importance of this
point, I ventured to ask what I should do next.

"Oh, look at your fish!" he said, and left me again to my own
devices. In a little more than an hour he returned, and heard my
new catalogue.

"That is good, that is good!" he repeated; "but that is not all; go
on"; and so for three long days he placed that fish before my eyes,

forbidding me to look at anything else, or to use any artificial aid. "Look, look, look," was his repeated injunction.

This was the best entomological lesson I ever had—a lesson whose influence has extended to the details of every subsequent study; a legacy the professor has left to me, as he has left it to many others, of inestimable value, which we could not buy, with which we cannot part.

A year afterward, some of us were amusing ourselves with chalking outlandish beasts on the Museum blackboard. We drew prancing starfishes; frogs in mortal combat; hydraheaded worms; stately crawfishes, standing on their tails, bearing aloft umbrellas; and grotesque fishes with gaping mouths and staring eyes. The professor came in shortly after, and was as amused as any at our experiments. He looked at the fishes.

"Haemulons, every one of them," he said; "Mr. _____ drew them."

True; and to this day, if I attempt a fish, I can draw nothing but haemulons.

The fourth day, a second fish of the same group was placed beside the first, and I was bidden to point out the resemblances and differences between the two; another and another followed, until the entire family lay before me, and a whole legion of jars covered the table and surrounding shelves; the odor had become a pleasant perfume; and even now, the sight of an old, six-inch, worm-eaten cork brings fragrant memories.

The whole group of haemulons was thus brought in review; and, whether engaged upon the dissection of the internal organs, the preparation and examination of the bony framework, or the description of the various parts, Agassiz's training in the method of observing facts and their orderly arrangement was ever accompanied by the urgent exhortation not to be content with them.

"Facts are stupid things," he would say, "until brought into connection with some general law."

At the end of eight months, it was almost with reluctance that I left these friends and turned to insects; but what I had gained by this outside experience has been of greater value than years of later investigation in my favorite groups.

Again achievement is followed by challenge. Agassiz is thoroughly pleased that Scudder has finally discovered that the fish has symmetrical sides. What shall he do next? "Oh, look at your fish!" "Go on." "Go on." Finally when the first fish is thoroughly studied another new challenge, a second fish, is placed before him for comparative study.

What is the effect of the continuing challenges upon Scudder? His interest in the subject is broadening, until finally the alcohol itself is a pleasant perfume and the old corks are producing fragrant memories.

The one theme that runs through Scudder's narrative is the ever-present direction of the professor. He may leave the laboratory completely while Scudder works on his own, but the student is constantly aware of his leadership. He points the way, sets the standards of excellence, insists upon the student persisting in his observations even though he is reluctant to do so.

Yet, he does not dominate Scudder. He does not give a lecture for the student to memorize and remember. He does not assign a chapter in a text. He does not give answers. Within his directed laboratory there is yet another kind of direction—self direction.

Scudder may have experienced less frustration had Agassiz used more conventional methods. Had Agassiz pointed out all of the characteristics of the haemulon in a lecture, Scudder's job would have been simpler: take notes, memorize, and rewrite the answers at examination time. But Agassiz's directions did not extend to this kind of control. His method gave Scudder freedom to find out for himself and thereby teach himself. It gave him more than freedom to find out (Emile had such freedom, too); it gave him the feeling that the professor *expected* him to find out and had confidence in his ability to do so. The professor was not reluctant to use the force of his influence to promote learning. He set high standards and was as eager as his students that they should reach them.

11. How about the series of hurdles which Agassiz places before Scudder? Do you think such hurdles should be a part of learning?

COMPARE AGASSIZ AND ROUSSEAU

In question number three you were asked which of these two men you would prefer as teacher. Let's draw them together for some brief comparisons and contrasts.

The student, to Agassiz, was important, but the thing to be learned was more important. In Agassiz's laboratory the thing to be learned was the center of interest. The focus was on the fish and its secrets. In Rousseau's outdoor laboratory the focus was on Emile. Agassiz believed that Scudder would grow through what he learned; therefore what he learned was crucial. Rousseau believed that it made little difference what Emile learned so long as he *understood* it and knew how to *use* it.

Agassiz set up standards of achievement. They were high. He expected his students to achieve those standards. Rousseau set no fixed standards for Emile, except those he set for himself. Rousseau was indeed interested in Emile's developing his own standards. He was opposed to setting them for him.

Agassiz believed that students generate interest as they are exposed to new experiences. These new experiences may not be interesting at first. They will be interesting later as the student gains insight. Scudder's boredom turned to interest only after he made some discoveries on his own. Rousseau believed that the student should never learn anything because he is told. Left upon his own with opportunity to explore and probe, he will develop interest when he finds use for the knowledge. Then he can be taught.

Agassiz didn't wait for this development. He believed it was the teacher's responsibility to provide those experiences, and then direct them. To do less would be to shirk his responsibility as an adult and teacher.

HOW IS DIRECTED LEARNING EVALUATED?

How is evaluation carried out in directed learning? How should grades be assigned? Look again at Agassiz's laboratory. The professor indicated to Scudder that there are certain things to know about the fish. All students of ichthyology should know them. The professor is the one who knows them already. The student does not. Who, then, can judge what the student has learned? The professor, of course.

Agassiz's method of evaluation is straightforward: "Well, what have you seen?" If the answer is right or wrong, he says so on the spot. He also evaluates what Scudder has not seen: "You have not looked very carefully . . ." He hopes that his evaluation will lead Scudder on to more diligent observations, and further discoveries.

There is another kind of evaluation in Agassiz's laboratory. Almost without his knowing it, Scudder begins to evaluate his own work. He is incapable of it at first. But under the professor's prodding he begins to understand how much there is to know about the fish, and how little he actually does know. "I see how little I saw before," he tells Agassiz. He is slowly gaining a position from which he can measure his own achievement. He is never asked by Agassiz: "How well do you think you're doing," or "What grade do you think you have earned?" He is simply gaining some of the professor's understanding and with it an ability to judge his own performance. In a sense he is becoming independent of the professor, upon whom he wished to lean so heavily at first.

12. Do you think Scudder would have achieved this growing independence if Agassiz had not first given him standards by which to measure his achievement?

Teacher-directed learning usually implies that the teacher will lead in evaluation, assuming full responsibility for assigning grades. The aim, however, is to give the student means of developing his own critical standards. With these he can eventually become his own best evaluator.

HOW SHALL WE JUDGE DIRECTED LEARNING?

As we said, teacher direction assumes that the teacher knows what students should learn. He expects that they will learn it. There is a risk here. The directing teacher may have structured so well what is to be learned that the student's own unique contribution to learning may be stifled.

Teacher direction needs to allow for individual differences. In setting a single standard of excellence, some students, incapable of achieving it, may revolt. Their revolt may take many forms. Some may withdraw from competition, some may look for diversion, some may become aggressive. The directing teacher must be prepared to watch the development of individual students and work out suitable programs for them.

Teacher-directed learning has attractive features. If the teacher has ordered the work well, the chances are students will understand their tasks. The work is well planned. A sensible sequence of learning activities is available to the student. Scudder first mastered the haemulon; only then he was given a second fish for comparative study. The general aim of the learning was always clear.

Teacher direction gives a student freedom to learn, but it also gives him support and guidance as he proceeds. The amount of direction given by the teacher can be adjusted to the student's needs at a particular time. The aim is eventual freedom for the student to carry on his own learning with only occasional reference to the teacher. Under good direction the student should grow away from the teacher and be less dependent upon him. Independence is the goal.

Good Follow-up Reading and Viewing

BOOKS

Aiken, Wilford M., *The Story of the Eight Year Study*. New York: Harper & Brothers, 1942. Chapter six presents evidence that there are many ways to help students learn what they need to know to be in college.
Association for Supervision and Curriculum Development, *Creating a Good Environment for Learning*, chaps. 1-6. Washington, D.C.: National Education Association, 1954. The work of teachers at various levels—primary, interme-

diate, junior high school, and senior high school—is presented in a realistic, interesting way.

————, *Leadership for Improving Instruction.* Washington, D.C.: National Education Association, 1960. Deals with leadership principles and methods which can be described and used by teachers in the classrooms of a democracy.

————, *Toward Better Teaching*, chap. 4, "Helping Pupils Develop Self Direction." Washington, D.C.: National Education Association, 1949. Ways and means by which teachers can get students to assume ever-increasing responsibilities for their own educations.

Boyce, Burke, *Miss Mallett*. New York: Harper & Brothers, 1948. The story of a teacher who made learning an adventure.

Cronbach, Lee J., *Educational Psychology*, chap. 15, "The Teacher As Classroom Leader." New York: Harcourt, Brace & World, Inc., 1954. Discusses undirected, teacher-controlled, and group-controlled activities, with illustrative cases. Good section on the effects of various control patterns upon students.

French, Will, and William L. Romson, *Evaluating the Curriculum for Provision for Meeting the Imperative Needs of Youth*, Bulletin No. 154, pp. 48-69. Washington, D.C.: National Education Association, 1948. Ten kinds of instruction and methods for evaluating each.

Grant, Madeleine P., "Learning in Biology," in *Essays in Teaching*, Harold Taylor, ed. New York: Harper & Brothers, 1950. The experience of a college teacher in using the questions and interests of students for the teaching of biology. "If we study the student as well as the subject we are more apt to promote learning."

Haskew, Laurence D., *This Is Teaching*, chap. 6, "What Teachers Do In School." Chicago: Scott, Foresman & Company, 1956. Discusses the different tasks teachers perform as they work with students.

Lippitt, Ronald, and Ralph K. White, "An Experimental Study of Leadership and Group Life," in *Readings in Social Psychology*, Guy E. Swanson, *et al.*, eds. New York: Holt, Rinehart & Winston, Inc., 1952. Summarizes a classic study of boy's clubs treated with different control techniques. Both the individual boys and the statistical results are discussed.

Van Dalen, Deobold B., and Robert W. Brittell, *Looking Ahead To Teaching*, chap. 15, "The Teacher At Work." Boston: Allyn and Bacon, Inc., 1959. Discusses how to establish objectives, translate objectives into plans, and develop unit and daily lesson plans.

PERIODICALS

Chamberlain, John, "Orville Platt High," *The Wall Street Journal*, February 13, 1959, p. 6. This is a description of the Orville Platt High School in Meriden, Connecticut, an industrial town with a population of 40,000. It also gives an account of the freshman English and Latin classes, the books used, the requirements for the courses and the teaching methods employed.

Dalton, W. Theo., "Classroom Atmosphere Reflects Quality of Learning," *Educational Leadership*, Vol. 9, April, 1951, pp. 429-33. This article shows how the attitudes of the teacher are reflected in the confidence of the children and what they learn.

Eby, Kermit, "A Tribute to My Teachers," *The Educational Forum*, Vol. 25,

January, 1961, pp. 215-20. A well-known social scientist recalls the great teachers who taught him.

Edmund, Neal R., and Charles Guzzetta, "The Democratic Classroom," *Peabody Journal of Education,* Vol. 38, July, 1960. One hundred and forty-five teachers list those conditions which are, or are not, necessary to the existence of a democratic classroom.

McNeil, John D., "Toward Appreciation of Teaching Methods," *Phi Delta Kappan,* Vol. 39, March, 1958, pp. 295-301. An evaluation of the directive and non-directive approaches to teaching, in the light of recent findings in social psychology.

Rushworth, Vivian, "Science is Exciting," *NEA Journal,* Vol. 47, May, 1958, pp. 328-29. A fascinating account by a sixth grade teacher relating how her students studied biology. Through thought-provoking questions the teacher directs the students to explore a wide variety of new vistas.

FILMS

Accent on Learning

A variety of teaching techniques to make learning effective. Teaching as effective communication involving good organization of materials, illustrations from everyday experience, constant re-examination of methods, and creative thinking. Value and use of varied teaching tools. (Ohio State, black and white, 30 minutes.)

Broader Concept of Method:

Part II—Teachers and Pupils Working Together

How group participation provides students with experience in thinking, self-expression and evaluation of results while the teacher functions primarily in an advisory capacity. (McGraw-Hill Book Co., Inc., black and white, 19 minutes.)

Fundamental Skills in a Unit of Work

How one teacher guided pupil effort in a unit of work on "How Man Keeps His Records." How opportunities were provided for functional use and development of reading, writing, arithmetic, and other study skills. Developmental approach to unit teaching; social values inherent in this method. (Bailey Films, Inc., black and white, 20 minutes.)

Profiles of Elementary Physical Education

Successful methods used in teaching physical education in the elementary grades. Importance of careful organization. Helpful ideas for the guidance of class activities. (Coronet Instructional Films, black and white, 32 minutes.)

CHAPTER 11

DOMINATED LEARNING

> In order to form the minds of children, the first thing to be
> done is to conquer their will.
>
> SUSANNA WESLEY

Teacher-dominated learning stands in sharp contrast to non-directed and directed learning. The teacher who employs non-directed learning stands at one end of the leadership spectrum. The teacher who dominates learning stands at the opposite end. The teacher who directs learning stands someplace near the middle of the spectrum, borrowing some methods and techniques from each.

Rousseau, employing non-directed learning, gave freedom to Emile. Agassiz, employing directed learning, gave limited freedom to Scudder, while at the same time structuring what he should learn. Susanna Wesley [1] taught her nineteen children under a rigid prescription which permitted little or no freedom of individual action. The child was to be submissive, listen to what he was told, and learn his lessons well. Within these adult-built walls he had freedom; outside these walls, he had little or none.

We warned in chapter nine that Rousseau, Agassiz, and Wesley were not to be thought of as models of ways of working with students. Their value as cases lies in their attitudes, beliefs, and feelings about how a teacher should relate himself to students. Susanna Wesley represents a way of viewing students. Her practice reveals certain fundamental assumptions about teacher-learner relationships. Her particular practice of these relationships may seem harsh to us, since they reflect her culture

---

[1] Nehemiah Curnack, ed., *The Journal of John Wesley* (London: The Epworth Press), Volume 3, pp. 34-39.

and time, eighteenth century England. But the values she held can be found in modern classrooms and their practice can take many modern forms. As you read the case, try your hand at this question:

1. Making allowance for Mrs. Wesley's eighteenth century language and customs, what place do you think teacher-dominated learning should have in our schools? (Later in the chapter we examine a case of teacher-dominated learning in a modern setting.)

SUSANNA WESLEY EDUCATES HER NINETEEN CHILDREN

Susanna Wesley has given us a personal description of her philosophy of teacher-dominated learning. In her case it was really parent-dominated learning, since she was both parent and teacher to her nineteen children. She explains her educational beliefs in a letter addressed to her son.

July 24, 1732

Dear Son,

According to your desire, I have collected the principal rules I observed in educating my family; which I now send you as they occurred to my mind, and you may (if you think they can be of use to any) dispose of them in what order you please.

The children were always put into a regular method of living, in such things as they were capable of, from their birth; as in dressing, undressing, changing their linen, etc. The first quarter commonly passes in sleep. After that they were, if possible, laid into their cradles awake, and rocked to sleep; and so they were kept rocking till it was time for them to awake. This was done to bring them to a regular course of sleeping; which at first was three hours in the morning and three in the afternoon; afterwards two hours, till they needed none at all.

When turned a year old (and some before), they were taught to fear the rod, and to cry softly; by which means they escaped abundance of correction they might otherwise have had, and that most odious noise of the crying of children was rarely heard in the house, but the family usually lived in as much quietness as if there had not been a child among them.

As soon as they were grown pretty strong, they were confined to three meals a day. At dinner their little table and chairs were set by ours, where they could be overlooked; and they were suffered to eat and drink as much as they would; but not to call for anything. If they wanted aught they used to whisper to the maid which attended them, who came and spake to me; and as soon as they could handle a knife and fork, they were set to our table. They were never suffered to choose their meat, but always made eat such things as were provided for the family.

Mornings they had always spoon meat; sometimes on nights. But whatever they had, they were never permitted to eat at those meals of more than one thing; and of that sparingly enough. Drinking or eating between meals was never allowed, unless in case of sickness; which seldom happened. Nor were they suffered to go into the kitchen to ask anything of the servants when they were at meat; if it was known they did, they were certainly beat, and the servants severely reprimanded.

At six, as soon as family prayers were over, they had their supper; at seven the maid washed them; and, beginning at the youngest, she undressed and got them all to bed by eight; at which time she left them in their several rooms awake—for there was no such thing allowed of in our house as sitting till it fell asleep.

They were so constantly used to eat and drink what was given them that, when any of them was ill, there was no difficulty in making them take the most unpleasant medicine; for they durst not refuse it, although some of them would presently throw it up. This I mention to show that a person may be taught to take anything, though it be ever so much against his stomach.

In order to form the minds of children, the first thing to be done is to conquer their will, and bring them to an obedient temper. To inform the understanding is a work of time, and must with children proceed by slow degrees as they are able to bear it; but the subjecting the will is a thing that must be done at once, and the sooner the better . . .

2. Contrast the life of Emile with that of one of Mrs. Wesley's children. Which do you think was the happier child? Which do you think learned the more?

Look at some of the salient features in Mrs. Wesley's approach. First, there was order, a schedule, which put all matters of daily living on a regular basis. The child knew what would happen, when, and how. There was a minimum of uncertainty and a maximum of certainty. The children also knew what the penalties were if they violated the well-ordered pattern. The rules and penalties for violating them were clear.

There are few problems here for children to solve. Contrast this with the problems set before Emile and Scudder. In the Wesley home the child's main problem was to learn the will of the parent and then comply with it. Major and minor decisions are made by adults. Learning consists in being able to understand their decisions and act in accordance with them.

Sometimes such compliance will be distasteful, as when taking bitter pills. A child might throw them up, but the important thing is that he can be taught to take them, distasteful though they be. Here is Mrs. Wesley's key belief: The prerequisite to learning is willingness to submit to authority. Once this child has developed an "obedient temper," a "great many childish follies and inadvertences may be passed by."

> 3. How do you think modern parents would feel about Mrs. Wesley's key belief? Take a survey of some of the parents you know. Share your findings with the class.

Here is how Mrs. Wesley practiced teacher-dominated learning.

None of them were taught to read till five years old, except Kezzy, in whose case I was overruled; and she was more years learning than any of the rest had been months. The way of teaching was this: the day before a child began to learn, the house was set in order, every one's work appointed them, and a charge given that none should come into the room from nine till twelve, or from two till five; which, you know were our school hours. One day was allowed the child wherein to learn its letters; and each of them did in that time know all its letters, great and small, except Molly and Nancy, who were a day and a half before they knew them perfectly; for which I then thought them very dull; but since I have observed how long many children are learning the hornbook, I have changed my opinion. But the reason why I thought them so then was because the rest learned so readily; and your brother Samuel, who was the first child I ever taught, learned the alphabet in a few hours. He was five years old on the 10th of February; the next day he began to learn; and, as soon as he knew the letters, began at the first chapter of Genesis. He was taught to spell the first verse, then to read it over and over, till he could read it off-hand without any hesitation; so on to the second, &c., till he took ten verses for a lesson which he quickly did. Easter fell low that year; and by whitsuntide he could read a chapter very well; for he read continually, and had such a prodigious memory that I cannot remember ever to have told him the same word twice.

What was yet stranger, any word he had learned in his lesson he knew wherever he saw it, either in his Bible or any other book; by which means he learned very soon to read an English author well.

The same method was observed with them all. As soon as they knew the letters, they were put first to spell, and read one line, then a verse; never leaving till perfect in their lesson, were it shorter or longer. So one or other continued reading at school-time, without any intermission; and before we left, each child read what he had learned that morning; and, ere we parted in the afternoon, what they had learned that day.

There was no such thing as loud talking or playing allowed of, but everyone was kept close to their business, for the six hours of school: and it is almost incredible what a child may be taught in a quarter of a year, by a vigorous application, if it have but a tolerable capacity and good health. Every one of these, Kezzy excepted, could read better in that time than the most of women can do as long as they live.

Rising out of their place, or going out of the room, was not permitted unless for good cause; and running into the yard, garden, or street, without leave was always esteemed a capital offence.

Here is teacher-dominated learning carried to its ultimate. The classroom is set in "order." The time for learning is precisely fixed. There are no interruptions. Each child knows what he is supposed to do. While learning, the children are forbidden to play or run about. No lesson is put aside until it is perfectly learned. At the end of each period, the child recites what he has learned.

The goals of learning are understood, also the time allotted for achieving them. In Mrs. Wesley's classroom a child of five years of age automatically was ready to learn to read. One day was spent in learning the letters, another period on spelling, another on reading. How about individual differences? And Mrs. Wesley's children did have individual differences! It took Molly and Nancy "a day and a half" to learn their letters. But Samuel learned the alphabet in a few hours! Or, take Kezzy. For some reason which isn't clear, Kezzy did not begin to read at five, and she was "more years learning than any of the rest of them had been months."

These individual differences did not keep Mrs. Wesley from pursuing her well-ordered pace for learning. Because Kezzy was slow she did not believe that all children should be taught at Kezzy's pace. Indeed, she took Samuel, her first child, and apparently one of the brightest, as her example. The rest of the children, she reasoned, should be brought along at his rapid pace.

Here she demonstrated her belief that children have infinite capacity to learn, if they are constantly challenged to outdo themselves. Her teaching pace was geared to her brightest child rather than her slowest.

4. In your own classroom, would you pace your program to the speed of the slowest child, the fastest child, or someplace in between? Explain your reasons.

5. Interview a teacher concerning his experience in dealing with children of widely differing abilities. Ask him at what level he pitches his program. Share your findings with the class.

Mrs. Wesley was pleased with the results of her method of teaching. Most of her children learned rapidly and well. As she said: "It is almost incredible what a child may be taught in a quarter of a year, by a vigorous application." The accent is on "vigorous." Teacher-controlled learning in the hands of a skillful teacher may produce remarkable results.

Unlearning May Take Place

One question keeps returning: Are children likely to revert under too long and intense learning pressure? Will they unlearn what they supposedly have learned? The teacher whose control and direction of learning is pervasive must watch for negative reactions. He accepts some of them as a normal part of learning. But if they reach what he considers critical proportions he acts. The emphasis is shifted to other learning activities to provide variety and relief.

Mrs. Wesley did not escape this problem. The family home burned and the children were scattered among several families. What happened she describes in the final paragraph which we quote from her letter. What do you guess happened when her children came under different influences? Let's see.

> For some years we went on very well. Never were children in better order. Never were children better disposed to piety or in more subjection to their parents, till that fatal dispersion of them, after the fire, into several families. In these they were left at full liberty to converse with servants, which before they had always been restrained from; and to run abroad, and play with any children, good or bad. They soon learned to neglect a strict observation of the Sabbath, and got knowledge of several songs and bad things, which before they had no notion of. That civil behaviour which made them admired when at home by all which saw them was, in great measure, lost; and a clownish accent and many rude ways were learned, which were not reformed without some difficulty.

It is obvious that Mrs. Wesley was disturbed by what happened to her children when they came under other influences. The learning which she thought had become habit turned out to be not so fixed after all. The good manners which she thought she had instilled gave way under pressure. It seems clear that her children had not made her standards of conduct entirely their own. Given the opportunity, they embraced other kinds of conduct.

What was the flaw in her teaching method? Rousseau would probably retort: "It's clear to see. Mrs. Wesley should have expected this to happen. You see, she paid too little attention to her children's real and present interests." Agassiz would probably say that Mrs. Wesley was doing sound teaching in expecting high standards of performance and conduct. That part is all right. "What she should have done was to give the children more freedom in activities leading to these goals. Set up activities in which they can find out for themselves what is right. Then they won't revert."

If Mrs. Wesley had her own reasons for the unlearning which took place she doesn't tell us in her letter. We can presume that she would have simply attributed it to bad influences in the new environments. She was still determined, however, that corrections could be made, though with "some difficulty." Her methods, she felt, were sound. They would simply have to be applied with new force and vigor.

In question number one we asked: What place do you think teacher-dominated learning has in modern schools? Let's now look at an example of it in modern practice.

MR. JACKMAN DOMINATES THE LEARNING IN HIS CLASSROOM

Bill Jackman is a fifth grade teacher who is making elementary education his profession. He is young, married to an attractive wife, and is the father of three children. His own children have reinforced his interest in the education of the young. He wants to become a specialist in the field.

Step into his classroom. It is quiet. The children are in their seats, obviously busy on the day's work. In the far corner a group of four children is working around the library table, the reward for having completed their seat work. The room is orderly and neat, free from the clutter of work which is often seen in more permissive classrooms. Children's work is neatly displayed on the bulletin board.

Mr. Jackman is walking up and down the aisles giving assistance on the assignment. A number of children raise their hands to get his attention. He gives specific directions in response to each question. The pupils expect him to guide them. They want to make sure that they are doing the assignment exactly as he wants it done. Some seem very anxious to please. A few are obviously trying hard to please but do not relish doing so. Two boys in the far corner seats have stopped trying and are engaged in a furtive fencing match when Mr. Jackman's back is turned.

The orientation in the classroom is toward the teacher. There is little consultation back and forth among pupils. Committee work is used sparingly. There are few group projects. Each child works, it seems, for the teacher. He is the dominant influence in the classroom.

As the classroom work proceeds, it is clear that most students are working hard, and apparently producing good results. Some students are not achieving according to Mr. Jackman's expectations. Several of these students wrinkle their brows and try a little harder. A few are obviously near the breaking point of interest and concentration and are looking for escapes. A little girl has withdrawn totally and is gazing out the window. Mr. Jackman accepts most of this behavior as normal under the conditions. He gives each child quiet help, and his manner indicates that he expects the child to finish the work successfully. The two boys in the corner get a firm look and a warning. They snap to attention with a brief show of interest, which soon lapses when the teacher is working with other students.

As recess time approaches, the children become restless, but they show remarkable discipline in staying at their work. It is apparent that Mr. Jackman's methods are working. It is also clear that a few of the students are rebelling against the teacher and are thinking of themselves as being in a pitched battle with him. This does not concern Mr. Jackman. He knows that learning is not always easy and that children must discipline themselves to do it. He must encourage such discipline.

Recess time has come. Mr. Jackman asks the students to pay attention to him and put their work aside. He looks at the boys in the corner. "You will stay for fifteen minutes," he says, "to continue your work." He names six other children. "You have a good start," he says, "and can continue on your own. You will take the project for homework tonight and I will see your work tomorrow." The class files out for recess. Outside the school door the quiet children erupt into bedlam as they race for the playground.

Inside the school room Mr. Jackman pulls up his chair beside the two boys. One looks genuinely penitent, the other resentful. To the penitent one he says: "Graham, I think you are learning that we mean business in this classroom. We are not here to play. Do you understand? As soon as you learn to do what I say rather than what James here says, the better off you'll be. Now I would suggest that you take your work to the library table and show me that you can do it."

James has been looking the other way during this conversation, pretending not to hear or to be affected by it. Turning to him Mr. Jackman says: "James, what do you have to say for yourself?" James shifts his shoulder away from the teacher. Silence. The teacher continues: "James, we're not going to get very far until you understand one thing. In school you can't just do as you wish. We're here to learn. When we grow up we have to do lots of things we don't want to do. It's a good time now to start. Big folks, too, have to take lots of instructions from other people and abide by the rules, like stopping at red traffic lights. If we don't

Agassiz. Agassiz told Scudder what to do and, to some extent, how, and how not, to do it. Beyond that he was free to explore and find out. When Scudder thought he had discovered something worth reporting, Agassiz was there to listen, encourage, and correct. Jackman, on the other hand, took full charge of the learning process from beginning to end. He made the assignments, kept close check of the work of each child, and shaped the final results.

HOW IS TEACHER-DOMINATED LEARNING EVALUATED?

Mr. Jackman and Mrs. Wesley held their students to strict accountability. They determined the standards and judged how well each child did in relation to those standards. The children knew these standards and were constantly aware of how well they were doing. There is little uncertainty in the teacher-dominated classroom.

The dominating teacher sets up a series of learning hurdles. The hurdles are explained and made clear. Then each child is encouraged to leap those hurdles. Some will leap them easily; others will just clear them. A few students may find the hurdles too high and attempt to find other ways around them, as in the case of James in Mr. Jackman's fifth grade. In assigning grades the teacher simply determines how well each child does in relation to leaping the hurdles.

HOW SHALL WE JUDGE TEACHER-DOMINATED LEARNING?

As we said at the beginning of our discussion of the three kinds of learning, it is easy to dismiss teacher-dominated learning as "old-fashioned" and not in tune with the newer democratic education. It should not be dismissed lightly. It has value.

It insists upon certain fundamental concepts in learning, achievement, and quality. It reminds the child of what he ought to be and what he can become. It holds standards and ideals constantly before him. It urges him to achieve them. At a time when a child is groping for values and direction, it provides them. It gives firmness and support when he needs them most.

Teacher-dominated learning need not be unkind to children. In the hands of skillful teachers it can be as kind as any other type of learning. Mr. Jackman demonstrated this. Harshness is a personal quality of the teacher and can express itself through almost any method of teaching. The teacher who refuses to give any guidance to children who need it may, indeed, be harsh and unkind in the estimate of his children.

Teacher-dominated learning fails children when it does not help

them to develop goals of their own. Self-teaching is a priceless achievement in education. Independence, not dependence, is the end of learning. The dominant teacher who has achieved no more than control of
children has cheated them. The good teacher wants his students to grow
away from him, fully capable of operating without him. Indeed, he is
happiest when they supersede him in daring, resourcefulness, and
achievement. To help his students achieve this, he helps them develop
good work habits, self-discipline, and ideas of excellence. His aim is to
teach so that these ends become their ends. If they remain his alone, he
feels he has failed.

WHAT KIND OF LEADERSHIP SHALL WE EMPLOY?

The teacher faces the questions: What kind of leadership is most becoming to me? Which of the three kinds of classroom learning can I best
employ? Which suits me?

It's best to keep the question on a personal basis. Leadership is a
personal matter. It cannot be purchased like a hat, or changed with each
new style or season. One's leadership ought to express his best self, wear
well, and be continually becoming. It cannot be someone else's. It must
be one's own.

It follows then that a teacher does not select, outside himself, the kind
of leadership he wishes to employ; he starts, rather, with himself. College
students who inventory their leadership experiences usually discover
that they have already developed a surprisingly rich background. Taking
your own experience in working with people, how do you think you
work best? If you've had the added advantage of working with children
and youth, your question can be more pointed: Under what conditions
do I give my best leadership? When do I get the best response? When
does the group accomplish most, work together best, plan best? Under
what conditions do I feel my work is most satisfying?

A little thought given to such self-analysis can tell us a great deal about
our own leadership. It can suggest our natural endowments and tell us
where to build.

There is another way to judge one's bent for leadership. We have
just discussed three rather distinct kinds of classroom leadership. As you
studied these three examples, to which one did you feel drawn? Which
one would you like to emulate? Which one in your judgment has the
most arguments in its favor? Your choice probably indicates the direction
of your own leadership strength. That is the strength you should develop.

The value in studying these examples is to permit you to see the im-

plications of each. There is no one absolutely right form of leadership
in classroom learning. Individual differences operate here, too. That
school is fortunate which has strong leaders of many bents. The children
will probably benefit by the experience.

Study living leadership. You can probably select certain characteristics
from your former or present teachers and place them on a spectrum that
runs from Rousseau on the left, through Agassiz, to Wesley on the right.

7. Select one of your former teachers for special study. If possible observe his
methods, his attitudes toward his profession, his work, his students. Interview him
to confirm your observations. What discoveries can you make about classroom
leadership?

8. Now write a reaction report to these three approaches to teaching and learning. Here is an opportunity to think through and express your own ideas about
teacher-pupil relationships. To start your thinking there follows a similar report
written by a student. Make sure you are expressing your own considered judgments, just as this student does.

*"I Haven't The Courage To Assume A Susanna Wesley Approach,
Nor Have I The Patience To Develop A Rousseau Method."*

STEPHANIE WALSH

Of greatest enlightenment in this section has been the fact that
there *are* different methods of working with students. Teacher-class
relationships were to me apparently the same throughout my years
as a student.

Because I am a mother, I discovered the account of Susanna
Wesley's teaching and rearing of her children to be almost unbe-
lievable. I found a great deal to be admired in her determination
and perseverance and could never criticize the amount of information she must have been able to force into them. Whatever she
must have felt when the family was dispersed after the fire would
have been negligible in comparison to what her reactions would
have been had those children been left entirely on their own, instead of given the support of another family. Since all decisions lay
in her hands and because she rendered her children submissive to
her own will, she gave them no chance for survival during any
crisis. They may have had understanding of their letters and numbers and been able to keep their emotions under control, but these
children were unprepared for "living."

Mrs. Wesley must have neglected her own pleasures in order to
adhere to such a rigid daily schedule. She is to be commended for
disciplining herself in this way. Yet, de-emphasizing worldly inter-

ests in order to devote her every waking hour to her family may have been her greatest fault. She appeared intolerant toward people who did not control their children as she did, and this was exemplified by her distaste when the children developed "rude ways" while living with the other families. I can only defend her way of thinking in this matter by saying she had set "high standards of performance and conduct" and was disheartened to see them failing under stress.

Yet, our term "old-fashioned" may be descriptive of her methods to a certain extent. Parents were more authoritarian in earlier years. Now, at the opposite extreme, leniency seems to be growing in popularity. If only there were a "happy medium" between the inflexible teaching method of Susanna Wesley and the "Bohemian" technique of Rousseau.

Louis Agassiz's leadership appears to offer a solution to this "happy medium" in teaching methods. There was Rousseau whose friendly counseling gave Emile an opportunity to learn those things which were of immediate interest to Emile, and then Susanna Wesley who conquered the will of her children before teaching them those subjects which she felt they must know. And in between stands Louis Agassiz, the friendly director, who points out mistakes, commands good efforts, and *points the way*. Agassiz plans the activities of his students, neither leaving them to their own devices as Rousseau nor forcing issues as did Wesley. His students will more closely achieve the aim of a good teacher; that is, to help them develop goals of their own. Agassiz did this by planning in advance what was to be taught and how. He then presented the subject or problem to the pupil, instructed him in the use of it, and told him to observe it. Agassiz checked progress, reminded the pupil of errors he might be making, and guided the student to develop an interest in the material which eventually led him to learn the "things important to know." The student is assured security by Agassiz's firm guidance, yet he develops independence by working out a solution to a problem with the teacher in the background.

I haven't the courage to assume a Susanna Wesley approach to teaching nor have I the patience to develop a Rousseau method. Therefore, I have chosen Louis Agassiz's ideas as a model upon which I'd like to base my work with students.

We now turn to a new section and a new topic: "The School and the Community." Mary Ellen Chase, you will recall, told us how the fishing community in which she taught influenced her work. The Utopians reminded us of the importance of the total community environment in learning. We are ready to look specifically at the relationship between the school and community.

Good Follow-up Reading and Viewing

BOOKS

Anderson, H. H., *et al.*, *Studies of Teacher's Classroom Personalities*, Parts 1, 2, 3. Stanford, Calif.: Stanford University Press, 1946. One of the classic studies on the influence of two kinds of teacher behavior upon students. "Dominative" and "socially integrative" behavior of teachers are studied for their affects upon learning.

Burton, William H., *The Guidance of Learning Activities*. New York: Appleton-Century-Crofts, Inc., 1952. Chapter eleven describes and evaluates various methods for organizing the daily classroom work.

Deasy, Mary, "The High Hill," in *Readings In Education*, Arthur Foff, and Jean D. Grambs, eds. New York: Harper & Brothers, 1956. Contrasts two teachers in their relationships with their students. Although our sympathies lie with one more than the other, they are both effective teachers.

du Nouy, Lecomte, *Human Destiny*, pp. 145-50. New York: New American Library of World Literature, Inc., 1949. The author believes that character can be formed only at the "most tender age," and that if the mother weakens only once, the child does not forget and soon becomes unbearable. Education must fashion the character of the child with firmness at the "moment when his brain is still free from any imprint and infinitely plastic."

Gouldner, A. W., ed., *Studies in Leadership*, Part 3, "Authoritarian and Democratic Leaders." New York: Harper & Brothers, 1950. Describes some of the characteristics and consequences of authoritarian and democratic leadership.

Lindgren, Henry Clay, *Educational Psychology in the Classroom*, chap. 10, "Teacher-Centered Approaches to the Learning Situation," chap. 12, "Discipline and the Learning Situation." New York: John Wiley & Sons, Inc., 1956. Chapter ten evaluates the teacher-dominated classroom in terms of its implications for the learning and growth of children. Chapter twelve is a valuable discussion of discipline: teacher-imposed, group-imposed, self-imposed, and task-imposed. Included is a good section on the teacher's anxiety about discipline.

Pressey, Sidney L., and Francis P. Robinson, *Psychology and the New Education*, chap. 8. New York: Harper & Brothers, 1944. The effects of differences in social climate, social structure, and teacher techniques within the classroom.

Smith, B. Othanel, *et al.*, *Fundamentals of Curriculum Development*, Part 3, "Patterns of Curriculum Development." Tarrytown-on-Hudson, N.Y.: World Book Company, 1957. Three types of curricula (subject, activity, and core) are described and evaluated.

Spears, Harold, *The High School For Today*. New York: American Book Company, 1950. Chapter ten gives a critical review of the characteristics of high school classrooms and suggests criteria for evaluating the daily routine.

Williams, Emlyn, *The Corn Is Green*. New York: Random House, 1942. The story of a Welsh school mistress and the young genius she discovers.

PERIODICALS

Collings, Ellsworth, "Democratic Learning in the Classroom," *Phi Delta Kappan*, Vol. 32, October, 1950, p. 40. Describes two methods of teaching; one requires pupils to repeat the subject matter they were learning, the other has them use the knowledge in everyday life.

Morse, William C., "The School's Responsibility for Discipline," *Phi Delta Kappan,* Vol. 41, pp. 109-13. The writer sees in the return to "basic" or "hard" education one more factor provoking disciplinary problems.

Sanford, Nevitt, "Dominance Versus Authority and The Democratic Character," *Childhood Education,* Vol. 23, 1946, pp. 109-14. A summary of research on class direction. Suggests a distinction between legitimate direction of activities and arbitrary suppression of the pupil.

Schmideberg, Melitta, "Training for Responsibility," *Phi Delta Kappan,* Vol. 41, December, 1959, pp. 90-93. The author contends that "while we should aim at creating the best methods and the best atmosphere for teaching, the simple and unpalatable fact must be accepted: In order to acquire knowledge, hard work, perseverance, and sacrifice of other pleasures are necessary."

Stansfield, Russell N., "The Human Side of Teaching," *Peabody Journal of Education,* Vol. 38, May, 1961, pp. 345-50. The author illustrates the importance of setting up the right kind of attitudes while teaching.

Thorndile, R. L., *et al.,* "Observation of the Behavior of Children in Activity and Control Schools," *Journal of Experimental Education,* Vol. 10, 1941, pp. 138-45. An experiment which reports the results of observations of "teacher controlled" classes and "activity" classes.

Tiedeman, Stuart C., "A Study of Pupil-Teacher Relationship," *Journal of Educational Research,* Vol. 35, May, 1942, pp. 657-64. This study is the result of questioning pupils of the seventh, eighth, and ninth grades in a junior high school which traits, characteristics, habits, and practices of their teachers they disliked greatly, and which they liked very much.

FILMS

Broader Concept of Method:
Part I—Developing Pupil Interest

Contrasts student attitudes and responses between teacher-dominated type of high school class and group-discussion type. (McGraw-Hill Book Co., Inc., black and white, 13 minutes.)

Children Are Creative

Two types of third grade art teaching with the results of each; teacher-dominated and pupil-centered with emphasis upon creative imagination. Motivation orientation and creative phases of instruction; accommodating individual differences. (Ellensburg; Bailey Films, Inc., color, 11 minutes.)

Developing Pupil Interest

Presents a traditional, teacher-dominated, lesson-hearing type of instruction and shows effects on student attitudes, responses, and learning. (McGraw-Hill Book Co., Inc., black and white, 16 minutes.)

Individual Differences

Two ways for a teacher to approach individual differences. Effects of subject-centered, standardized type of teaching on a shy sixth-grade boy. In contrast, the analysis and individualized treatment employed by good teachers in such cases. (McGraw-Hill Book Co., Inc., black and white, 22 minutes.)

THE SCHOOL AND COMMUNITY

CHAPTER 12

WHAT IS THE TASK OF THE SCHOOL?

*The schools are far outdistancing other local organizations in
bringing new ideas to Tepoztlan.*

JAMES G. MADDOX

Sometimes we can understand our own schools better by looking at
other people's schools. That's what we are going to do in this case. We
are going to visit a school in the Mexican village of Tepoztlan. James
G. Maddox,[1] a correspondent for the American Universities Field Staff,
will conduct us to the graduation ceremonies and tell us about the relationship of the school to the community around it.

Before we travel abroad, however, we should fix in mind some of the
fundamental aspects of the relationship which exist between a school
and its community. To help us do this we turn to the experience of an
American educator who taught us much about the task of a school in
the community.

BOOKER T. WASHINGTON STUDIED THE COMMUNITY AROUND HIS SCHOOL

When Booker T. Washington founded Tuskegee Institute, he spent a
month traveling through Alabama, living with the people whom the
school was to serve. "The most of my traveling was done over the coun-

---

[1] James B. Maddox, "Education in Tepoztlan," JGM-1-1955, New York: American
University Field Staff.

try roads," he tells us in his autobiography,[2] "with a mule and a cart or a mule and a buggy wagon for conveyance. I ate and slept with the people, in their little cabins. I saw their farms, their schools, their churches. Since, in the case of most of these visits, there had been no notice given in advance that a stranger was expected, I had the advantage of seeing the real everyday life of the people."

Booker T. Washington wanted to learn all he could about the people he hoped would attend Tuskegee Institute. So he traveled, observed, and lived among the people. He observed their everyday way of life.

> The common diet of the people, was fat pork and corn bread. At times I have eaten in cabins where they had only corn bread and "black-eye peas" cooked in plain water. The people seemed to have no other idea than to live on this fat meat and corn bread—the meat, and the meal of which the bread was made, having been bought at a high price at a store in town, notwithstanding the fact that the land all about the cabin homes could easily have been made to produce nearly every kind of garden vegetable that is raised anywhere in the country. Their one object seemed to be to plant nothing but cotton; and in many cases cotton was planted up to the very door of the cabin. . . .

Mr. Washington also observed the schools. "I recall that one day I went into a school house—and found five pupils who were studying a lesson from one book. Two of these, on the front seat, were using the book between them; behind these were two others peeping over the shoulders of the first two, and behind the four was a fifth little fellow who was peeping over the shoulders of all four . . ."

From his observations, Booker T. Washington drew certain conclusions about the relationship of Tuskegee to its community.

> Of one thing I felt more strongly convinced than ever . . . and that was that, in order to lift them up, something must be done more than merely to imitate New England education as it then existed . . . to take the children of such people as I had been among for a month, and each day give them a few hours of mere book education, I felt would be almost a waste of time . . .
>
> In fact, one of the saddest things I saw during the month of travel which I have described was a young man, who had attended some high school, sitting down in a one room cabin, with grease on his clothing, filth all around him, and weeds in the yard and garden, engaged in studying a French grammar.

---

[2] Booker T. Washington, *Up From Slavery*. Reprinted by permission of the publisher. (Garden City, New York: Doubleday and Company, 1951), pp. 111-116, 118, 121-122.

WHAT SHOULD BE THE RELATIONSHIP BETWEEN THE SCHOOL AND THE COMMUNITY?

What Booker T. Washington is talking about is the kind of relationship which he believed should exist between his school and community. What did he think about this relationship? Let's look at some of the implications of his narrative.

The School Has A Task To Perform In The Community

As a tool of society the school has a function to perform. It does not exist for itself, its administration or staff. It is an institution through which society achieves certain of its ends. It is an agent for both preserving the culture and bringing about change.

The school has particular kinds of tasks to perform. It has its specialized jobs. In the case of Washington's Tuskegee the job was to help "lift them up." He believed that the school should tackle such practical matters as diet, health, and the wise use of money. The task isn't the same for each community. Perhaps in your own community the task of the school is quite different from that of Tuskegee.

The tasks should fit the needs of the particular community. Washington did not want New England education in rural Alabama. Not that he was against New England education in New England. He simply concluded that it did not fit the needs of the people Tuskegee was to serve.

Decisions must be made regarding what the school should do about the needs. For Washington and Tuskegee the answer was a program of practical uplift. It's quite possible that someone other than Washington, making the same tour through Alabama, would have drawn different conclusions about what Tuskegee should do. In any case, such a decision must be made. In the public school the decisions must be made by the community.

1. In case of the school you attended, what kinds of tasks does it perform in the community? Can you name five?

2. Do you know how the decisions are made regarding the tasks which the school is to perform? Who makes these decisions? Check the references at the end of this chapter to help you find answers to these questions.

Booker T. Washington's experience sets the stage for a closer examination of the relationship between school and community. Let's now turn to our case study.

COME TO THE FIESTA IN TEPOZTLAN

As a correspondent for the American Universities Field Staff, James G. Maddox is a specialist in Mexico and her culture. In this case he takes us to the graduation exercises at the village school in Tepoztlan. He describes vividly the colorful setting, the students, their parents, and relatives. Then he raises significant questions about the relationship of this school to the Mexican community of which it is a part. You will discover that the questions apply equally well to the relationships between our own schools and communities.

Here are some questions worth pondering as we read this case:

3. What tasks does this school perform in the community of Tepoztlan?

4. Are these tasks related to the vital needs of Tepoztlan? For example, does the curriculum of the school "fit" the community?

5. How do the people look upon the school? Is it incidental or vital to their lives?

At 8:30 Friday evening, November 25—exactly one-half hour behind schedule—the formal graduation festivities began. They were to celebrate the end of the year in Federal Primary School "Escuadron 201" in the village of Tepoztlan, Mexico. Two hours later, 41 boys and 16 girls had received certificates which informed the world that they had finished the requirements of legally-approved primary schools in Mexico and were entitled to enter a secondary school of their choice. The following Tuesday evening, 16 boys and 10 girls were graduated by the secondary school in the same village. These were big and important days in the lives of pupils, teachers, and parents.

Throughout Mexico, similar ceremonies were being held. Let's take a closer look at the graduation exercises in Tepoztlan, and ask ourselves a few questions about their significance.

When we walked through the entrance of Primary School "Escuadron 201," we were certainly not prepared for the scene that met our eyes. I had previously talked to a couple of the teachers, a few pupils, and three or four parents. I had assured my wife and sixteen-year-old daughter, who accompanied me to the fiesta, as it was called locally, that this would be a dull, uncomfortable affair. I had visions of being crammed into one of the classrooms, along with a bunch of nervous, boisterous children and a few parents. Instead, we found ourselves in a large open patio—the playground for the school—which had been especially decorated for the occasion. A tremendous aid to the artificial flowers and crepe-paper streamers which constituted the decorations was a bright, beautiful moon overhead. It gave almost as much light as

the three dozen 40-watt bulbs that had been strung across the
playground and which received only intermittent surges of "juice"
from a portable generator out in the street. Benches from the
schoolrooms had been placed four rows deep around a rectangular
area in the center of the courtyard which, with its more brilliant
lighting and numerous streamers of crepe paper hanging from overhead wires, was obviously the stage where the festivities of the
evening were to take place.

More surprising than the bedecked and moonlit patio was the
large number of people present. By the time the program was ready
to begin, there were at least 1,000 people on hand. I made several
counts of various sections of the crowd, and tried to estimate the
total. This was difficult, however, because the courtyard was soon
overflowing, and scores of men and teenage boys were seated on a
little parcel of hillside which slopes gently from the courtyard wall.
It is possible that those in attendance included one-third of the
5,000 residents of Tepoztlan. A few persons came from neighboring
villages.

The first row of seats around three sides of the rectangle was re-
served for the members of the graduating class. At one end was the
speaker's table and about a dozen chairs for visiting dignitaries,
most of whom were faculty members from nearby schools or officials
from the Department of Education offices in Cuernavaca, the capital city of the state of Morelos in which Tepoztlan is located. The
Maddoxes, however, were soon escorted to three of these chairs,
when the principal of the school noticed that we were becoming
the center of attraction. Numerous youngsters were pressing in from
all sides to get a close look at the strange gringos. Women with children in their arms and grandmothers had first priority on the seats
immediately behind the graduates and the visiting dignitaries.
Squeezed in among them were the four to eight-year-olds. Then
came a mixed layer made up of godparents of the graduates, a few
elderly men, a sprinkling of well-dressed women in their twenties
who had obviously returned from the city to see a younger brother
or sister graduate, and other close friends and relatives of the class
of 1955. These took most of the available seats. Behind them stood
the men, each of whom was wearing his newest white straw hat.

It was these hats, as they reflected the soft light of a full moon
and formed a wide moving border around the crowd that was seated
in the patio, which awakened me to the obvious: we were deep in
the earthy heart of Mexico. We were no longer part of sophisticated
modern Western culture. Yet neither were we among the Aztecs.
We were in rural central Mexico; one of those hazy cultural zones,
where the modern and national is interacting with the traditional.
We were seeing a part of what Cline calls "the third world," that

great stratum of population which is culturally somewhere between the "modern" and the "Indian." Everything around us was typically Mexican—the dirt-floored patio, from which a light breeze would occasionally pick up swirls of dust and deposit it on the crowd; the artificial flowers and crepe-paper streamers decorating the courtyard, when a half-mile away there were small fields of the most beautiful gladioli and daisies that one would want to see; the dozens of barefoot women, each with a long dark shawl around her shoulders which was folded in front to form a small hammock for the ever-present baby; the multitude of children hanging on to the loose flowing skirts of their mothers; the sprinkling of over-dressed young women; and the men in the shadowy background with their white straw hats so heavily filled with starch that the salesmen in the local markets fit them to the buyers' heads by pounding them to the desired shape with a hammer and a small circular piece of iron held inside of the crown. This was rural Mexico—a crazy quilt of the old and the new—and this cross section of it was assembled in the patio of a school, the important local institution which is theoretically trying to merge the two cultures, but which is very probably one of the most potent forces for destroying the old and enthroning the new.

6. How do you think the school is destroying the old and enthroning the new? Is this what the school in Tepoztlan should be doing? Where do you think it gets the authority to do it?

When the nine-piece student band, just a few feet behind us, started to blare out the national anthem, the graduating class marched briskly into the open rectangle. In the forefront was the tallest girl in the class, carrying the Mexican flag. The color guard was made up of five boys, dressed in blue serge trousers and white shirts. About ten paces behind came the column of classmates. The girls were dressed in ballerina-length evening gowns, which my wife said were orchid-colored. I would have called them a hybrid of old-rose and purple. They glistened in the light, and created an atmosphere completely foreign to the sleepy rural village of Tepoztlan. The blue serge trousers and white shirts of the boys were more in keeping with the local setting. The girls' dresses had all been made by the same dressmaker in Cuernavaca. Literally they were not a part of this world, that is, the world of Tepoztlan. They were specks of that brisk new modern culture which one finds around Mexico City and a few other urban centers in the nation. The cost of these dresses represented a real sacrifice to the barefoot shawl-covered mothers and white-hatted fathers, who were seated a few feet away, beaming with pride at the splendid appearance of their offspring. Here was the Old and the New in bold contrast. Moreover, the New was of the very newest, and it was unmistakably the center of attraction.

7. We are told that "the girls' dresses had all been made by a dressmaker in Cuernavaca," the cost representing "a real sacrifice to the barefoot shawl-covered mothers and white-hatted fathers." Considering the general poverty of the parents, was the school justified in fostering a fiesta demanding such sacrifice? Would it have been more appropriate for the school to teach the girls to make their own dresses?

Much of the program reminded me of graduation exercises in the United States—a short speech of farewell to the outgoing graduates by one of the teachers; several songs, dances, and recitations by youngsters from each of the six grades in the school; a good-by speech by a member of the graduating class; a lengthy report by the principal to the school, in which she took a lot of time to say that 1955 had been a good year but that much remains to be done to make "Escuadron 201" the kind of institution that Tepoztlan deserves, and of course admonished the graduates to continue their education by attending a secondary school. After this, a district inspector of the Department of Education spoke, and finally the youngsters were given their certificates. It was a touching scene. As each youngster's name was called, he came to the speaker's table where he received his certificate, and as he returned to his seat he was met midway by one of his godparents who presented him with a gift and a huge bouquet of flowers and embraced him with the feeling which only a Latino can put into the *abracijo*. This was a real show of affection. It was one of those little niceties of life which North Americans rarely expect from people who live in extreme poverty, and who often appear to neglect the material welfare of their children. Yet the public demonstration of affection and giving of gifts were characteristic; Mexican peasants unquestionably have strong affection for children, and they also must show that they are keeping up with their neighbors.

The exercises at the secondary school, four nights later, were essentially the same as those held for the primary grades. The girls wore beautiful ballerina-length bluish-green evening dresses that had been made in Cuernavaca. About half of the boys wore blue serge trousers and white shirts, while the others wore blue serge suits. I was told that the parents of all of the boys had bought them suits for the occasion, but "some of the boys were just too stubborn to wear a coat and a tie as they were supposed to do." The speeches were a little shorter; the songs and dances were a little better; and representatives of the Lions Club in Cuernavaca were on hand to present a medal to the graduate who had the highest grades. Otherwise, the program was a replica of the one at the primary school. Here, too, each graduate received from one of his godparents a present, a bouquet, and a hug. The effect, however, was somewhat less touching, because the graduates were virtually full-grown men and women, and they obviously were not as thrilled to receive presents and flowers as the younger ones had been.

In a moment Mr. Maddox will conclude his story. Let us pursue another matter, however, while it is fresh in mind. The graduation is called a fiesta. The girls are in their brightest dresses, the mothers in their prettiest shawls, and the fathers in their best white straw hats. Artificial flowers and crepe paper decorate the scene, and a third of the 5,000 inhabitants are present. How do you react to the following questions which grow out of this festive scene?

> 8. What does all this tell you about the role of the school in Tepoztlan? Does it tell you anything about the task it performs?
>
> 9. Up to this point, how well do you think the school is serving Tepoztlan?

Let's now return to Mr. Maddox and his view of the contribution of the school to the community.

> Following the formal graduation exercises, both at the primary school and at the secondary school, the seats and chairs were hastily pushed out of the way, a local orchestra set up its instruments, and a dance was soon underway. I wilted at about midnight and did not stay for the end of either affair. I was told, however, that at the primary school dancing continued until two o'clock in the morning, and that it lasted an hour longer at the secondary school. It is commonly said that Mexicans dance whenever there is the slightest opportunity, and this, no doubt, is one explanation of why so many people attended these festivities. It is also clear that the schools are not blind to the need for good public relations. The teachers looked on the dance as one way of "winning the hearts of the people." Few teachers, however, have a clear-cut practical concept of how the schools might be made effective institutions for contributing something to the community beyond teaching the children the regular routine subjects.

> 10. Do you think a school should be concerned "with winning the hearts of the people"? Did your own school carry on programs which had "public relations" aspects? If so, what were they and what affect did they have?

This brings us to a fundamental question: how well prepared are the graduates of the Tepoztlan schools to face the life ahead of them? The question is not easy to answer, but one thing is clear. The curriculums of the Tepoztlan schools are not designed to train the students for the life of small farmers and shopkeepers in a rural setting such as the village of Tepoztlan. The schools and the courses of study they offer seem to be set apart from the village community, where the over-crowded adobe houses lack running water and electric lights and have so little furniture that sometimes there are not even beds. The schools have done little to foster home and community sanitation in a village where pigs, chickens, and dogs freely run in and out of many of the houses, and the toilet facilities of a house usually amount to no more than a half-hidden nook in the corner of the yard or adjoining the corral. Nor is there anything in the curriculums that would help a graduate to make a better living on one of the 5 to 15 acre farms on which most of the families depend for the major part of their income.

The first four years of the primary school are, of necessity, devoted mainly to teaching the simple skills of reading, writing, and arithmetic. In the sixth and final year, the basic curriculum is as follows:

Spanish	.5 hrs/wk
Arithmetic and geometry	.5 hrs/wk
Natural sciences	.5 hrs/wk
Geography	.3 hrs/wk
World history	.3 hrs/wk
Civil government	.2 hrs/wk
Total	.23 hrs/wk

In addition, at least three hours per week are given to such subjects as vocational studies, drawing, music, and sports. The vocational studies include a little sewing, cooking and child-care for girls, and carpentry, painting, and some horticulture for boys. These are the types of activities which could conceivably make a real improvement in the level of living of the community. In reality, however, they are of little significance. The children of the primary school are too young to be taught very much in the way of vocational skills; the equipment for teaching is almost nil; and the teachers are short of ideas for constructive projects geared to local ways of living.

In the secondary school, which consists of three years beyond the first six years of primary instruction, the curriculum is as follows:

Spanish literature	3 yrs	World History	2 yrs
Mathematics	3 yrs	History of Mexico	2 yrs
Biology	3 yrs	Drawing and modeling	3 yrs
Geography	3 yrs	Carpentry and printing	1 yr
English	3 yrs	Sports and music	3 yrs
Chemistry and physics	2 yrs		

There are 30 hours of classes each week, and the school year is 36 weeks, when allowances are made for vacations and holidays. Most of the subjects are taught three times each week for a 50-minute period, but in a few courses there are classes every day, with the result that others are cut to one or two class periods per week. There are no laboratories; the carpentry shop is practically without tools; and the printing press—the smallest I have ever seen—is about the size of my portable typewriter. Clearly nobody can learn to be either a carpenter or a printer with the equipment and material available. Biology is taught by a local doctor—there are also several other part-time teachers—but from what I could learn it is mainly "textbook teaching." There are rare trips to the surrounding countryside so that students can become acquainted with local plants and animals, but these usually are in the nature of "excursions" away from the tedium of the classroom. By and large, the school is something apart from the village and fields of Tepoztlan. It is only distantly related to the myriads of rustic, almost primitive, activities in which both the children and the parents are customarily engaged. The school is a place where city ideas (maybe they are cosmopolitan ideas) prevail. Mexico does not yet have an organized and respected body of rural knowledge, nor a corps of trained instructors to teach agricultural and allied sciences to the children of farm families.

It would be easy for those who cherish rural values, and who believe that education should be functional and utilitarian in content, to be highly critical of the schools in Tepoztlan. The cultural gulf between the schoolroom and the community gives rise to a situation that is far from ideal. At the same time, those of us from the United States need to look closely in our own backyards to determine just how well we have related education to our processes of living and making a living before we express too much disappointment in regard to our neighbors. To a person like me—reared in an isolated backwoods area of southern Arkansas; with vivid memories of the one-room school house in which I finished ten grades; and with even clearer recollections of the three-teacher high school where five subjects were taught (English, history, mathematics, Latin, and one year of physics), where a converted clothes closet doubled as both laboratory and library, and where "book l'arnin" was definitely suspect by a large proportion of the parents —the schools of Tepoztlan look pretty good. That my memories are four decades old is of little importance. It was not until the early 1920's that the people of Mexico really gained control of their educational institutions, and forced the Federal Government to take major responsibility for them. Since that time, tremendous progress has been made. This is not the place to review the whole story of the struggles, strifes, and sacrifices that have gone into the national effort to promote education in Mexico, but one can easily get a distorted picture of the situation in both Tepoztlan and the nation if he does not recognize that this effort is only a generation old, and that it has had all sorts of handicaps—ranging from the general poverty for the country through a gamut of factors, such as lack of teachers, lackadaisical attitudes of parents, romantic ideals of leaders, and outright opposition of some conservative elements in society. As I read the history of this effort, I am surprised that the schools of Tepoztlan are doing as well as they are.

That they are making progress is attested by the steady increase in physical facilities, as well as by the growth in enrollment. It was not until the middle 1930's that Tepoztlan had a primary school which went beyond the fourth grade. Now it has a kindergarten, four primary schools—three of which are small and teach only the first two grades—and a secondary school. The latter is only three years old. If, therefore, one looks at the past 20 years, there has been a decided increase in educational facilities. Enrollment in the central primary school in 1955 was 693. This was almost 30 percent higher than ten years earlier, although the three new primary schools had opened in the meantime. The secondary school had an enrollment of 129 in 1955, and a larger number is expected next year. It is obvious that only a small proportion of the students who finish the primary grades continue their education in secondary school. However, the principal of the primary school proudly points out that enrollment in the secondary school is not a good index of the number who continue their studies; a goodly number, she says, enter professional schools to become secretaries, bookkeepers, or teachers. A few go to Cuernavaca, or other cities, to continue their secondary education. She estimates that 95 percent of the children in Tepoztlan between 6 and 16 years old were enrolled in school in 1955. This figure may be a bit high, and it is certain that attendance was far from perfect. Nevertheless, all the evidence points to the conclusion that the schools of the village are significant institutions of growing importance. They are far outdistancing other local organizations, such as the Church and the municipal government, in bringing new ideas and broader visions to Tepoztlan.

Their teachers, most of whom receive salaries of only $50 to $75 per month, are dedicated public servants. Their training is not always the best (although 10 of the 14 teachers in the primary school have finished their studies at a recognized normal school) and their equipment is meager. Nevertheless, in the village they represent one of the strongest forces for cultural change. And the pressure they exert will almost surely have a cumulative effect. As

of the present, the barefoot, shawl-covered, white-hatted peasants
—many of whom can neither read nor write—dominate the local
scene, but their days are numbered. Their faces beamed too brightly
at the recent graduation exercises, and their sacrifices for those
fancy dresses were too great. Their commitments to the schools are
deep. They can't turn their backs on them now, and yet the schools
are potent forces for destroying some of the most cherished values
of the man under the white hat and woman in the blue shawl.

As Mr. Maddox points out, "The school is something apart from the
village and fields of Tepoztlan. It is only distantly related to the myriads
of rustic, almost primitive, activities in which both children and parents
are customarily engaged. The school is a place where city ideas (maybe
they are cosmopolitan ideas) prevail." What would you do about this
problem?

11. Would you propose a program something like Booker T. Washington proposed for Tuskegee, reject "mere book learning" and establish a curriculum related to everyday needs "in order to lift them up"?

12. Or, are "city ideas" more appropriate for Tepoztlan, since some of the young
people go there, and since "city" clothes and the "new" generally are sought
after in Tepoztlan?

13. Or, should the school attempt to have a "multiple-track" program which
serves both the immediate needs of those children who will stay in the rural
community as well as the needs of city-bound children?

SEEK TO UNDERSTAND THE PURPOSE OF THE SCHOOL

It must be clear from this case that the relationship between a school
and a community is not a simple matter, easily reduced to principles and
rules. Communities and schools are complex living organisms, subject
to all the changes which occur in living things. If we expect that so
lively a relationship can be reduced to easy rules which, once learned,
will forever hold, we shall be disappointed.

We can, however, build up ways of viewing the problems in this relationship and evolve our own judgments, knowing that in the life of a
teacher this is an ever-continuing process.

Tepoztlan suggests that we may profitably form judgments about certain vital issues on the subject of school and community. These are
worthy of our persistent attention.

The school is set in a community for some purpose. What that purpose
is may differ widely from community to community. It may be simply
to preserve the old ways, or it may be to create new ways. The purpose

may be solely to teach the simple skills of language and arithmetic, or it may be to develop ability in complex skills in science and technology. Some schools set out to create in students whole new attitudes and forms of behavior suited to new and changing times. Sometimes the purposes of the schools are sharp, generally understood and agreed upon. This is more apt to be true in a relatively static community. In a changing community, the purposes may be blurred because of changing expectations of the people. Some people will feel that the school should reinforce the old and traditional ways; others will demand that the school prepare youth for the new demands which will be put upon them. Conflict and controversy over the school may result.

Sharp or blurred, understood or not understood, agreed upon or not agreed upon, the school's purpose is there. It is a tool of the community, from which it must draw its ultimate authority to act.

THE TEACHER HAS A RESPONSIBILITY

What does this fact mean to a teacher? It means that a teacher has a responsibility to develop competence in school-community relations. Like Booker T. Washington, the teacher needs a knowledge of the community around him. He should study it with the same care that he studies his teaching area. The students he teaches are a product of the community. He will understand them better if he understands the community. Parents and other citizens hold certain aspirations for their schools. The teacher needs to know what these aspirations are. Frequently, the teacher needs to interpret the school and its program to citizens. The teacher who understands the community is in a better position to communicate with it.

Good Follow-up Reading and Viewing

BOOKS

Bathurst, Effie, *Where Children's Lives Affect Curriculum,* Bulletin 7. Washington, D.C.: U. S. Office of Education, 1950. Explains how community surroundings can be utilized in the school curriculum.

Campbell, Ronald F., and John A. Ramseyer, *The Dynamics of School-Community Relationships.* Boston: Allyn and Bacon, Inc., 1955. Shows how citizen participation can be a dynamic force in school improvement.

Carter, Hodding, "Charlie Burton's Field Day," in *Where Main Street Meets The River.* New York: Holt, Rinehart & Winston, Inc., 1953. An account of a Negro teacher and a county agent's program for educating Negro farmers to improve their agricultural methods.

Cook, Lloyd Allen, and Elaine Forsyth Cook, *A Sociological Approach to Education.* New York: McGraw-Hill Book Co., Inc., 1950. Presents reviews of studies, projects and research in the school and community area.

Darling, Edward, *How We Fought For Our Schools.* New York: W. W. Norton & Company, Inc., 1954. A documentary novel on some of the issues in school conflicts in which the central character finds himself thrust into the heat of a school controversy.

Educational Policies Commission, *Education For All American Youth—A Further Look.* Washington, D.C.: National Education Association, 1952. Chapters four through eight present case-like studies of a rural and a metropolitan community, their characteristics and youth needs, their schools, curriculum plans and activities, organizational plans and purposes.

Lynd and Lynd, *Middletown in Transition,* pp. 231-41. New York: Harcourt, Brace & World, Inc., 1937. A searching study of the conflict in values between schools and community. This section analyzes the question: Whose purposes are the schools fulfilling?

Olsen, Edward G., *School and Community Programs.* Englewood Cliffs, N.J.: Prentice-Hall, Inc., 1949. Present examples of numerous successful community-school projects in various fields and at all academic levels.

Tireman, L. S., and Mary Watson, *A Community School in a Spanish-Speaking Village.* Albuquerque, N. M.: University of New Mexico Press, 1948. The story of a New Mexico village and its school. An excellent example of how lessons can be learned from the resources of the community, to the benefit of both school and community.

Van Dalen, Deobold B., and Robert W. Brittell, *Looking Ahead to Teaching,* chap. 17, "The Community and the Teacher." Boston: Allyn and Bacon, Inc., 1959. Deals with learning about the community, the importance of community analysis, and good school-community relations.

Washington, Booker T., *Up From Slavery.* New York: Doubleday & Company, Inc., 1927. This autobiography, from which the Washington excerpt in this chapter is taken, illustrates many significant ideas about teaching.

PERIODICALS

Banks, Waldo Rice, "The School and its Neighborhood: A Program of Human Relations for the Urban Community," *Peabody Journal of Education,* Vol. 37, No. 1, July, 1959, pp. 15-25. The author demonstrates the need for good relations between the urban school and community. "Although progress has been made in developing programs of human relations in smaller communities, there has been an ironic lack of precisely such development where it is, perhaps, needed most of all: the city 'community,' or neighborhood."

Carter, Richard F., "Voters and Their Schools," *Phi Delta Kappan,* Vol. 42, March, 1961, pp. 244-54. This is a summary of a survey conducted in more than 1,000 school districts to get answers to these questions: What does the voter think of his schools? How do voters participate in school affairs? Who are the critics of the schools? What are the roots of greater participation? How does the family affect participation? How do the schools communicate to the voters? The conclusions of this study do not present an encouraging picture.

McClusky, Howard Y., "Some Propositions in Support of the Community

School—A Summary," *The Journal of Educational Sociology,* Vol. 33, December, 1959, pp. 179-183. Eight valuable propositions which support the community school concept.

Melby, E. O., "Citizen Action in Education-Centered Communities," *Phi Delta Kappan,* Vol. 39, October, 1957, pp. 2-5. The survival of modern free society depends, this noted educator thinks, upon the development of education-centered communities.

"School Public Relations," *NEA Journal,* Vol. 49, February, 1960, pp. 15-30. A valuable series of articles on school public relations. Articles deal with the purposes and methods of good school-community relations.

Strub, Grace F., "Building Better Communities—How The Schools Can Help," *The School Executive,* Vol. 76, September, 1956, pp. 81-111. Case studies of twenty-two communities in which schools are helping to improve the quality of living.

U. S. Office of Education, *Education for Better Living,* U. S. Department of Health, Education, and Welfare Bulletin 1956, No. 9, 1957. This small volume describes how education is helping to improve community living in 15 foreign countries.

FILMS

Children Must Learn

The unsatisfactory relationship between the education of children and the needs of the community which existed in the mountain country of the South. A program designed to revise curricula so as to educate children in solving their problems. (New York University, black and white, 14 minutes.)

Conversation With James B. Conant

Interview with this noted educator who speaks with Nathaniel Ober about the essential problems of American educators. Dr. Conant discusses the conclusions of a study of American public high schools for the Carnegie Foundation. (Encyclopaedia Britannica Films, Inc., black and white, 28 minutes.)

School and the Community

Comparison of the isolated school and the community-type school. Advantages and examples of cooperation between school and community. (McGraw-Hill Book Co., Inc., black and white, 25 minutes.)

Schools March On

Work of a citizens committee in reorganization of school districts in a midwestern county; benefits to students. Improvements in furnishings, teaching materials, and services. Place of good schools in a democracy; necessity of democratic processes in reorganization. (March of Time; McGraw-Hill Book Co., Inc., black and white, 18 minutes.)

Way of Life

Story of school at Beaverton, Michigan; how problem of finance was solved and broader educational opportunities for whole community provided. (Harvester, color, 21 minutes.)

CHAPTER 13

THE TEACHER IN THE COMMUNITY

> Every man, woman, and child in this community is part of
> Landsburgh High School.
>
> JESSE STUART

Jesse Stuart,[1] Kentucky novelist and poet of the mountain country, has spent a great part of his life teaching. His teaching experiences, vividly described and interestingly told, give inspiration to much of his writing and speaking.

As a teacher he made decisions about the vital relationships between a teacher and the community. "What is the teacher's responsibility to the community?" he asked. He found his personal answer. "What is the community's responsibility to the teacher?" he inquired. He developed a point of view. "Is the school an isolated cell or a vital organ in the living community?" He found an answer which seemed right to him. "How can a teacher develop skill in recognizing the community aspects of school problems?" He worked hard at this one. "How can a teacher muster community support for the solution of school problems?" In this chapter we shall observe how he went about building such support.

EACH TEACHER MUST DECIDE

Like Jesse Stuart, most teachers confront these vital questions. They must find the kinds of answers which, to their best judgements, are right. Jesse Stuart's answers are his own. They may not be appropriate for others. Ultimately, each teacher must make his own decisions about the

---

[1] Jesse Stuart, *The Thread That Runs So True* (New York: Charles Scribner's Sons, 1950), pp. 123-128.

dynamic human relationship that should exist between himself and the community about him.

We can with profit use Mr. Stuart's experience as a case study to assist us in making our own decisions. We can confront these basic questions with him, observe the principles he uses in getting answers, look at the reasoning behind the principles, examine the risks involved in his approach, and ask finally: Had I been in Stuart's position, what would I have done?

First let us have Stuart tell us about the setting for the problem. Then we can pause to sharpen the issues, after which we shall hear him explain how he chose to handle the problem. The action takes place in Landsburgh High School, in Stuart's native state.

THE TEACHER INTERRUPTS A POKER GAME

The parent-teacher organization was the best organization we had to present the Landsburgh problems that affected our high school. It was not a large organization. Not half the parents whose sons and daughters attended Landsburgh High School belonged to the P. T. A. None of the parents of our country pupils attended since they lived miles away and were without, for the most part, convenient methods of travel. Our P. T. A. was, and had been, more or less a social function where parents and teachers got together and drank tea and ate cakes at the end of each meeting. I thought it time to do something besides drink and eat. It was time we did something constructive for the high school and community. But I didn't know how to go about presenting my problem to these mothers, for seldom did a father attend one of the P. T. A. meetings, and the husbands of these women were, in many cases, involved in the vices we had to eliminate.

Then something happened that gave me the chance. I had been going to the hotel for lunch. We had arranged a schedule whereby two teachers remained at the high school during noon hour while the others went downtown for their lunches. We rotated this schedule. My turn came to be at the high school during the noon hour. I had heard gambling had been going on beyond the high board fence that surrounded the athletic field. I made it a point to start walking leisurely around this fence. Autumn was in the air and the sycamores, birches, and willows between the schoolhouse and the river were flaunting their bright-colored leaves to the autumn wind. The air was crisp and fine to breathe. It was a beautiful day.

When I walked around the corner of the high board fence, I came upon the young card players. A topcoat was spread on the ground. Cards, silver, and folding money were lying on the coat.

Four young men were sitting on the ground around the coat, with cards in their hands. Fifteen or twenty young men were standing around watching this poker game. I had walked around the fence corner and was standing in their midst unnoticed, for everybody was watching the cards and money.

"Who's winning and who's losing, fellows?" I asked.

One of the young men playing poker was the son of a Landsburgh minister. One was the son of a rural schoolteacher. Two were the sons of a Landsburgh merchant. When they saw me, their faces turned sliced-beet red. They couldn't speak. They looked at each other. The young men who had gathered to watch the poker game began to scatter. I didn't bother the cards or the money, or tell them to take them up or quit playing poker. I walked on. I left this problem in the pupil's hands—for them to worry about. I walked on around the board fence, where the sycamore, birch, and willow leaves were drifting like golden birds with every gust of autumn wind. When I reached the far corner of the fence, I looked back and the gamblers, money, and coat had disappeared.

That afternoon these young men expected me to have them in my office. But I was going futher than just reprimand them for a temptation placed before them. We had to have the ounce of prevention to effect the pound of cure. I knew my catching these young men playing poker would be news in Landsburgh. I knew that everybody would know it, for there were too many young men standing around not to tell it, and I knew it was not good publicity for our school.

Now let us pause to analyze this bit of human drama.

SIGNIFICANT IDEAS GOVERN TEACHER-COMMUNITY RELATIONSHIPS

What does Jesse Stuart believe about teacher-community relationships? Can we make a list of the principles upon which he is operating? Let's state some of the significant ideas which seem to govern his thinking.

Events Which Take Place In The School Significantly
Affect The Home And Community

Stuart sensed that the gambling incident is not an isolated event which is the concern alone of the school. He knows that the boys learned to gamble in the community. He knows that parents and other citizens are concerned. They would soon know about it, and the news would not be good for the school. Events which take place in the school do involve the community.

Can the same be said for all the life which goes on in the school? Is it not all community business with community implications? The problem confronting Stuart happens to be one of behavior and conduct. What about other matters? Take, for example, the academic program. A student does well in school, achieves, matures, and becomes a useful citizen. Something of value is added to the community. Or, a student fails to achieve and realize his full potential. The community is the loser. The school is a public place. Who can draw the boundary line between it and the rest of the community?

Events Which Take Place In The Community Significantly Affect The School

Stuart feels sure that gambling is a school problem because it is first a community problem. To solve the problem in the school means that it must first be solved in the community.

Experienced teachers frequently sense in their students that something is "wrong" in the home or community. The home or community problem significantly changes the student's behavior, his attitude toward the teacher, and school work. When what is "wrong" is corrected, teachers note an improvement in attitudes and behavior. Similarly, parents readily sense when things aren't going well at school. School problems affect home life. The flow of influences between school and community is circular; they flow both ways.

A Teacher's Handling Of School Problems Should Take Into Account Their Community Aspects

Stuart might have called the boys into his office, reprimanded them, and dropped the matter. But could he do this and be consistent with his belief that the problem was a community one? Believing this, he had to act in order to get at the real cause of the boys' behavior. Had he held the view that what happens in school is school business only, his problem would have been made easier. The problem would then be only between himself and the boys. Dealing with them, he would have discharged his responsibility. He chooses a different course of action.

School Problems Provide The Teacher With Opportunities To Work With The Community

Stuart chooses to pursue this problem to gain still another end—constructive school-community action. He wants to turn the problem into a positive benefit. He will use it to strengthen the community's ability to solve its own problems. Here he sees an opportunity to contribute as a teacher to the total community.

*School-Community Organizations Can Enrich Both School
And Community*

In Landsburgh, the P. T. A. provides, as we shall see, an opportunity for the parents to raise questions about the gambling incident. Such opportunities for communication are important in school-community relationships. They can help keep the relationship free of misunderstandings. They can help to build constructive programs.

Stuart believes that the P. T. A. is good for the school and community. He isn't happy with the way it is working. He believes it should do more than provide an opportunity for parents and teachers to drink tea and eat cakes. It should, he thinks, deal constructively with significant matters.

*Wide Citizen Participation In School Affairs Strengthens
The School*

Jesse Stuart is concerned about the narrow appeal of the P. T. A. The school is community business, he reasons. It deserves the best attention of all citizens of the community. Fathers should contribute. Parents who live out in the country some distance from the school should be represented. Broad participation makes for a better school.

COMMUNITY PARTICIPATION INVOLVES SOME RISKS AND PROBLEMS

How shall we judge Stuart's thinking on teacher-community relationships? Is it sound? Or, has Jesse Stuart left unsaid some things which ought to be said? Are there risks and pitfalls of which teachers should be aware? What does Stuart's approach demand of teachers? Before accepting his principles, let's ask ourselves some further questions.

*What If The Community Says: "School Problems Are
Your Problems, Stuart; You Take Care Of Them"?*

Would this not be a legitimate way for the community to react? The modern community consists of specialists, each carrying out specialized functions. The police, sanitary engineers, tax collectors, and judges all perform those duties assigned to their positions. "This is a school problem," the community may reason. "We pay the teachers to handle such problems. They should settle it." The community may not accept Stuart's concept of joint responsibility.

In what kind of position would this reaction place the teacher? Might not the community think that he isn't equal to the task for which it employed him? If it does, his usefulness as a teacher is diminished. He cannot afford to appear weak in the face of difficult problems.

If he maintains his position that this is a community problem, he must be prepared to convince the community first that it has a stake in the problem. This effort will take him far beyond his classroom work and call for leadership skill of the highest kind. The job will not be easy and he can anticipate some opposition and misunderstanding.

What If The Community Applies One Standard Of Conduct To Itself, But Expects A Higher Standard Of The School?

This double standard is well known to teachers. Parents who drink excessively at home may blame the school when their child drinks at a school party. Children who come from homes devoid of scholarly interest are expected by their parents to become honor students.

In a sense the community may be entitled to expect more of the school than it does of itself. The school, it may be reasoned, is created by the community in order to improve the community. It should hold itself to a higher standard in order to set an example. The point is this: The teacher who holds to Stuart's principles may have to reckon with this double standard. He will have to work hard with the community to secure a better understanding of the true nature of school problems.

What If The Community Says: "Stop Intruding; We'll Handle Our Own Problems"?

Assume that Stuart were to approach the parents about their sons' behavior. How do you think the parents would react? Is there a chance that they might be defensive and resent the intrusion into what they consider family affairs? How can he approach the problem in order to avoid this reaction? Here the teacher is required to exercise skills in diplomacy.

What If Wider Community Participation Imposes New Responsibilities On The Teacher?

What do you think would happen if twice as many parents in Landsburgh took an active part in the P. T. A.? Would the teachers' jobs be made easier or harder? Would more people think of more problems, resulting in more committee work for more teachers?

Let's assume that a high school teacher in Landsburgh has 125 students in a given term. These 125 students, under normal circumstances, have 250 parents. What if a substantial percentage of these parents suddenly take a personal interest in school affairs, especially as they relate to the progress of their children? They all want a thirty minute conference with the teacher. What will this mean? It may mean that the teacher may have to confront a basic question: How much community participation in education do I really believe in?

Stuart made his decision on this issue and had apparently thought through the consequences. He believed that to do the teacher's job as he viewed it, he had no choice but to push for the widest possible community participation. Ultimately, he felt that the school would have fewer vexing problems and the teacher's job would be more satisfying if more citizens contributed. He had faith in the democratic way.

This faith calls for a large view of teaching. The teacher, in this view, is more than a classroom specialist, operating solely within the walls of the school. He is, rather, a skilled group leader, helping students, parents, and other citizens build a better community.

In this dynamic role the teacher's life may not be easy. He must be a student of group behavior. He needs to understand the sociology of communities. He must develop skill in working with many different people. His job is large and complex. It is also rewarding.

Now let us return to Jesse Stuart's narrative. Let us observe (1) how he applies his own principles to the problem and (2) how he handles the risks and responsibilities involved in community leadership.

> The first person to ask me about her son's gambling was Mrs. Hunter, wife of the Methodist minister. She asked me what punishment I was going to inflict. I replied I hadn't made up my mind. I told her, on second thought, I probably wouldn't punish any of them. She couldn't believe me.
>
> "Do you believe in letting your pupils gamble?" she asked, staring at me wildly.
>
> "No, I don't believe in letting pupils gamble," I told her.
>
> "Then, why don't you do something about it?" she asked me.
>
> I didn't say anything more. I wanted her to talk. I wanted her to tell other women, and I knew she would. I wanted them all to talk.
>
> The mother of each son caught in this act came to ask me what I was going to do about the gambling at Landsburgh High School. I didn't give one of them a satisfactory answer. I let them talk and tell others.

1. Here is the "you-take-care-of-it" attitude. Had you been in Mr. Stuart's position, how would you have replied to the mothers?

Finally these women must have decided I approved of gambling, for the members of the P. T. A. took the responsibility upon themselves to bring it up at our next meeting. I had not punished any offender. Each one of these young men was worried, too, for he had come to me more than once and apologized and wanted to know what his punishment was going to be. He was getting his punishment, but he didn't know it. Suspense is a great punishment.

At our first P. T. A. meeting after the gambling incident, I noticed that the members of the P. T. A. were very somber. They didn't laugh and talk as they had done at our former social meeting. The Methodist minister, Reverend Hunter, was among the P. T. A. members. Several fathers had come to this meeting. After the meeting had come to order, Mrs. Albert Davis, president of the P. T. A., soon finished with the organization's business. Then she said: "Something has been going on at the high school I would like to bring up. It is a sad reflection but a true one, and it is the talk of the town. It is the gambling that has been going on here. Pupils were caught in the act and have never been punished. We would like to hear from Mr. Stuart if he has anything to say regarding this situation."

"I have a lot to say," I said, rising to my feet. "First, I want to tell you why I haven't punished these young men. I don't see any use in punishing them until a few temptations are removed. I happen to know about these temptations."

Then I told them how my clothes had been criticized and how I had moved to the Landsburgh Hotel. I told them their criticizing my clothes was the reason for my knowing all about the town. That in my room in the Landsburgh Hotel, I could see over the town in all directions but one. And that if anyone didn't believe me, he should come to my room and switch off the lights and look over the town at night. I told them I had the room the town's police ought to have. Then I said to the mothers and fathers in the P. T. A. that I had seen their sons and daughters walking the streets until midnight. I asked them if they knew where they were at night. If they knew what time they got in off the streets.

Women whispered to each other. Their faces reddened and they looked down at their desks. I told them their sons were able to buy illegal whiskey, and there was not one among them that didn't know where they could get it. That to stop the sale of whiskey to their sons was their business. It was the town's business and not the teachers! Yet it did concern the high school, for our young men had gotten drunk on river-boat excursions and the school had been blamed for it. Now it was their duty to eliminate the temptations.

2. Here is an example in which the community applies a higher standard of conduct to the teachers than it does to itself. Make an analysis of your own community in this regard. Would you say that your community expects a higher standard of conduct of teachers than it does of "average citizens"?

"And another thing—" I said. "Gambling is carried on in many of the homes in this town. Poker for money is played before your sons and daughters. You know who these people are. Fathers of the young men on our football team, wearing derby hats, with long cigars in their mouths, walk up and down the side lines with a bank roll in their hands and bet as much as fifty dollars on one of our football games! You know this is true! It is said that the men in this town will gamble over who can spit the closest to a knothole on the wall or a crack in the floor. The parents in this town must have a change of heart if we are to break up gambling in this school. I'm certainly glad, Mrs. Davis, you brought this up.

"And another thing—" I continued. "Somebody had better pass the word to the town's favorite bootlegger to be careful to whom he sells his whiskey. Remember, he has five pupils in this school! If you want to watch him sell some evening, come up to my room. If you want to know his customers, be sure to come to my room."

"One thing more and this is all I have to say," I concluded. "Landsburgh High School is not a separate unit from you. We are part of you. Every man, woman, and child in this community is a part of Landsburgh High School. Your ways of life in your homes and in the town reflect here in the school. You can help us or you can hurt us. Our success here depends largely on you. I used to think when I first started teaching school that it was up to the teachers and the pupils. I have changed my mind. The little island of humanity that is each one of you must unite with other islands and become a mainland if we are to have a successful school."

3. Two sentences sum up Jesse Stuart's philosophy: "You can help us or you can hurt us. Our success depends largely on you." Here is an opportunity to test Stuart's conclusions. Interview a teacher to find out if he agrees with Stuart. For comparison, interview a parent. Does the parent agree that the teacher's success "depends largely" on him?

The results of this P. T. A. meeting solved the problems in Landsburgh. I never again saw any parents betting on football games. Something suddenly happened to the little racehorse slot machine. The jukebox dancing ended gracefully at nine o'clock, for the city's board of aldermen imposed a curfew to ring at nine, and every pupil enrolled in school had to be in off the streets. Drinking suddenly ended among our young men. Not one person was arrested. Our school had caused a moral reformation among the citizens of Landsburgh. Gambling never occurred again, at our high school. And the only punishment I gave the four young men caught in the act was suspense. They waited and waited for something to happen but it never did.

In six weeks we gladly showed members of our P. T. A. what their cooperation had done in their sons' and daughters' grades. Many of their sons and daughters who had been failing were now making passing grades. Many pupils who had been passing with low marks had lifted their average a letter higher. The unexcused tardy and absence marks had diminished approximately 70 per cent. School-work had been made easier for us. The pupils were happier and loved school more. This was the result of cooperation between parents, citizens, teachers, and pupils. "This P. T. A. has taught us something," Bill Hadden remarked later at a teachers' meeting. "All you have to do to solve a town problem that hurts your school is to get the women on your side. Show 'em what's wrong, and they'll clean it up."

4. Do you believe that students make better grades, "are happier and love school more," when there is close cooperation between teachers and parents?

HOW SHALL WE ACCOUNT FOR STUART'S SUCCESS?

How shall we explain the apparent success which resulted from Jesse Stuart's appeal to parents? Several factors are worth considering:

(1) Stuart refused to deal with the problem as an isolated school problem. He saw it for what it was—a community problem.

(2) He took the leadership in telling the community that it was a community problem.

(3) The community accepted the responsibility, changed its attitude from "what are *you* going to do about it?" to "what are *we* going to do about it?"

(4) The combined influence of school and community was brought to bear on the problem, constituting a much stronger force than either alone.

This is Stuart's story, based upon his own teaching experience. It is dramatic, and we would not expect that similar problems in other communities could be solved in exactly the same way. Each community is different.

The valuable point for us is this: There are some fundamental questions which each teacher must confront as a public servant. How he answers these questions will help to determine his influence with students, parents, and other citizens. They are big questions, never fully answered, because they are life-time questions. We start where we are and continually enlarge upon our answers. This is the excitement of teaching.

Here are some of these life-time problems:

(1) As a teacher, how can I help the school to become a tool for achieving desirable community goals?

(2) How can I help to weld together the forces of school and community to achieve better learning and living?

(3) How can I keep professionally aware of my ever-widening responsibilities of school-community leadership?

The modern teacher's task is large, and ever-growing larger. He is more than classroom teacher; he is community leader and educator. The work he does in the school spills over into the community around him. The events and attitudes of the community come pouring into the classroom with the students. To be a teacher he must know both school and community and be willing to work in both to advance the cause of education.

Good Follow-up Reading and Viewing

BOOKS

Fox, Robert S., ed., *Teaching in the Small Community*. Washington, D.C.: National Education Association, 1956. For the prospective teacher who would like to teach in a rural community. A good discussion of how the teacher can make fullest use of the community in the classroom.

Gollomb, Joseph, *Albert Schweitzer: Genius in the Jungle*. New York: Vanguard Press, 1949. Schweitzer exemplifies social responsibility on an international scale, the kind of responsibility which good teachers should demonstrate on a local scale.

Grobman, Hulda, and Vynce A. Hines, "Teacher as a Citizen," in *The Teacher's Role in American Society*, Lindley J. Stiles, ed. New York: Harper & Brothers, 1957. A comprehensive discussion of teachers' fulfillment of their responsibilities as citizens, blocks to citizenship activity, and ways to improve the citizenship of the teacher.

Haskew, Laurence D., *This Is Teaching*, chap. 4, "Here Live the Learners." Chicago: Scott, Foresman & Company, 1956. Some graphic particulars on how the whole community serves to educate.

John Dewey Society, *The Teacher and Society*. New York: Appleton-Century-Crofts, Inc., 1937. A statement of the teacher's rights and responsibilities in a democracy.

McCloskey, Gordon, *et al.*, *Introduction to Teaching in America*, Part 4, "The Teacher in School and Community." New York: Harcourt, Brace & World, Inc., 1954. This section focuses on the teacher's relation to the school and his relations with adults both in the school and the community. Also treated is the teacher's routine of weekly work.

Richey, Robert W., *Planning For Teaching*, chap. 15, "Community Aspects of Education." New York: McGraw-Hill Book Co., Inc., 1958. Deals with the forces in the community which serve to educate and how the teacher can help the community to find a place for its youth.

Smiley, Marjorie B., and John S. Diekhoff, *Prologue to Teaching*, Part 4, "The School in Context." New York: Oxford University Press, 1959. Readings deal with the environmental setting of education. Topics include the influences of culture, family, religion, communications, and the social order.

Stuart, Jesse, *The Thread That Runs So True*. New York: Charles Scribner's Sons, 1949. The excerpt in this chapter is representative of the interesting quality of Jesse Stuart's entire book. Profitable reading for teachers and prospective teachers.

Yates, Elizabeth, *Nearby*. New York: Coward-McCann, Inc., 1947. An exciting and realistic novel about a young teacher's experiences in a small town. It provides discussion topics regarding the teacher's relations with students, parents, and community.

PERIODICALS

Burton, Dwight L., "The Tumult and the Teacher," *Phi Delta Kappan*, December, 1955, pp. 109-11. A discussion of the tumult in public education and how it affects the teacher. It is not new, but today the controversy has some unique earmarks.

Chilcott, John H., "Community Restrictions on Teacher Behavior," *The Journal of Educational Sociology*, Vol. 33, March, 1960, pp. 336-38. Residents and teachers of a western town are queried about their expectations for teacher behavior in the community.

Conner, Forrest E., "Bring Thy People In," *The Nation's Schools*, Vol. 65, March, 1960, pp. 57-60. A superintendent of schools makes a strong plea for educator-citizen cooperation in order to meet the crisis in education.

Priwer, Jane, "Strengthen the Schools Through Citizen Activity," *NEA Journal*, Vol. 49, March, 1960, pp. 59-60. The story of how greater St. Louis is using lay groups to strengthen the schools. The importance of cooperation between professional educator and lay citizen.

Ravenbolt, Albert, "Miss Stewart—Our Teacher," *American University Field Staff Letter*, No. AR6-58, August 8, 1958, New York. Correspondent Ravenbolt interviews Elvessa Ann Stewart who spent forty-five years teaching home economics in the Philippines. An excellent example of how teaching can be adapted to community needs.

Taylor, Joy J., "A Learning Laboratory," *NEA Journal*, Vol. 47, October, 1958, pp. 475-76. Relates how an entire city is a learning laboratory for teachers and students.

FILMS

American Teacher

Relationship of education to the nation's economic and cultural strength. Comprehensive explanation of progressive, or modern, education in present society. Responsibility of public school teachers; downward trend of recruits. Explanations by Kilpatrick, Dewey, Bagley. (March of Time; McGraw-Hill Book Co., Inc., black and white, 15 minutes.)

Assignment: Tomorrow

Vital role of the teacher; the place of teachers as citizens in the community; their contributions as members of professional organizations. (National Education Association, black and white, 31 minutes.)

Near Home

How a group of English school children studied their community's history, industries, public utilities, government, geography, and other important features. The field trip as an integrated experience. (International Film Bureau, black and white, 27 minutes.)

Passion for Life

Dramatic and moving story of the transformation of a community and its school by a dedicated and inspired teacher. The meaning of real teaching. French dialogue, English subtitles. (Brandon Films, black and white, 85 minutes.)

CHAPTER 14

THE TEACHER AND PARENTS

Every parent has a tremendous prejudice in favor of his or her
offspring, and the world would be a dreadfully cold place to live
if this were not true.

HORACE DUTTON TAFT

Horace Dutton Taft [1] was for almost fifty years headmaster of the
Taft School for boys. In his story of these years he remarks, "A school-
master can hardly indulge in reminiscences without giving a chapter to
parents." The same may be said for public school teachers. Wherever
they gather, the conversation is likely to get around to parents.

Teachers, like most people, enjoy talking about unusual parents. They
speak of the mother who thinks that the teacher should devote all of his
time to her child, or of the father who begins by saying, "No one is in
favor of school discipline more than I am," and then proceeds to defend
his son who has just started a fire in a classroom wastepaper basket. Most
teachers at one time or another get sick of "parental jaw," and are ready
to agree that "parents are the last people on earth who ought to have
children." (And more than one parent has felt that teachers are the last
people on earth who ought to *teach* children.)

WORKING WITH PARENTS IS A PART OF TEACHING

Taft recalls the kinds of experiences with parents which are familiar to
most teachers. Let's look at several of them. First, he remembers an over-
solicitous mother.

---

[1] Horace Dutton Taft, *Memories and Opinions* (New York: The Macmillan Company,
1942), pp. 200-04, 210-11.

One dear friend of mine, who had been most reasonable about her boy and was emphatically on the list of good parents kept bothering me morning after morning. Her boy had been kicked in the end of the spine and retired to the infirmary. Dr. Martin assured me that with a little rest and refraining from exercise he would be all right, and that there was nothing to worry about; but she kept calling me up at the busiest time of the morning, until I said: "Mary, you make me tired. You are wasting valuable time every morning for me. I will tell you the boy is all right. I will only add that it's the other end of his spine about which I am worried." She laughed and reported that to her family, and that was the end of it.

Then there are the parents who can't agree among themselves about what is best for the child. Sometimes the teacher is placed in the "middle."

School masters are made aware of differences of opinion in families in regard to the education of their children, and sometimes this is embarrassing. Some twenty-five years ago I had the unpleasant duty of dismissing a boy for very substantial reasons. A few days afterwards his father came in to ask whether I could not take the boy back. I told him that would be quite impossible; the boys themselves would be shocked to hear of his return. He said, "Well, what am I going to do with him?"

"The only thing to do is to find him a good hard job and put him to work. He will waste his time in school and go to the devil in college. Hard work out in the world will probably sober him up."

"I believe you are dead right. That is what I will do."

When he reached the door, however, he turned around and said, "But you remember that I have made a hell of a fight to get him back into this school!"

Also, there is the parent who shifts responsibility to the school.

Sometimes it is amazing to see the way in which the parent will shift responsibility to the school. The father of a boy who was attending a private day school was very indignant because the boy was expelled for gambling. He wrote to the head of the school that he did not object to the rule against gambling or think the punishment excessive. He only felt that the school was at fault for not instructing him about the evils of gambling, adding, "If a boy is not going to learn at school the evils of dishonesty, immorality, and gambling, where will he learn?"

These cases, of course, are the unusual kind that teachers like to recite when comparing notes. They certainly do not represent all parents. The great majority of parents exercise good sense and restraint in their relationships with teachers and endeavor in every way possible to help them. Experienced teachers know what powerful allies parents are in the schooling of children. And teachers frequently find good friendships with parents—friendships which last far beyond the time the child is a student.

Let's look further at the relationship between teachers and parents.

THE RELATIONSHIP IS FREQUENTLY CLOSE

When a new teacher steps into his first classroom he may think of his job as one of working exclusively with students. He soon finds out differently. He hears a child say, "My Dad says . . . ," or "My mother says . . . ," and he is aware of the parental influence behind each child.

The telephone rings. "Why didn't you collect the milk money, today?" a mother wants to know. And then it suddenly dawns on the new teacher why little Bobby was able to treat the other children to candy that particular morning.

The first P. T. A. meeting arrives and a dozen parents suddenly surround the new teacher, wanting to meet him, making sure he knows their names, and listening for any scrap of information which will let them know how their child is getting along.

Then comes the first parent-teacher conference. The parent is armed with all kinds of questions about his child. How is he doing? Is he keeping up with the rest of the class? What about his reading? Does he behave himself? Why can't he get arithmetic? What happened to his leather glove? Will he get into college?

From experiences like these the new teacher begins to sense the closeness of his relationship with parents. He comes to know that his work is reported each night at the dinner table, sometimes accurately, but frequently garbled to suit the child. He learns that parents judge his work far more than he would like by what the child reports at home. He learns that some parents speak only praises for the teacher, and if they have differences they will bring them directly to him without the child's knowing. In this home the teacher gets support. He also learns that in other homes parents discuss their differences with teachers freely with the children. He learns to tell from the behavior of children what attitude the parents hold toward the school and toward him. He discovers how important a good parent-teacher relationship is in the education of the child.

The relationship of the teacher and the parent is especially close in American schools. As we observed in the last chapter, American schools are close to the community. They belong to the people. Citizens, not educators, build them, pay for them, and employ professional people to teach in and administer them. For the most part, these schools have been open to all. Our public schools are very public.

By contrast, many foreign schools do not have this kind of close relationship with the people. Many foreign public schools are operated by central bureaus where major decisions are made and teachers employed. In a sense, these schools do not "belong" to the community around them. Some places there is a tradition that the school teacher's word is supreme and takes precedence over that of even the parent. In such communities parents are frequently discouraged from visiting the school or taking part in its program. On the other hand, American schools are often the social and recreational center of the community. In them there are many opportunities for parents and teachers to work closely together.

> 1. What kinds of opportunities are provided in your own community for parents and teachers to work together? Is the relationship "close" or "distant"?

MUCH DEPENDS UPON THE RELATIONSHIP

Not only is the relationship between teachers and parents close; much depends upon it. It is a partnership in the interest of the child. If the partnership is mutually supporting, the child benefits. If there is conflict or misunderstanding, the child suffers. As we indicated before, the teacher can usually tell by the behavior of the child the regard with which the parent holds the work of the teacher.

Likewise, the parent can usually tell by observing the child the regard in which the teacher holds the work of the home. The matter flows both ways. A teacher who expects cooperation from parents must be expected to give it. In word and deed he must let the student know that he regards himself as a partner with the parent in the best interest of the child.

PREPARE TO WORK WITH PARENTS

In view of the closeness of this relationship and the importance of it, the teacher has no choice but to prepare himself to work effectively with parents. He will find deep satisfaction in doing so. Working as he does with children and adolescents most of the time, the teacher usually finds contact with the adult world of parents a refreshing change. Further, such contacts help him in working with children. As the teacher's acquaintance with the parent grows, so does his ability to work with and understand the parent's child.

Let us turn now to two vital questions growing out of this relationship:
(1) What do parents expect of teachers?, and (2) What do teachers expect
of parents? Certainly a parent has the right to expect certain things of
a teacher. Conversely, a teacher has a right to expect certain things of a
parent. Let's look first at the parent's expectation.

WHAT DO PARENTS EXPECT OF TEACHERS?

For several years I have invited parents to speak to classes of prospective teachers on the topic: "What I expect of my child's teacher." The
tapes of these discussions make revealing listening. They are most instructive to beginning teachers, for the parents are willing to say in these
discussions many things which they probably would not say directly to
their child's teacher—not that what they say is derogatory; they are
simply frank and straightforward.

Most of all, these discussions reveal how much importance parents at-
tach to the work of the teacher, and how much they expect of him. Their
own expectations for the child are understandably great. They want the
teacher to help the child fulfill these great expectations. Most parents
feel some sense of failure in rearing a child. Somehow, they hope that the
teacher will be able to succeed where they have failed. They want the
teacher to extend the limited horizons of the home, open new doors and
aspirations. At the same time they want the teacher to reinforce the
home.

Sometimes parents' expectations may conflict. Some parents place
highest priority on the child's moral and spiritual behavior. Others place
highest importance on the child's academic development. Still other
parents want the child to be able to "get along" and "be able to work
with people." Some parents insist on homework for the school child;
others oppose it. Somehow, the teacher must learn to work with students
whose parents may hold widely different aspirations for them.

Let's listen now to what some of these parents have to say.

Parents Expect Teachers To Be Committed

Parents like to feel that their children are being taught by people who
enjoy teaching and are dedicated to it. They want the teacher to take his
job seriously; he is, after all, dealing with their most precious possession.
They are happy when the teacher's enthusiasm for learning is com-
municated to their children. Here a mother expresses these expectations:

> In reflecting about what parents expect of teachers, I think of two
> teachers in particular who are doing fine jobs with our children.
> These teachers have one thing in common: they like to teach. They

want to teach more than they want to do anything else. They are really excited about their jobs. I am thinking particularly of a mathematics teacher who thinks that mathematics is a fascinating subject; and she is leading my children to see that mathematics is fascinating. That is what I think parents want—professional people who are proud of their profession. They want you to show enthusiasm and excitement that is contagious.

Here is another parent who expresses a similar expectation.

The profession of teaching is one that is often interrupted, especially with many of our young girls going into it. Often, of course, they come back to teaching after marriage, and this is good. But I want a girl to go into teaching because she really wants to, and not simply as something to do until she gets married. I want her to have an enthusiasm for teaching. I want her to be able to say that teaching is what she wants to do professionally, that it is work she loves. I am wondering if too many young people don't choose teaching simply as something to do until they get married or until they move on to something else.

2. Do you agree with this parent? What is the quality of the commitment among those you know who are preparing to teach?

Parents Expect Teachers To Challenge Their Child

The teacher sees the needs of 30 or 40 students in his room. His attention and skill must be given to all. The parent is likely to think of the teacher's job in terms of one child, his own. He wants this child to develop to the limit of his capacity. A good teacher, of course, is as interested as the parent in developing the unique capacities of each child. But the situation requires that the teacher decide how he will spread his time among all of the children in terms of their particular needs. The way he makes this important decision may not always please certain parents. Here is an expression of such dissatisfaction:

We have two girls and two boys, ranging from the nursery school to junior high school. In my opinion the thing that is basically wrong is that teachers spend too much of their time with slow students and with the students who have personality problems. If you happen to be blessed with an intelligent child, one without special personality problems, the only reaction you ever get from a teacher is "Oh, aren't you lucky. I don't have to worry about your child." This is completely frustrating from a parent's point of view. After one week in school our junior high school girl finds she doesn't have to bring home any homework because there is so much time wasted

in class that she can do her homework there and still have time
left over for day dreaming. Then at home she can spend four hours
watching television. I am very critical of the teacher because she
doesn't give my child sufficient work. I believe we have got to do
something to keep children occupied in the schoolroom. We are so
concerned about well-adjusted students that we don't give them
enough work to keep them well adjusted. Frankly, the schools creep
along at such a slow pace that it makes you feel that your children
are just wasting their time.

3. As a prospective teacher you should learn all you can about how parents
"feel" about teachers. Interview several parents to some depth regarding their
opinion of the work of their children's teachers. Share your findings with the class.

Parents Expect Teachers To Teach Basic Knowledge And Skills

Parents want their children to "know something," to have a good grasp
of the subjects offered in the public school. They want them to be able
to handle the basic skills and academic subjects. These matters are now
assuming more significance than ever before. With college becoming a
common goal of great numbers of high school students, these matters will
be given even more stress in the future. Parents expect teachers to give
their children the necessary knowledge for college entrance. Not all high
school graduates go on to college. For them, however, the basic skills are
equally important. Here is the view of a parent who happens also to be
an employer of high school students:

I am an employer and own and operate a retail drug store. We
normally employ two or three high school students on a split-shift
basis throughout the week. I notice so many of the students who
work for me have difficulty with the three R's. Take, for example,
the spelling of common names and common words which are
required in ordering and reordering. Many of the students who
work for me have great difficulty in arithmetic in such matters as
figuring taxes on items. It is necessary to divide and multiply, and
many can't do it accurately. They also have trouble with writing.
Penmanship is very poor. I think that I probably notice these basic
things more than some other people, since all of them affect my
business. If, for example, a customer comes in and says "This
column is not added correctly," I risk losing that customer.

Parents Expect Teachers To Pay Attention To Moral
And Spiritual Values

Learning and religion have historically been closely associated in the minds of many Americans, even though constitutionally we maintain a separation of church and state. It was quite common for early school masters to teach school during the week and conduct religious services on Sunday.

Our early school architecture reflected a close identification of learning and religion. Many school buildings, especially on college campuses, used Gothic architecture as a natural expression of a place of learning. These outward forms of expressing the close relationship of learning and religion have largely disappeared from the modern scene. The expectation which parents hold, however, has not. Most parents, following our constitutional separation of church and state, do not want sectarian religion taught in the public school. But they do expect the teacher to give support and encouragement to those broad moral and spiritual values which undergird our society. In fact, some parents give these matters top priority, as for example, this mother:

> In thinking of what I expect of teachers I place moral values first. To me these are the most important. It makes a great deal of difference how a teacher feels about moral principles. If he is willing to teach moral and spiritual values, I think he is a much better teacher. To me this is vital. We must have it. We can learn and pick up basic information in many ways, but we must have moral values to start with.

Parents Expect Teachers To Share Their Concern For the Child

A teacher stands in the place of a parent. This is true legally, but it is more than legally true. In terms of aspirations for the welfare of the child, parents like teachers to stand in their place. They like to think the teacher will have the same concern for the child they have. A good teacher, in their judgment, wants their child to grow and achieve just as they want him to grow and achieve. Parents expect in the teacher a parent's concern for children. This mother expresses this expectation:

> When I think of what I expect of a teacher I put it like this: Especially in elementary and high school I want a good parent substitute. Perhaps I can illustrate what I mean by telling of an incident. Last month I was visiting a public school with a distinguished scientist and teacher. Students were walking around us when suddenly he stopped and looked about. Then he said, "You know, every boy and girl who passes us here is somebody's darling. Somebody's hopes and aspirations are all bound up in this one person who is passing us now. No matter how cross-eyed he or she may be, how bow-legged, how scrawny, he or she is somebody's

darling." I like the teacher of my children to feel that way and to appreciate how parents want their children to get on and achieve.

Parents Expect Teachers To Keep Them Informed

Not only do many parents expect teachers to understand the home background, they personally want to be informed about what the child is doing. They also like to be called upon to give assistance when such assistance can be meaningful to the child. Not all parents, of course, take this personal interest in the child's education, but most of them do, as is the case with this parent:

> Normally in our experience the teacher does not take the parent into his confidence. He doesn't tell parents what is going on. You don't know what subject matter, for example, is being taught, unless you sit down with your child for half an hour each night. You haven't the foggiest notion of what the child did in class or what the subject is about. There is considerable interplay that would be possible between the teacher and the parent if only the parent knew approximately what was going on. Maybe the school should have a syllabus of the course of study for the parent. I am not sure. But in any event, it seems to me that parents could help out in the problem of motivation if they know more about what is happening.
>
> Let me give you just one example. The other night I talked to our junior high school girl about what she was doing. She said she was studying blueprints of houses and thought this was strictly a waste of time. She wasn't going to learn anything from it. Well, had we known about this topic, we could have shown her our own house plans and blueprints, and told her how they were developed, and how important they were in building our house. It seems to me that there is a great opportunity for cooperation here which is not being used.

PARENTS MAY HAVE CONFLICTING EXPECTATIONS

As we indicated earlier, teachers who work closely with parents frequently discover that they have conflicting expectations regarding their children. Recall, for example, that one parent wanted highest priority given to the basic subjects, another to moral and spiritual views. It is natural that parents' aspirations for their children should differ, since their own aspirations differ. Here are the comments of two parents which reflect a conflict in respect to assigning homework:

> My four children go to a small school. One of my four children has graduated and another is in pre-school; so I have a child in

almost every department. I think that teachers give students too much work to do outside of school. I think if you plan better and if you teach children how to study better in school, it won't be necessary to give so much homework. I would prefer that you would utilize their school time better and eliminate homework completely. My children are active, as most children are, in many activities outside the school. They have such things as sporting events, girl scouts, boy scouts, and church activities. Their schedules pile up and up, even though we do our best to keep them from doing so. I believe that if a child is in school from 8:30 in the morning until 4:00 in the afternoon, that is enough. After that they should have some time with the family. Bringing home volumes of books does not necessarily make them good students.

Here is a parent who disagrees:

I think homework is fine discipline for the child. I feel that a child should take the responsibility for some amount of preparation for the following day's classes. It's good discipline. Our children have homework quite regularly from the second grade on. The second grader has a small amount, taking no more than 15 to 20 minutes to do. I feel he must do it, however, and apparently his teacher feels so too. I feel that it is very good for him to have it. He should know that before he goes to school the next morning he has that little assignment to finish. I wouldn't like it if my boys' teacher arranged things so that they had no school work.

4. Let's assume that you are the teacher of the children of these two mothers. One wants her child to have home work. The other opposes it. What would you do?

The list of parents' expectations is a long one, and it could be much longer. In a way, the length of the list is a tribute to teachers. If parents had less confidence in teachers, they probably would not expect so much. The list also indicates that many parents feel the need for help in the complex and difficult business of rearing children. They want the teacher to be a cooperative and productive partner in this enterprise.

WHAT DO TEACHERS EXPECT OF PARENTS?

Teachers expect certain things of parents. This list of expectations could also be long. We shall, however, confine our discussion to two broad expectations which are basic to a good working relationship between teachers and parents.

First, the teacher has the right to expect that parents will not shift responsibility. Certain responsibility, of course, is legally shifted to the teacher—responsibility to teach the prescribed curriculum and to give reasonable attention to the child's health and welfare while he is in school. But here we are speaking of shifting another kind of responsibility. We are speaking of the kind referred to by Horace Dutton Taft in the case of the father who, when his son was expelled for gambling, asked *where* a boy would learn acceptable behavior, if not in school?

Second, the teacher has a right to expect that parents will cooperate with him and give full support in those matters which affect the educational welfare of the child. Let's look at these two matters more closely.

Teachers Expect Parents Not To Shift Responsibility

It is not uncommon for parents to expect miracles of teachers. Parents who never read a book at home may expect the child to become an expert reader. Parents who never talk about wind and weather, heat and cold, or other matters of scientific interest may expect their child to become a scientist. And parents who never examine with a child a map or a globe, or carry on a family discussion about rivers and mountains, may expect their child to do well in geography.

Sometimes students do well in spite of these handicaps. But they do considerably better when the home supports what is being done in the school. Taft tells the story of the father who criticized the school for the way it was teaching English. The story illustrates how a sincere and intelligent parent can unwittingly expect the school to accomplish what he has been unwilling to encourage at home.

A college graduate, a man of considerable ability, was visiting the school to see his boy and walked in on me. He said, "I do not think much of the way you teach English these days."

"Neither do I."

"When I was a boy, I used to browse in my father's library."

"So did I."

"I read Cooper and Scott and Dickens and Thackeray with no prodding or compulsion."

"So did I."

Then we two foolish men proceeded to match books we had read, whereupon he said, "I would rather have done that reading on my own than have the compulsory reading which is involved in your English course."

"So would I."

He then looked at me as though he thought it was my move.

"You realize, of course," I said, "that browsing is a voluntary thing that depends on the boy himself, on his whole environment, but especially on his home influence. You have had that boy of yours 15 years all to yourself, with the influence of the entire family brought to bear on a single boy. I have it from his own lips that he never read a single book except for what he was compelled to read by school authorities. For 15 years! And yet you send him to me, one of 250 boys, and expect me to teach him to browse! Could anything be more absurd?"

5. Within your own experience, can you cite an example in which parents shifted responsibility to the teacher?

6. What do you think a teacher can do when he has determined that parents are expecting something of him which they do not expect of themselves.

7. Had you been Taft, how would you have replied to the father who criticized the teaching of English?

This father was probably unaware, until Taft reminded him, that he was expecting the school to accomplish something which he had not encouraged at home. Other parents may be fully aware of it and may honestly wish to support their child's school work in every way possible. They simply don't know how to do it.

The teacher, in these cases, can be helpful. The teacher has many opportunities to explain his work to parents, and suggest ways in which they can reinforce classroom activities. If the teacher asks the parent not to shift responsibility, he must be prepared also to help parents when they sincerely want to reinforce school work at home.

Teachers Expect Personal Support From Parents

Does any single factor make a greater difference in the education of a child than the support the teacher gets at home? On the other hand, can anything undercut the efforts of the teacher better than the lack of support at home? Let's make the matter more specific. As some children go about their school activities their home influence seems to be saying to them: "What I am doing is important. My parents expect me to do well. The teacher is an important person and I can learn from him. For now, getting an education is the most valuable thing I can do." On the other hand, the home influence may be saying to the child: "School isn't important. Who cares whether or not I get my work? Dad doesn't think much of the teacher anyway. He never says so, but I know he doesn't. Besides, what difference is this going to make five years from now?"

Teachers can usually tell how the home influences the child. What that influence is makes a tremendous difference in the work of the teacher. It can make a tremendous difference for good or ill, success or failure. Because of this crucial importance the teacher has a right to expect that parents who send their children to him will give their best efforts to support his work.

Taft underscored the importance of this expectation by drawing on his long experience in working with parents. Here are his comments:

> Few parents have any idea what hearty cooperation with the school means. We can never have in the country even if we wish it, assistance such as obtained in Germany, before the World War and in France, where the school authorities had power, not only over the boy, but over the entire family.
>
> Two or three things, however, are of vital importance. The first is that the home, and therefore the boy, should take school seriously, should consider it the business of the boy's life for the present. Lecturing and preaching will do little good. The boy will know quickly whether his parents regard his work and conduct at school as a serious matter. Another condition that is absolutely requisite is that the home, and therefore the boy, should consider the school authorities supreme in their own sphere. I do not mean merely that a boy should go to recitations, be regular in attendance, and obey the rules, but that his frame of mind should be sympathetic and respectful and serious towards his work, and towards his school authorities.
>
> The free-for-all discussions at home of the discipline of the school or of the value to the boy of what he is studying, a discussion which the American boy hears and often takes part in, is a singular thing known only to America to any extent. I have wrestled with many boys in the study of Latin and have been well aware that they have listened to comments at home on the utter futility of that particular study. This is a splendid preparation for the beginning of the work that is necessary for the mastery of a difficult study. It is as though the parent should send the boy to the doctor and say, "His medicine is of no use, and I would not take any more of it than he compelled me to take." The question before the parent in the cases I referred to was not the value of the study of Latin. They knew that he was going to study it. Surely any study is better for the boy's development, both mental and moral, if he devotes himself to it honestly and consciously; and any teacher, competent or incompetent, is a better teacher if he has the moral advantage of that attitude toward school which ought to exist in every home.
>
> Criticism of individual teachers, of school rules, or of the course of study is not only allowed, but encouraged in many a family. It would surprise the heads of these families to know that those criticisms and condemnations and the ridicule often involved have lowered the standards of the school, has made the work of the

234

The School and Community

teacher more difficult, and have [done] a great injury to all the boys of this school, including their own. Criticism of school matters, while often amply justified, should be confined to the discussion of the grown-up members of the family, but the school has a right to much more than silence. The whole influence of the home honestly and positively, should be exercised to uphold and increase the power of the school authorities.

A good teacher can do much to make it easy for parents to give their influence "honestly and positively" to the school. Through good teaching, through personal interest in the child, and through direct acquaintance and communications with parents, the teacher encourages positive personal support. Parents respond to those teachers who genuinely indicate that they want and need parental support in their teaching.

Let us turn now to specific things a teacher can do to stimulate a close and supporting working relationship with parents.

WHAT CAN A TEACHER DO?

A good relationship with parents obviously begins in good teaching. Without this the basis for a good relationship is flimsy indeed. The first thing a teacher can do to encourage a wholesome relationship with parents is to teach well in the classroom. A good teacher can do other things. Here are six specifics:

Look For Opportunities To Get Acquainted With Parents

Many opportunities will come your way in the normal course of your teaching. P. T. A., school committees, and parent-teacher conferences all offer opportunities to get acquainted with parents. Other opportunities come through outside social and civic events in the community. Through these contacts both parents and teachers become "real persons" to one another. A "real person" relationship affords a good basis for mutual understanding.

Seek Extra Opportunities To Report To Parents

Parents expect the usual reports on the child's progress: report cards, conferences, and routine notices. They doubly appreciate the personal, extra reports from the teacher. Say, for example, that Mary has shown unusual progress in reading during recent weeks. The teacher takes pen in hand and writes a short note:

"Dear Mrs. Reed: Have you noticed how Mary has spurted ahead recently in reading? She's finished two 'enrichment' books and is working on a third. I know you're as pleased as I am. Cordially, Miss Dixon." Such extras take extra time. They also pay extra dividends in teaching.

Consult With Parents About Little Problems Before They Become Big

Too frequently a first-rate crisis brings parent and teacher together. Emotions may run high at a time where there is no basis for an understanding. A perceptive teacher catches problems before they become critical and consults with parents in a calm and informal atmosphere. Let's assume that the history teacher has noticed that Burt's grades and interest are slipping. He is usually a good student, and the teacher is at a loss to explain the turn of affairs. After school he calls Burt's mother.

"This is Mr. Stuckey," he says. "I've noticed that Burt's grades have been slipping in history, and I thought maybe you could help me. I don't think it's anything serious, but I know he wants to go to college, and I'm sure you don't want to take any chances. Could you come in for a chat about it after school some evening this week?"

Perhaps together the teacher and parent can get at the problem. How much better is this approach than to wait until Burt has been refused admission to college. At that time the parents could rightfully say to the teacher: "Why didn't you tell us?" The perceptive teacher seeks to forestall crises before they happen.

Be Frank And Honest About Children With Parents

Parents, of course, like to hear good things about their children. But above all they want the teacher's appraisal to be frank and honest. They are suspicious of the teacher who constantly says "everything is just fine." They expect a person with professional training to be able to be specific and forthright in his evaluation of the child, glossing over neither the good nor the bad. The teacher's approach should always be sympathetic and kind, of course. At the same time it should be straightforward and honest.

With Parents, Do Not Compare One Child With Another

Parents naturally want to know how their child is doing in relation to other children, and in most cases no harm is done by comparing the child's achievement with that of the group. "Your child is working in the upper third of the class," will answer the question for most parents. Some parents, however, may persist. For example, "Is he doing better than the Chandler boy?" Responding to this question can be tricky. If the teacher says "Yes," he has gratified the parent's ego; if he says "No," he has hurt it. In either case he runs the risk of gossip about a confidential matter. Should Mrs. Chandler hear about it, she can rightfully ask the teacher why he was talking to another mother about her boy.

In this case the teacher is probably in a professionally stronger position if he replies simply: "I really don't compare children that way, because each is so individually different. They all have their strong and weak sides. I think you will be glad to know, however, that your boy is improving steadily in relation to his own past performances, and that is what really matters."

Keep Superiors Informed

Parents frequently like to confer with school people other than the teacher. They may call the curriculum coordinator, the building principal, the superintendent, or any other person within the system whom they happen to know. The teacher's superiors can talk more intelligently with parents if they know the background from the teacher. They are also in a better position to interpret the teacher's actions to parents if they are fully informed about the situation. Relations with parents are frequently a team affair, with several people representing the school. Members of the team need to keep one another fully informed.

In the quotation at the beginning of this chapter, Taft makes two comments: (1) "Every parent has a tremendous prejudice in favor of his or her offspring," and (2) "The world would be a dreadfully cold place to live if this were not true." These two thoughts have real significance for teachers. The first thought conditions the relationship between the teacher and the parent. It can never be a casual relationship because the teacher is dealing with the parent's most treasured possession. The teacher must always remember that there is someone who has still a stronger, more personal interest in the child than he.

The second thought points to the possibilities for cooperation between the teacher and the parent. If the teacher can use the parent's warm concern for the child to reinforce his school learning, all parties benefit. When parents and teachers work together, school will not be a "cold place" for the child, but rather a good place in which to work and achieve.

8. Prepare a case report on some aspect of a school-community relationship. You may wish to select your own community and school because you know them best. Or, for greater objectivity, you may decide to select another community and school. Focus on some particular problem, project, or aspect, rather than on the total. For example, you may wish to deal with school-community action leading up to the building of a new school, the consolidation of two or more school districts, or the introduction of a new curriculum. To stimulate your thinking about

a topic here is such a report written by a student who tells how her own school is meeting a serious community problem.

The Principal Wanted Everyone To Think Of Central As
"Our School," And Not "That School."

Reported by
EARLYNN BYAS

Early in 1954 Central High School began to experience a change in the community around it. Negroes began moving into the all-white neighborhood. The whites and negroes were of all social classes. The school had problems of adjustment to make, for it was not ready or prepared to serve and accept negroes. There were also class struggles among the negroes. These struggles created more tensions.

As the years passed, the school's reputation and rating suffered. The Central which was looked upon for its high scholastic achievement before was now being frowned upon. Delinquency developed. It was necessary to have police patrol the school during class hours. Vandalism in the neighborhood and school was at its peak. Night games in the city were abolished because of an incident in which Central was involved.

The school spirit was completely lost. The faculty, I believe, lost most of its interest. Classes were disorderly. Parents and students were not interested in the school. The school existed only as an institution of compelled attendance.

This was the attitude taken by almost everyone. There were many drop-outs and cases of students expelled from school. Something had to be done.

Then a new principal was assigned to the school who had previous dealing in situations of this nature. He was willing to give his time and advice in a most sincere manner. He brought the school and the community together in trying to solve the problem, by working with the faculty and parents personally. Several meetings were called to discuss in detail the problems at hand, and to stress the importance of cooperation of the parents with the faculty.

It was discovered that the feeling would have to be developed in each child that Central was his school, and he should be proud of his school, academically and socially. The principal wanted everyone to think of Central as "our school," and not "that school."

Committees of students, faculty, and parents worked on projects to develop unity in the school. The P. T. A. sponsored bake sales and various drives to get money to improve the school. They purchased such things as a trophy stand, gym equipment, and stage props. Other committees gave dances and encouraged plays and programs which would offer students a chance to exhibit their talents. Students were encouraged to join extracurricular clubs and to attend sports events.

The school began to serve the community by offering night school to the adults. Classes were taught in academic, practical, and recreational subjects. Citizenship honors were given for students who took part in extra activities or who were recommended by teachers. It was a great honor for both parents and students to receive citizenship awards. The object was to get six consecutive awards for the six terms normally spent at Central. A special program was given to honor those persons. Everyone looked forward to the graduation exercises to see who would get the scholarships and other recognitions.

The school had open house once a year in order that the parents might see the school in action. Parents were urged to go on the senior trip. The school sponsored a "let's fix up our community" campaign every spring.

I went back to Central recently to observe the progress which they are making. I found that Central High has managed to create a democratic atmosphere of adult-youth interaction. At Central High this kind of atmosphere has been achieved in part through various devices that enable young people to share in the planning and management of curriculum and in the regulation of student activities and discipline. These efforts have paid off because the school and community have come together to help young people develop maturity and independence.

This case report by Earlynn Byas suggests the question posed in the next section: Who should be educated? Underlying the new principal's action at Central High School was his conviction that all the children and young people in the community should receive the best possible education. What are the implications of this philosophy for the teacher? We find part of the answer in our changing American creed about educational opportunity.

Good Follow-up Reading and Viewing

BOOKS

Gabbard, Hazel F., *Working With Parents,* U. S. Office of Education, Bulletin No. 7. Washington, D.C.: Government Printing Office, 1948. Enumerates the values and methods of parent-teacher cooperation.

Hymes, James L., Jr., *Effective Home School Relations.* Englewood Cliffs, N.J.: Prentice-Hall, Inc., 1953. Explains various ways of bridging the gap between the home and the school.

Langdon, Grace and Irving W. Stout, *Helping Parents Understand Their*

Child's School. Englewood Cliffs, N.J.: Prentice-Hall, Inc., 1957. In this excellent study the parents of 865 families were asked in individual interviews, "What would you like to know about your child's school?" The replies present refreshing and enlightening information for both prospective and experienced teachers.

———, *Teacher-Parent Interviews.* Englewood Cliffs, N.J.: Prentice-Hall, Inc., 1954. A comprehensive analysis of teacher-parent relations with special focus upon teacher-parent interviews.

Lindgren, Henry Clay, *Educational Psychology in the Classroom,* chap. 4, "The Learner and His Family." New York: John Wiley & Sons, Inc., 1956. A discussion of the family's contribution to the learning situation.

Patton, Frances, *Good Morning, Miss Dove.* New York: Dodd, Mead & Co., 1954. The effect of a teacher on the people of a small Southern town.

PERIODICALS

Bain, Leila D., "I Put Parents To Work," *NEA Journal,* Vol. 49, January, 1961, p. 49. A first grade teacher checks her records for occupations of parents and finds that many have special skills they are willing to share with the class.

Calatrello, Robert L., "Parent-Teacher Conferences," *Peabody Journal of Education,* Vol. 38, March, 1961, pp. 259-64. A statement on the importance of the short parent-teacher conference which keeps parents informed about the progress and achievement in the school situation.

Cunningham, Earl C., "My Child's Teacher and I," *Phi Delta Kappan,* March, 1956, pp. 254-58. A discussion by a parent of "qualities that I have a reasonable right to expect from the teacher, and what the teacher has a reasonable right to expect of me."

Ford, Thomas R., "Social Factors Affecting Academic Performance: Further Evidence," *The School Review,* Vol. 45, Winter, 1957, pp. 415-22. A research study which demonstrates that parental interests in, aspirations for, and relations with their children exert a powerful influence on the child's schoolwork.

Mayer, Frederick, "Parents as Teachers," *Phi Delta Kappan,* Vol. 41, February, 1960, pp. 216-19. A discussion of how basic changes in the family system influence how parents teach their children.

Sloan, Fred A., Jr., "Helping Parents To Help Their Children," *NEA Journal,* Vol. 49, March, 1960, pp. 49-51. Tells how a teacher used parents as resource persons in a science experience, making them coeducators with the teacher.

FILMS

Parents Are People Too

How good understanding with parents is essential to emotional health of teen-agers. How it can be achieved. How privileges can be earned through proof of ability. How to evaluate points which parents seem to "nag" about. (McGraw-Hill Book Co., Inc., black and white, 15 minutes.)

School Social Worker

Cooperative effort of the social worker with teachers, parents, and others, in helping children resolve the social problems that interfere with their school adjustments, learning, and attendance. Several case problems with children of different ages. (University of Southern California, black and white, 25 minutes.)

Teen-Agers As They Are (Kinescope)

A parent, an educator, and a psychiatrist discuss complexities which face adolescents in their school, home, and community life. (University of Michigan, black and white, 30 minutes.)

PART **7**

WHO SHALL BE EDUCATED?

CHAPTER 15

THE CHANGING AMERICAN EDUCATIONAL CREED

> She picked up a stick and marked off a square on the ground,
> and told him he would have to stay there.
>
> T. R. CARSKADON

T. R. Carskadon tells a story [1] which illustrates the problem posed in these three chapters: Who should be educated? In the story some neighborhood children are playing school under a pear tree in the backyard. The "teacher" excludes one child from the group, scratches a square on the ground, and tells him to stay there. Within this play school not everyone is to be educated.

WHO SHOULD BE EDUCATED?

Should *everyone* be educated? Or should only those who can make some *special claim* be educated? For example, we know that some children are brighter than others. Are these promising children the ones in whom we should invest most heavily? Some parents have greater ability than others to pay for the education of their children. Should wealth or the lack of it determine who should be educated? People have different colored skins and ethnic features and came to America from different parts of the world. Should skin pigmentation or ethnic background determine who should be educated? How about the matter of class status? We know that in our democratic society classes do exist. Our

---

1 T. R. Carskadon, *Story in America, 1933-34,* Whit Burnett and Martha Foley, eds. (New York: The Vanguard Press, 1934), pp. 267-273.

classrooms are filled with children from widely different social classes. Should a child's social class determine his educational opportunity?

Some school districts are wealthy and can afford to hire the best teachers and build glass-and-garden schools. Other districts are poor, with little or no taxable wealth. Their schools are old, their teachers and resources second-rate. Should the school district in which the child happens to reside determine the extent of his educational opportunity?

Recall, if you will, your own school days. Were some children treated somewhat like the child in Mr. Carskadon's story, set apart, out of things, denied for some reason the educational opportunities available to the majority of the students? Did the children from poor homes benefit from school as much as those from better homes? Did you know children who were capable of attending college but could not because of lack of funds? How about the children who dropped out of school? Do you know why they dropped out? Was it because they did not feel that they "belonged" to the school? If so, what gave them this feeling? Were there capable students in the school who somehow didn't "get into things?"

These questions pose a problem which every teacher confronts. Does our educational system set certain children apart, for whatever reason, mark off a square around them, and deny them equal educational opportunity? If so, what can a teacher do to help equalize educational opportunity for students?

THE PROBLEM CAN BE A PERSONAL ONE FOR THE TEACHER

The intellectually bright teacher will feel drawn to those students who are gifted, possibly to the neglect of the other students. The teacher whose intellectual achievements are only average may feel an unconscious antipathy for the bright and precocious child and sympathy for the plodding and average child. The bright child may be as easily discriminated against as the slow child. In fact, the current work with gifted students indicates a rather widespread neglect of those with special capabilities. Most teachers come from the middle class and share middle class values and beliefs. Teachers have a natural sympathy for middle class children and less understanding of children from the lower or upper classes. Thus, the teacher, who should be a part of the solution, can instead be a part of the problem.

1. We can now see the problems which cluster around the central question: Who shall be educated? Take a fellow class member as a team mate and interview one another on the question: How equal are the educational opportunities in your community? Compare your findings with other teams.

THE AMERICAN CREED CALLS FOR EQUAL EDUCATIONAL OPPORTUNITY

Few people have applied themselves as diligently as Americans to the problem of providing equal educational opportunity for all. Ours is the oldest public school system in the world. Many nations are only now extending educational opportunity in a manner which has been common in America for years. Hardly had the first Americans become settled along the Atlantic coast when they began to build schools. In the Massachusetts Bay Colony the Old Deluder Satan Law of 1647 set up a system of community-supported schools. Such schools were without precedent in world history. This little frontier colony, with scarcely fifteen or twenty thousand residents, within a few years had established a Latin School, Harvard College, and a system of public education. The Americans put their faith in education early.

Why? Was it because they had unusual respect for learning and scholarship? Some did, but most did not. Learning and scholarship were not the prime reasons for extending educational opportunity. Americans saw in education the opportunity to bring closer to reality the dreams of the good life for all. It was this promise that spread across the land and led Americans to pay for education out of their public and private pocketbooks.

REVIEW A FEW HISTORICAL HIGHLIGHTS

The Northwest Ordinance Extended The Common Schools

The great Northwest Ordinance of 1787 expresses the American belief in the connection between education and the good society: "Religion, morality, and knowledge, being necessary to good government and the happiness of mankind, schools and the means of education shall forever be encouraged." This ordinance, requiring that proceeds from grants of land be used for education, established common schools in the Northwest Territory and helped to put a "little red school house" in every community.

The Morrill Act Extended Education To The Working Class

The American faith in equality of educational opportunity was expressed in other legal acts. The Morrill Act of 1862,[2] signed by President Lincoln, provided for the establishment of land grant colleges which ex-

---

2 United States Congress, *Statutes at Large,* Chapter 130 (1862) (Boston: Little, Brown and Co., Inc., 1863), XII, pp. 503-4.

tended educational opportunity to sons and daughters of working people
and taught the practical arts of agriculture and mechanics. The Morrill
Act stated that the money obtained from the sale of certain public lands
should be invested in order to support and maintain in each state "at
least one college where the leading object shall be . . . to teach such
branches of learning as are related to agriculture and the mechanic
arts . . . to promote the liberal and practical education of the industrial
classes in the several pursuits and professions in life . . ."

The Kalamazoo Case Extended Education To High School

In 1874 the famous Kalamazoo Case [3] ruled that a local board of education could use tax funds to provide educational opportunity beyond
primary school. Some citizens had opposed the school board's use of funds
for educating children beyond primary school. The court ruled in favor
of the board, saying that as an elected body charged with providing
educational opportunity for the citizens, it could use those funds in the
way it best saw fit. The Kalamazoo court ruled: "We content ourselves
with the statement that neither in our state policy, in our constitution,
or in our laws, do we find the primary school districts restricted in the
branches of knowledge which their officers may cause to be taught, or the
grade of instruction that may be given, if their voters consent in regular
form to bear the expenses and raise the taxes for the purpose." The way
was open for the establishment of high schools throughout the land.

The Supreme Court Decision On Segregation Defined Equality
Of Educational Opportunity

The Supreme Court decision of 1954 ruling against racial segregation
in public schools [4] is another chapter in the long and continuing story
answering the question: Who should be educated? The Supreme Court
said in its historic decision:

> In these days it is doubtful that any child may reasonably be ex-
> pected to succeed in life if he is deprived the opportunity of an
> education. Such an opportunity, where the state has undertaken to
> provide it, is a right which must be made available to all on equal
> terms.
> We come then to the question presented: Does segregation of
> children in public schools solely on the basis of race, even though
> the physical facilities and other "tangible" factors may be equal,

---

[3] Stuart v. School District no. 1 of Kalamazoo, 30 Michigan 69 (1874).
[4] Brown v. Board of Education 347 US 483 (1954).

deprive the children of the minority group of equal educational opportunities? We believe that it does.

THE AMERICAN CREED IS BEST SEEN IN PEOPLE

These legal acts make an impressive catalogue to the credit of the American people. It was, however, in the stories of the people themselves that we see American educational opportunity at work. Here we find what it meant to the people to have a system of free public education.

Mary Antin: It was with a heart full of longing and hope that our father led us to school.

An American classic is the experience left to us by Mary Antin, a Russian immigrant girl, in her autobiographical novel, *The Promised Land.*[5] Her father was unsuccessful in his native land, not much more successful in his adopted land. He came to America to find a new home for his family. What attracted him most to the new world was the opportunity to give his children an education, something denied to them in his native land. Mary Antin describes the thoughts and feelings stirred up in her father by the educational opportunity offered in America; then she relates how her father presented her, her sister, and her brother to the teacher on that memorable first day of school.

So it was with a heart full of longing and hope that my father led us to school on that first day. He took long strides in his eagerness, the rest of us running and hopping to keep up.

At last the four of us stood around the teacher's desk; and my father, in his impossible English, gave us over in her charge, with some broken word of his hopes for us that his swelling heart could no longer contain . . . I think Miss Nixon guessed what my father's best English could not convey. I think she divined that by the simple act of delivering our school certificates to her he took possession of America.

So it was that thousands of new citizens took possession of America through its free public school system.

To people whose educational opportunities had been few the school became a symbol of opportunity. It may have been but one room standing in the lonely countryside, but it served the countryside's children well and brought new life and hope which would not otherwise have been there.

---

5 Mary Antin, *The Promised Land* (New York: Houghton Mifflin Company, 1912), pp. 202-205.

Hamlin Garland: It was a barren temple to the arts, even to the residents of Dry Run.

Hamlin Garland, novelist of the American prairie, has described his own one room school in Iowa with realism and good feeling.[6] He remembered that the little school stood on the bare prairie and "had not a leaf to shade it in summer nor a branch to break the winds of savage winter." It was nevertheless the "center of our social life" and "a barren temple to the arts, even to the residents of Dry Run." Mr. Garland's vivid descriptions give us the flavor of the school life in this drab little symbol of America's interest in educational opportunity. He also remembered:

> It was always too hot or too cold in our school room and on certain days when a savage wind beat and clamored at the loose windows, the girls, humped and shivering, sat upon their feet to keep them warm, and the younger children with shawls over their shoulders sought permission to gather close about the stove . . . Happily all days were not like this. There were afternoons when the sun streamed warmly into the room, when long icicles formed on the eaves, adding a touch of grace to the desolate building, moments when the jingling bells of passing woodsleighs expressed the natural cheer and buoyancy of our youthful hearts.

But Garland remembered more than just the hardships in his prairie school. It was there that his first literary interests were stirred. He describes it like this.

> Our readers were almost the only counterchecks to the current of vulgarity and baseness which ran through the talk of the older boys, and I wish to acknowledge my deep obligation to Professor McGuffey, whoever he may have been, for the dignity and literary grace of his selections. From the pages of his readers I learned to know and love the poems of Scott, Byron, Southey, Wordsworth, and a long line of the English masters. I got my first taste of Shakespeare from the selected scenes which I read in these books.

Clarence Darrow: The things we were taught seem very absurd.

Not everyone shared Garland's view regarding the value of the education offered in the common school. Clarence Darrow,[7] the famous trial

---

6 Hamlin Garland, *A Son of the Middle Border* (New York: The Macmillan Company, 1922), pp. 95, 112, 115.

7 Clarence Darrow, *Farmington* (New York: Charles Scribner's Sons, 1932), pp. 53-54.

lawyer, reflected on his one room school in Ohio and concluded: "The things we were taught seem very absurd as I look back." Using the gentle satiric skill for which his jury speeches were famous, he poked fun at the subjects taught and methods employed in the little school of his childhood. Several chapters of his lively autobiography are exciting educational history. He describes the feelings of the boys and girls as they dallied along the road on the way to school, watching the birds in the trees, kicking stones on the road, observing little fish in the brook. With all this, he says, "No boy could ever manage to go straight to school, or straight back home after the day was done." Inside the school, he remembered, what he was taught didn't make much sense. It wasn't of much use in later life. This is the way he describes his recollections.

> Most of us boys could learn arithmetic fairly well—in this, indeed, we always beat the girls. Still, some parts of arithmetic were harder than the rest. I remember that I mastered the multiplication-table up to "twelve times twelve," backwards and forwards and every other way, at a very early age, and I fancy that this knowledge has clung to me through life; but I cannot forget the many weary hours I spent trying to learn the tables of weights and measures, and how much vexation of spirit I endured before my task was done. However, after weary weeks and months I learned them so well that I could say them with the greatest ease. This was many, many years ago; since that time I have found my place in the world of active life, but I cannot now remember that even once have I had occasion to know or care about the difference between "Troy weight" and "Apothecaries' weight," if, in fact, there was any difference at all.

In these examples we see how the American common school, free and open to all, had its impact on citizens. Let us turn now to some of the men who helped to make the American creed a reality.

THESE MEN HELPED SHAPE THE AMERICAN EDUCATIONAL CREED

The American educational creed did not spring to life fully grown. Many people opposed each new extension of educational opportunity. Fortunately, free public education had its strong friends who made their voices heard, sometimes at personal cost to themselves. We shall not here recount the contributions of the host of men who supported equal educational opportunity. We shall, however, listen to a few of them recite their faith. In these recitations we can feel the deep faith which Americans expressed in equal educational opportunity. We can also see the reasons with which they supported their faith.

Thomas Jefferson: We hope to avail the state of those talents which nature has sown so liberally among the poor as the rich.

Among Thomas Jefferson's wide ranging interests few stood higher than education.[8] Founder and first chancellor of the University of Virginia, he liked to stand at Monticello, his mountain top home, telescope in hand, and watch the construction program on the new buildings of the University in Charlottesville off to the west. But he did more than look from afar. On the campus he personally supervised the construction of the buildings and took an active hand in the management of the new school.

Thomas Jefferson was a democrat in education as he was in politics. While he did not foresee full and equal educational opportunity for all, he was so far ahead of his times that it would be difficult to overestimate the impact of his ideas on education. And in some respects we haven't yet caught up with him. An example is his proposal for the free education of poor but bright students at state expense all the way from primary school through college.

Thomas Jefferson had a well thought out answer to the question: Who should be educated? Everyone, he said, should be given primary schooling at state expense. Those who could afford it should surely go on as far as they wished. Among those who could not afford it and who were bright, the state should select the most promising and send them through grammar school and college without cost to themselves.

What were Jefferson's real reasons for making this daring proposal? In his reasons we get further insight into his answer to the question: Who should be educated? Jefferson advanced two reasons. First, he believed in extending educational opportunity to the poor as well as the rich. Said he: "By that part of our plan which prescribes the selection of youths of genius from among the classes of the poor, we hope to avail the state of those talents which nature has sown as liberally among the poor as the rich, but which perish without use, if not sought for and cultivated." Jefferson believed that intelligence and ability were not the sole property of the wealthy. These qualities are found in the poor people as well. Those children who possess them should be sought out and educated. Why? Because the state benefits thereby.

Jefferson's second reason for his proposal is even more far-reaching. It was, he said, impossible to have democratic government without having educated citizens. Only educated citizens can guard their own liberty.

---

8 Thomas Jefferson, *Notes on the State of Virginia* (Chapel Hill: University of North Carolina Press, 1955), pp. 146-49.

Educational opportunity, therefore, should be widely spread among the people. He commented: "But of all the views of this law none is more important, none more legitimate, than that of rendering the people safe, as they are the ultimate guardians of their own liberty."

Running through Jefferson's plan is an expression of his deep belief that the children of the poor could benefit from education as well as children of the rich. Further, it was the obligation of the state to develop their talents. Democracy depended, he was convinced, upon enlightened citizens.

> 2. Scholarships are sometimes given on the basis of "need," sometimes on the basis of "merit," sometimes upon a combination of the two. Which basis do you think is the most appropriate for awarding scholarships? Why?

Benjamin Rush: These institutions will lessen our taxes.

Dr. Benjamin Rush was a friend of Thomas Jefferson and a fellow signer of the Declaration of Independence. Considered by many to have been the great physician of his time, this Philadelphia doctor was equally well known for his achievements outside the field of medicine. He was a close friend of Thomas Paine and matched him in his uncompromising revolutionary spirit. In his varied interests he has been compared with another friend of his in the young United States, Benjamin Franklin.

Benjamin Rush's articles, letters, and speeches number in the thousands.[9] He fought for the abolition of slavery, pled for removal of the death penalty, argued for more civil treatment of prisoners, and built hospitals for the insane. Many worthy causes benefited from his warm support.

He was continually active in support of the advancement of human learning. He was instrumental in establishing colleges and other schools of higher learning in his native state of Pennsylvania, and he advocated the establishment of free public schools in every township of the state. "Let there be free schools established," he said, "in every township, or in districts consisting of one hundred families."

Rush was prepared to deal with those who put forth arguments against the extension of educational opportunity. He was told that the people could not afford free schools. He said:

> I answer that these institutions will lessen our taxes. They will en-
> lighten us in the great business of finance—they will teach us to
> increase the ability of the state to support government, by increas-

---

[9] Dagobert D. Runes, *The Selected Writings of Benjamin Rush* (New York: Philosophical Library, 1947), pp. 98-99.

Header: "252" and "Who Shall Be Educated?"

ing the profits of agriculture, and by promoting manufactures. They will teach us all the modern improvements and advantages of inland navigation. They will defend us from hasty and expensive experiments in government, by unfolding to us the experience and folly of past ages, and thus, instead of adding to our taxes and debts, they will furnish us with the true secret of lessening and discharging both of them.

3. We frequently hear complaints about high "school taxes." Do you agree or disagree with Rush's argument that schools "lessen taxes"? What are your reasons for your position?

Horace Mann: Education is a great equalizer of the conditions of men.

Few men in our history have done more to spread educational opportunity than Horace Mann. As Secretary of the Board of Education of the State of Massachusetts, he championed educational reforms from which we still benefit. He saw education as being vital to the progress of the industrial state of Massachusetts.[10] The state, he said, is exposed to the "fatal extremes of overgrown wealth and desperate poverty." Such a condition is dangerous to the state, leading to discontent among the masses, violence, sometimes bloodshed. The only answer is to give the poor a chance to raise themselves and share the good fruits of their labor. Otherwise, the rich who are educated will continually hold domination over the poor who are uneducated. The only answer is equally diffused education. Here is the argument in Mann's own words:

> If one class possesses all the wealth and the education, while the residue of society is ignorant and poor, it matters not by what name the relation between them may be called: the latter, in fact and in truth, will be the servile dependents and subjects of the former. But, if education be equally diffused, it will draw property after it by the strongest of all attractions; for such a thing never did happen, and never can happen, as that an intelligent and practical body of men should be permanently poor . . .
>
> Education then, beyond all other devices of human origin, is a great equalizer of the conditions of men—the balance wheel of the social machinery. I do not here mean that it so elevates the moral nature as to make men disdain and abhor the oppression of their fellow men. This idea pertains to another of its attributes. But I mean that it gives each man the independence and the means by

---

10 "Education is the Balance Wheel of The Social Machinery" in *Living Ideas in America,* Henry Steele Commager, ed. (New York: Harper and Brothers, 1951), pp. 566-68.

which he can resist the selfishness of other men. It does better than to disarm the poor of their hostility toward the rich: it prevents being poor.

4. What do you think Mann means by his statement that education "prevents being poor." Do you agree?

Jefferson saw equal educational opportunity as essential for political democracy. Mann saw it as essential to economic democracy. Educated people help to create wealth and prosperity. The nation cannot remain prosperous without widespread educational opportunity. Education is "the balance wheel of social machinery."

Who should be educated? According to Mann, it is to the advantage of the rich as well as the poor to have the benefits of education widely spread. It is good business for the state.

Thaddeus Stevens: Those who support general education can acquire some portion of honor.

In 1834 the Pennsylvania legislature passed a free school law which gave reality to the dreams of Dr. Benjamin Rush. It had not yet gone into effect when a storm of popular protest rose against the bill, stirred up by some of its original opponents. There was strong sentiment in the next session of the legislature to repeal the law. Several members, who had supported the measure originally, were defeated at the polls when they refused to change their stand for free schools. Other members owed their elections to their opposition to free schools. It was a critical time in the history of education in Pennsylvania. Feeling was running high as Thaddeus Stevens took the floor to defend the bill. Stevens was known for his eloquence, courage, and forthright positions. He was determined to do everything he could to save free schools for the state. In his defense we see a restatement of the American educational creed as well as a point by point defense of it.[11]

In the following section of his speech, he is dealing with an amendment introduced to change the free school law. The amendment would restrict free schooling to the children of proven paupers. Stevens lashed out at it.

The amendment which is now proposed as a substitute for the school law of last session, is, in my opinion, of a most hateful and degrading character. It is a reenactment of the pauper law of 1809.

---

11 "A Plea For The Public Schools," in *Report Of United States Commissioner of Education,* 1898-99, Volume 1, pp. 519-520, 522-23.

It proposes that the assessors shall take a census, and make a record of the poor. This shall be revised, and a new record made by the county commissioners, so that the names of those who have the misfortune to be poor men's children shall be forever preserved, as a distinct class, in the archives of the country! The teacher, too, is to keep in his school a pauper book, and register the names and attendance of poor scholars; thus pointing out and recording their poverty in the midst of their companions. Sir, hereditary distinctions of rank are sufficiently odious; but that which is founded on poverty is infinitely more so. Such a law should be entitled "An act for branding and marking the poor, so that they may be known from the rich and proud."

An argument put forth by the opponents of free schools was that taxpayers without children receive no benefit. Stevens turns to this argument.

Many complain of this tax, not so much on account of its amount, as because it is for the benefit of others and not themselves. This is a mistake; it is for their own benefit, inasmuch as it perpetuates the Government and insures the due administration of the laws under which they live, and by which their lives and property are protected. Why do they not urge the same objection against all other taxes? The industrious, thrifty, rich farmer pays a heavy county tax to support criminal courts, build jails, and pay sheriffs and jail keepers, and yet probably he never has, and never will have, any personal use of either . . . He cheerfully pays the tax which is necessary to support and punish convicts, but loudly complains of that which goes to prevent his fellow-being from becoming a criminal, and to obviate the necessity of those humiliating institutions.

5. School bond elections frequently fail in communities where a large portion of the citizens have no children. Do you think that this argument which Stevens encountered could help explain such failures? Is his reasoning as valid today as it was then?

Finally, Stevens turns to those members of the legislature who owed their election to their opposition to the free school bill and to others who were politically sensitive to the popular clamor for its repeal.

Those who would repeal this law because it is obnoxious to a portion of the people would seem to found their justification on a desire of popularity. That is not an unworthy object when they seek that enduring fame which is constructed of imperishable materials. But have these gentlemen looked back and consulted the history of their race to learn on what foundation and on what materials that popularity is built which outlives its possessor, which is not buried in the same grave which covers his mortal remains? Sir, I believe that kind of fame may be acquired by deep learning, or even the love of it, by mild philanthropy or unconquerable courage. And it seems to me that, in the present state of feeling in Pennsylvania, those who will heartily and successfully support the cause of general education can acquire at least some portion of the honor of all these qualities combined, while those who oppose it will be remembered without pleasure and soon pass away with the things that perish.

The record of this session of the legislature tells us that loud and prolonged applause burst upon the chamber as Thaddeus Stevens finished his plea for the extension of educational opportunity in Pennsylvania. The amendment was defeated and the free school law went into effect.

Our purpose in this section has not been to give a detailed summary of the development of the American educational creed. We have sampled it enough, however, to know its flavor. The official acts and the men who helped to make it were driven by certain ideals. First, their views of education were large. They included the rich and the poor, the high and the low, capital and labor, and the newly arrived immigrants. Second, they believed that talent, wherever it is found, should be developed in the self-interest of the state. The child, whatever his origin, is entitled to an education, and the state stands in need of the fruits of his education. Democracy depends upon wise and educated citizens for its proper functioning. Only such citizens are capable of safeguarding their liberty.

Last, the American educational creed has faith in the practical benefits of education. Widely diffused education can lead people to the good life —better homes and communities, more respect for law and order, more progress. Education became the American way of achieving the good life.

HAVE THE SCHOOLS LIVED UP TO THE AMERICAN CREED?

To what extent have the schools succeeded in justifying the faith placed in them by the American creed? Has the wider diffusion of education lived up to expectations? One of the best answers to this question has been given to us by historian Henry Steele Commager in his worthy article, "Our Schools Have Kept Us Free." [12] Commager believes: "No

---

[12] Henry Steele Commager, "Our Schools Have Kept Us Free," *Life Magazine,* October 16 (1950).

other people ever demanded so much of education as have the Americans. None other was ever served so well by its schools and educators."

Historian Commager points out that Americans gave four large tasks to their schools: (1) "to provide an enlightened citizenry in order that self government might work"; (2) "to create national unity"; (3) "to foster Americanism"; (4) "to create a spirit of equality among the people."

Let us look briefly at these historical tasks of the free American public school.

"To Provide An Enlightened Citizenry In Order That Self-government Might Work"

We have already observed what tremendous emphasis Jefferson and others gave to this matter. With the coming of independence the problem of self-government became urgent. The key to the problem was heavy investment in education.

Did it work? "None can doubt that it has," comments Commager. Americans made democracy workable. Then he adds: "Only a people taught self-government could record these achievements."

"To Create National Unity"

In 1789 the American nation consisted of four million people thinly spread over an area of continental dimensions. Few ties bound them together. Differences were great. Yet out of this diversity grew unity and nationalism. There were material forces helping to unite the nation, such as canals, railroads, turnpikes, and cheap land. Then there were the songs and the pictures, too.

In school and lyceum, children came to learn and remember at least snatches of the "Concord Hymn" or "Old Ironsides" or the "Midnight Ride of Paul Revere." From famed paintings they learned to recognize Wolfe dying on the Plains of Abraham, Penn making a treaty with the Indians, Washington crossing the Delaware, Boone pushing his way through the Cumberland Gap. Through its young people, America came to see itself as one nation.

"To Foster Americanism"

When Mary Antin's father presented her to Miss Nixon, he "took possession of America." The responsibility of helping to make Americans of immigrants from many lands lay heavily upon the schools. As Commager points out:

> How, after all, were these millions of newcomers to be "Americans"—in language, in ways of life and thought, in citizenship? The

nation's first and main answer was the public school. Most of the
new millions, eager though they were to be Americanized, were too
old for school, but their children went to the public schools, adapt-
ing themselves with children's speed to American ways, and taking
home with them the idiom, the habits, the very thoughts and
standards they picked up in the schoolroom and on the playground.

"To Create A Spirit Of Equality Among The People"

America was and is a heterogeneous society. We are varied in our racial
backgrounds, religious beliefs, social and economic interests. Such societies are frequently "the most easy prey to forces of riotous privileges
and ruinous division." Have these forces prevailed in America? Commager thinks not.

> These forces have not prevailed; they have been routed, above
> all, in the schoolrooms and on the playgrounds of America. In the
> classroom, the nation's children have lived and learned equality—
> all subject to the same educational processes and the same disci-
> plines. On the playground and the athletic field, the same code has
> ruled—with the reward of honor and applause heartfully given
> to achievements to which all could aspire equally. The roster of
> "foreign" names of our high school and college football teams has
> seemed worth a feeble joke to many an unwitty radio comedian.
> Who can seriously doubt that the cause of democracy is served
> when it is a Murphy, a Schwartz, a Groglio, or a Levitsky that the
> cheering stands applaud?

6. Can you name those programs in your high school which tended to "create
a spirit of equality" among students? Can you also name programs which tended
to create a spirit of *inequality*?

The intent of the changing American educational creed is clear. It is
to extend to every child full educational opportunity regardless of ability,
class, or creed. Here we have dealt with just a few of its historical aspects.
But it is more than historical. It is as modern as the school which you
attended. Many of its programs were there because of the American belief
in equal educational opportunity. Take, for example, double and triple
track high school programs designed to provide for children with different life goals, special education programs to accommodate students with
both special handicaps and special abilities, cooperative programs with
business and industry, adult education programs, community college programs and many others. All these programs are designed to extend further
educational opportunity to those with special problems, interests and
abilities. They are fruits of the American Creed.

It must be clear from what we have said that we Americans have applied ourselves better than most other people to answering the question: Who should be educated? It must be clear, too, that the question has never been fully answered. Each new gain has been difficult to win. And there are always those under one guise or another who would restrict educational opportunity.

We must return in honesty to the question posed by T. R. Carskadon's story. Are we now taking some stick of bias and marking off a square around certain children and restricting their educational opportunities? It is clear that we are. It is also clear that teachers must face this problem and prepare themselves to deal with it.

Good Follow-up Reading and Viewing

BOOKS

Brogan, D. W., *The American Character,* Part 2, chap. 5. New York: Alfred A. Knopf, Inc., 1944. An eminent Briton describes the function of the school in America's development. "The main political achievement of the high and grammar schools is to bring together the young of all classes and all origins, to provide, artificially, the common background that in an old, rural society is provided by tradition."

Butts, R. Freeman, and Lawrence A. Cremin, *A History of Education in American Culture.* New York: Holt, Rinehart & Winston, Inc., 1953. A scholarly work which illuminates the development of education in America, based upon the best available primary and secondary sources.

Counts, George S., *Education and American Civilization.* New York: Bureau of Publications, Teachers College, Columbia University, 1952. A cultural historian traces the development of our society and describes the heavy role education must play in helping to solve the problems confronting us.

Educational Policies Commission, *Public Education and the Future of America.* Washington, D.C.: National Education Association, 1955. The rich educational heritage of America is described in this statement by distinguished educators.

Fenner, Mildred S., and Eleanor C. Fishburn, *Pioneer American Educators.* Washington, D.C.: National Education Association, 1944. These biographies of eighteen of America's most distinguished educators help to personalize our educational history.

Knight, Edgar W., and Clifton L. Hall, *Readings in American Educational History.* New York: Appleton-Century-Crofts, Inc., 1951. A valuable collection of writings which have helped to shape our educational development.

Meyer, Adolphe E., *An Educational History of the American People.* New York: McGraw-Hill Book Co., Inc., 1956. A historical discussion of the role of education in the social order.

National Citizens Commission for the Public Schools, *How Have Our Schools Developed?* New York: 1954. A case history of how the York, Pennsylvania school system developed. Described against a background of general educational development in America.

Smiley, Marjorie B., and John S. Diekhoff, *Prologue to Teaching*, Part 2, "Schooling for All." New York: Oxford University Press, 1959. Contains a rich collection of historical documents which support the extension of educational opportunity in America. Includes the Rockefeller Report on "Excellence in a Democracy."

Tharp, Louise Hall, *Until Victory*. Boston: Little, Brown & Co., 1953. A biography of Horace Mann.

Wynn, Richard, *Careers in Education,* chap. 2, "Our Educational Heritage." New York: McGraw-Hill Book Co., Inc., 1960. A survey of the development of American schools and their present operation.

PERIODICALS

Butts, Freeman R., "Search for Freedom," *NEA Journal,* Vol. 49, March, 1960, pp. 33-48. The story of American education and a plea that it continue to be "the unflagging search for freedom."

Commager, Henry Steele, "A Historian Looks At The American High School," *The School Review,* Vol. 46, Spring, 1958, pp. 1-8. A distinguished historian traces the development of the American high school. He suggests that the modern high school continues practices which were once justified, but which no longer are, and proposes changes for the future.

Corey, Arthur F., "The Real Attack Is On Education For *All* The People," *The Nation's Schools,* Vol. 62, July, 1958, pp. 38-39. How would the current proposals for applying more rigid academic standards and a narrower curriculum affect educational opportunity? The author contends that such proposals would deny a high school education to many youths.

Densford, John P., "The Educational Philosophy of Thomas Jefferson," *Peabody Educational Journal,* Vol. 38, March, 1961. A concise statement of Jefferson's educational philosophy.

Dorough, C. Dwight, " 'Preach, My Dear Sir, A Crusade Against Ignorance,' " *Phi Delta Kappan,* Vol. 40, April, 1959, pp. 272-76. A timely reminder of certain principles which Jefferson regarded as of paramount importance.

Wimpey, John Andrew, "Horace Mann's Influence in Today's Schools," *Phi Delta Kappan,* Vol. 40, February, 1959, pp. 206-08. The author shows how Mann's ideas remain pertinent to today's educational issues.

FILMS

Born Equal
Interprets the United Nations Declaration of Human Rights with special emphasis on rights for children. (Library Films, black and white, 10 minutes.)

Democracy in Education: John Dewey (Kinescope)
The great traditions of American education. The words of Dewey illustrate the principles of education in a democracy. (University of Michigan, black and white, 29 minutes.)

Desk for Billie
The search for a better life through education. True story of a "hobo kid"

who persisted in re-entering school as her itinerant parents moved from town to town. The great American dream epitomized. (National Education Association; Agra Films, Inc., black and white, 55 minutes.)

Dilemma of Thomas Jefferson (Kinescope)

How Jefferson's vision of universal education helped establish foundations of the American school system. The dilemma of local versus federal aid. (University of Michigan, black and white, 29 minutes.)

Education in America: Seventeenth and Eighteenth Century

Beginnings of American education from the early New England school laws to the provisions of the Northwest Ordinance. (Coronet Instructional Films, black and white, 17 minutes.)

Education in America: Nineteenth Century

Northwest Ordinance westward movement; change to secular education; influence of American textbooks; use and decline of district schools; struggle for tax support and state control; Webster and Mann; the Civil War; compulsory attendance laws; teacher education. (Coronet Instructional Films, black and white, 16 minutes.)

Education in America: Twentieth Century Developments

Effects of the industrial revolution on education; influences of Herbart, Binet, Dewey, Thorndike; building of consolidated schools; federal aid to schools during the Depression; the G.I. Bill; recent Supreme Court decisions. (Coronet Instructional Films, black and white, 16 minutes.)

Freedom To Learn

Dangers to democracy because of regimentation of teaching, and of avoidance of controversial subjects in schools. Teacher called before board of education because communism is studied in her social studies class. Her defense: freedom to learn the facts is basic to intelligent decision and consequent defense of our democratic way. (Agra Films, Inc., black and white, 28 minutes.)

Horace Mann

Episodes in the life of the "father of the common schools" and his influence on education. Efforts to get education; political activities toward social reform; fights for a better educational system. (Encyclopaedia Britannica Films, Inc., black and white, 20 minutes.)

Secure the Blessings

Dramatizes the important role that public schools have played in the history of American democracy. (National Education Association, black and white, 27 minutes.)

Segregation in the Schools

Problems raised by non-segregation decisions of Supreme Court in May, 1954. Views of newspapermen, businessmen, PTA's, ministers, high school students— both colored and white—in two Southern communities. (McGraw-Hill Book Co., Inc., black and white, 28 minutes.)

CHAPTER 16

THE TEACHER EXTENDS
EDUCATIONAL OPPORTUNITY

The frustrations experienced by most lower-class children in their daily school situations force them to give up the struggle for advancement.

W. LLOYD WARNER

The goal of the American creed is to provide equal educational opportunity for all children. Each child, it proclaims, should be permitted to develop his own unique ability to the fullest possible extent. The child's life is thereby made richer, his contribution to his fellow men greater, his citizenship stronger. Education, it confirms, is an investment in the nation's good.

Our thousands of schools and classrooms are little societies of America. Here the American creed touches people, boys and girls, parents and teachers. If the American creed lives, it must live in the attitudes and behavior of real people.

In the school the teacher is the key person through whom our American faith finds expression. It would be difficult to overestimate the importance of his position in helping to bring equal educational opportunity to each child. Probably each of us knows teachers who, with skill and understanding, give educational opportunities to children who would not otherwise have them. These are the teachers who take a special interest in the child, who, for one or many reasons, does not find satisfaction in school. Such teachers have skill in diagnosing these problems, plus sympathy and dedication in working with children and youth.

These are the teachers who spot the bright child whose capacities are

261

going unused, the timid child who is held back by lack of confidence, the rebellious one who has troubles at home, the excluded one who lives in the "bad" part of town. Like a good medical doctor who is skilled in diagnosis this teacher has a "sense" about such problems, can detect them, understand them, and lead the child to fuller realization of his capacities. In thus bringing new educational opportunity where it was previously denied, the teacher achieves his finest hour.

How can a teacher realize this fine hour of accomplishment? One must begin with the understanding that some children face a terrific struggle in school. Through conditions with which we shall deal in this chapter, they are literally denied full educational opportunity. As W. Lloyd Warner states in our chapter theme: ". . . their daily school situations force them to give up the struggle for advancement." For these children, the American educational creed, hard won over many years, is meaningless.

WE VISIT JONESVILLE

In this chapter we shall be conducted by social scientist W. Lloyd Warner into a real American school and its classrooms.[1] The name of the town is fictitious, but the town and the school are real; the students are real. You may regret that what we find there is real. But it's the kind of reality with which teachers must deal. Therefore this chapter may be more meaningful to you if you place yourself in the position of a teacher in Jonesville. Both elementary and high school situations are described. Select your job. What would you do if confronted with these conditions? As a teacher you may be.

We see in this school what would seem to be a normal collection of American children. The casual observer would rightly conclude that these children are like most school children in American schools. But a teacher must be more than a casual observer. This classroom, like most classrooms, is made up of children who are greatly different from one another. These differences regulate their attitudes and behavior toward one another. To an alarming degree these differences influence their satisfaction or dissatisfaction with school.

What basis do Jonesville students use for judging their fellow students? As we shall learn in a moment, they reflect the adult values of Jonesville and judge one another much as the adults of Jonesville judge one another. They make their determinations along social class lines. Those

---

[1] W. Lloyd Warner, *Democracy in Jonesville* (New York: Harper and Brothers, 1949), pp. 78-81, 85-87, 88.

children in upper social classes are judged to be well dressed, good looking, popular, clean, and friendly. Those in lower social classes are judged
to be poorly dressed, not good looking, unpopular, dirty, and with few
friends. Upper class children uniformly are credited with favorable
characteristics while lower class children draw the unfavorable characteristics.

The relationship of the problem to teaching has not escaped you. One
child has satisfying relationships in school; he stands to make most of the
learning opportunities provided by the school. Another child's relationships bring only unpleasant experiences; he cannot similarly benefit.
For these two children educational opportunities are not equal. They are
grossly unequal. In the case of the lower class child the American educational creed, as we said earlier, is meaningless.

What can the teacher do? That is the problem of this chapter. As we
proceed with the case, you can profitably keep certain questions in mind.
What answers can you develop by the time you have finished this
chapter?

1. If you were a teacher in Jonesville, what would you do for those children who
are denied full educational opportunity? (Your answer to this question will assist
you in studying the case of Priscilla in the next chapter.)

2. How would you revise the school program of Jonesville to make for greater
educational equality? In your judgment, what kind of curriculum provides the
fullest equality of educational opportunity?

3. Have you known teachers who could extend educational opportunities to the
children of Jonesville? What are these teachers like? What would they do? Can
you cite some examples from experience?

A Social Scientist Tackles The Problem

Let us turn to W. Lloyd Warner's study of Jonesville. First he tells us
how the study was conducted.

To check our observations, a systematic study was undertaken of
all the children in the fifth and sixth grades of the public school—
a number totaling 174, ranging in age from ten to twelve years.
In Jonesville, beginning with the fifth grade, all public school
children are in one building and have the same teachers. From the
fifth grade on, the child comes into daily contact with all the other
children of his age in the community (with the exception of those
few who attend parochial school).

After several months of the school year had passed, allowing time
for the children to become well acquainted, they were asked for
their evaluations of each other. They were told, first, to name their

best friends, and then to name the boys and girls with whom they did not want to associate. They were then asked to name those children who they thought were well dressed and those who were not well dressed; those who were good-looking and those not good-looking; those who were fighters; those who were popular and those who were unpopular; those who seemed to like school and those who seemed to dislike school; those who were leaders; those who always were clean and those who were dirty; those who seemed always to have a good time and those who never had a good time; those who had good manners and those who were not well-mannered; those who always played fair and those who did not play fair.

The children wrote this information in prepared booklets, under circumstances which insured the greatest possible freedom from restraint—in their regular classrooms, with the investigator the only adult present; with the assurance that not a person in Jonesville would have access to the booklets; and with the instruction not to sign their names to their papers.

On the basis of previous research, each child's family had been class-typed. The investigator could thus group the names of the boys and girls according to the five social classes of Jonesville and could find what proportion of the votes went to children of each social class. Furthermore, the booklets had been coded beforehand in such a way that authorship of each was known, and the investigator could study how each social class cast their votes.

Here Is The Social Class Structure Of A Jonesville Classroom

The results of the study we have already previewed. Here they are in more detail. It is important to keep in mind in reading the results that Warner had, on the basis of research, divided the town of Jonesville socially into five classes: (1) upper class, (2) upper middle class, (3) lower middle class, (4) upper lower class, and (5) lower lower class.

It happened that there were no children of upper-class families in the fifth or sixth grades; six percent of the group came from upper-middle class families; 17 percent from the lower-middle; 62 percent, from upper-lower; and 15 percent, from lower-lower.

If social status was *not* influencing the way in which the votes were distributed, then it was to be expected that each group would receive approximately the same percentage of votes as the proportionate size of the group in the total population of the fifth and sixth grades.

The percentages actually obtained, however, were markedly different from these proportions. On the ten positive, or favorable, items ("best friend," "well-dressed," "good-looking," "popular," and so on) the upper-middle-class children, with 6 percent of the total population of the two grades, received from 11 percent to 29 percent of the total vote for each item, or an average of 19 percent. On the ten negative, or unfavorable, items ("don't like," "not well-dressed," and so on) the upper-middle-class group received less than three percent of all votes.

The lower-middle-class group, constituting 17 percent of the population, received 27 percent of all favorable votes and only 6 percent of all unfavorable.

The upper-lower class, 62 percent of the population, received approximately 50 percent of all votes on both favorable and unfavorable items.

The lower-lower class children, 16 percent of the population, received less than four percent of all favorable votes, but received an overwhelming share of all unfavorable votes—over 40 percent . . .

We find a striking degree of relationship between social status and social participation. The lower the social class of the child, the fewer times he is mentioned as a "best friend" and the more times he is mentioned as "don't like to be with."

Perhaps the most significant fact about the data is the consistency of the ratings given to children of the four social classes. Without exception, upper-middle-class children are ranked highest on every favorable item; lower-middle-class children are ranked second; upper-lower-class, third; and lower-lower-class children are given the lowest ranking. Similarly, without exception, lower-lower class children receive the largest proportion of votes on every unfavorable item.

There is a mirror-like relationship between the positive and negative characteristics being rated; as status decreases, the number of votes on positive characteristics decreases, and the number of votes on negative characteristics increases. The obvious contrast is between the child who comes from an upper-middle-class family, the Level Above the Common Man, and the child who comes from a lower-lower-class family, the Level Below the Common Man."

How Does Social Class Influence Children?

Let us now look at this data in terms of its effect upon children. What impact does this class bias have upon the individual child? How does it affect his learning opportunity? Here are Warner's conclusions regarding the meaning of this data for individual children.

Consider the position of the lower-class child in Jonesville. He has the reuptation of being poorly dressed, unattractive, unpopular, aggressive; of not liking school; of being dirty and bad-mannered; of never having a good time; and of not playing fair. Few lower-class boys and girls are exceptions to this rule.

It is safe to assume that a child of this age soon becomes aware of his position in the group and makes his adjustment to a psychological climate which he recognizes as cold and unfriendly. There is a circular relationship between the psychological environment of an individual and the behavior he exhibits. The child's behavior has an effect upon his reputation, of course; but his reputation also has an effect upon his behavior. Many lower-class children, facing so difficult a situation, become increasingly hostile and aggressive; and many welcome the first opportunity to drop out of school and limit their associations to members of their own social class.

In our society, education offers the best route to social mobility. But the frustrations experienced by most lower-class children in their daily school situations force them to give up the struggle for advancement. In the literal sense, they know what the score is. And with the bitter poignancy of children who have been deeply hurt by the rebuffs and veiled insults of their playmates, they are trying to put their feelings into words the adult might understand. They are learning, the hard way, that "this is the way it is," and "life is like that."

4. Have you known of schoolmates who were forced "to give up the struggle for advancement?" How do you characterize these persons? Do you know why they gave up the "struggle"?

What About Educational Opportunity In Jonesville High School?

What happens by the time boys and girls reach high school? When all the sophomores and juniors in the Jonesville high school (over two hundred, averaging sixteen years old) were asked to evaluate their age-mates, we obtained data similar to those obtained from fifth- and sixth-graders. Adolescents select their friends largely from the same social class as their own. The boy or girl from an upper-status family is mentioned most often on the "best friend" item; the lower-class boy or girl, least often. Regarding reputation, the upper-middle-class adolescent is ranked highest on every favorable item; the lower-middle-class, second; the upper-lower, third; and the lower-lower, fourth . . .

There is evidence which shows that, of the boys and girls who drop out of school from the eighth grade on, the great majority are lower-class. There is a heavier weighting of lower-status groups in the elementary school of Jonesville than in the high school. At the fifth and sixth grades, 62 percent of the children are upper-lower-class; 15 percent are lower-lower. At the tenth and eleventh grades, these proportions drop to 46 percent and 6 percent, respectively. Thus, the high school population in Jonesville is selective in relation to not only academic ability but also social status.

If a boy or girl whose family occupies the lowest social position in the community has continued in school to the tenth or eleventh grade, he is likely to have certain characteristics which set him apart from other lower-class boys and girls. He is probably more studious, more ambitious, more persistent. He may have certain special abilities—prowess on the athletic field, or usual academic aptitude, or a talent for art or music. He is sure to have greater social adaptability than the average boy or girl of his age. He is, in brief, the mobile member of his social class; and, as such, his appearance and behavior do not differentiate him markedly from the boys and girls with whom he is trying to "make the grade . . ."

The number of lower-class boys and girls who manage to force their way up the social ladder are few; and the price they pay is usually dear. For in a society where middle-class values are dominant, the lower-class child, if he is to be successful, must manage to discard the pattern of living and the pattern of thinking that he has learned from his family. He must fight the social-class stereotypes which operate so forcefully against him from earliest childhood. He must win the favor of his social superiors, and, in doing so, he must establish a reputation for himself different from that of the rest of his class. He is expected to accomplish all this, in most cases, unaided. It is little wonder that, faced with so formidable a task, few are successful.

5. Have you known lower-class schoolmates who managed to force their way up the social ladder? Can you explain how they achieved this "upward mobility"?

HOW DOES CLASS BIAS INFLUENCE LEARNING?

Our central aim in presenting this case is not to demonstrate that class bias operates in classrooms. Our main interest is to understand how this class bias influences the learning of students and how the teacher can counteract its negative influence.

Recall our discussion of learning in Chapter 7, in which we observed how a little boy learned to print his name. We said that three elements made this learning possible: (1) the little boy who was full of learning potential, (2) the total environment which enveloped and stimulated him to his accomplishment, and (3) the free interaction between the boy and the environment.

Apply these three elements to the lower class children of Jonesville.

Their physical potential for learning is probably as great as that of the children of higher social classes. But when these physically able children are placed in the school environment, they lose their equal chance for learning.

Look at some of the particulars. The total environment of the little boy who learned to write his name reinforced his learning. He was given a number of emotional and social rewards. Further, the home and the school helped together to stimulate his learning. They reinforced one another. Each was rich in learning opportunity.

How different the situation is with lower class children in Jonesville! The chances are that lower class homes in Jonesville do not reinforce what the school is doing. Nor does the school reinforce the home. Lower class parents probably participate very little in school affairs, are not represented on the Board of Education, and know few of their children's teachers. We can conclude that the relationship from the school's side is just as distant.

When one of these Jonesville children leaves his home for school, in a sense he enters another world with strange and foreign values. The chances are that his home is concerned mainly with work-a-day attitudes. Books are unimportant. Ideas, as such, are not discussed. The cultural horizon is low. The language used in his home is different from that used by teachers and upper class children. Aspirations are of a lower order. His clothes are different. His family eats different food and their table manners are different. His parents may be very anxious for him to get an education. But their own examples argue against it.

In short, his home and school environments not only fail to reinforce one another, they are at odds. The child feels unable to give himself fully to the values of either one. How can he possibly learn well under these circumstances?

In Chapter 7 we said that learning takes place best when there is free interaction with the environment. The lower class child in Jonesville has little opportunity for free interaction with his environment at school. He has few friends. He probably thinks his teacher is against him. His most appropriate reaction to his environment is to fight and rebel against it. As soon as he is old enough, he will drop out of school and escape it, return to the environment he knows and understands. In his particular case the American public school does not present him with an educational opportunity equal to that of other children.

In addition to these three elements—the child, the environment, the interaction—we learned that other factors are crucial in stimulating learning. Motivation provides the steam which causes children to persist to successful learning. There are few incentives in the lives of these Jonesville lower class children to learn. Satisfaction, we said, is important in learning. That, too, is denied these children. The feeling of security stimulates learning. These children carry more than their share of insecurity. They may experience it both at home and at school.

What does it add up to? Probably this: Learning opportunities in Jonesville are not equal. The situation stifles learning for particular students. On the other hand, students in the higher social strata have considerable opportunity to take advantage of what the school has to offer. The school is geared more to their status, interests, and needs.

HOW MANY JONESVILLES ARE THERE?

Perhaps you are thinking: "How many Jonesvilles are there?" Maybe your own school and community bear little or no resemblance to Jonesville. Or, upon reflection, perhaps you *do* see some ways in which your own school and community restrict the educational opportunity of certain children and young people.

The value in studying Jonesville is that it puts these questions squarely to us: *Are* we making progress? Or, has social class discrimination simply taken new ways of expressing itself in today's schools?

At the conclusion of the next chapter you will be given an opportunity to prepare a report on: "How equal are educational opportunities in the school I attended?" You might keep in mind some comparisons and contrasts between your school and Jonesville's. If you conclude that social class discrimination does restrict educational opportunity, you may wish to determine how such restriction expresses itself, and how it affects learning opportunity.

WHAT IS THE SCHOOL'S RESPONSIBILITY?

Let us first ask the basic question: Does the school have a responsibility for seeing that each child is given an opportunity to develop his talent to the fullest extent? Would it not be easy to argue, for example, that the conditions which deny such opportunities in Jonesville are created by the community, not the school? The children simply bring to school the biases which they learn at home. Why should the school stand against the community and attempt to practice the American Creed when the community itself compromises it?

There is also another question: Can the school alter the situation, even if it wants to? There are strong arguments supporting the position that a school cannot have a strong impact upon a community's value structure. The school is a tool of the community, the reasoning goes. The community pays for it through taxes and controls it through the Board of Education. Conclusion: The school is in a good position to reaffirm community values, but in a poor position to change them.

The argument is formidable, and experience confirms it. Too many schools simply hold a mirror up to the community and reflect what they think they see there. They add nothing new to the community, nor do they enrich community thinking on crucial matters. Except for those existing values which are reinforced by the school, the community would be about the same as it would be were the school not there.

Many schools, however, take a different view. They take seriously their responsibility to extend educational opportunity to all children.

Today many adults were, as children, in the same position as the lower class children in Jonesville. Their economic and social status made for limited opportunity. The school made the difference. There, through the efforts of perceptive and sympathetic teachers, these children were given courage to rise above their frustrations to new and satisfying achievements. In these cases, the teacher accepted full responsibility for doing what he could to spread educational opportunity.

The point is this: Where the school and teachers count it their job to extend educational opportunity to those denied it, opportunity is extended. A young doctor takes the Hippocratic Oath binding him to minister to the sick one whatever his circumstances. Sickness is its own sufficient reason for the doctor's care. A teacher does not take such a formal oath. But great teachers have always practiced their art as though they had. The need to learn, whatever the status of the child, is its own sufficient reason for teaching. Quintilian, that remarkable teacher of first century Rome, once remarked that the great teacher was one who could take the littlest child by the hand, and, shortening his stride, lead him along.

Schools must take the leadership in stimulating community interest in educating *all* children and youth. Whenever the schools go to the community, explain the problem, and point out what should be done, citizens usually respond. The result: enriched school programs which serve children and youth of widely different backgrounds, abilities, and vocational goals. Here are a few such programs which extend educational opportunity:

> Guidance and counseling programs
> Cooperative programs with trade and industry
> Technical and vocational programs
> Programs for the gifted

College preparatory programs

Commercial programs

Special education programs for the crippled, mentally retarded, speech defective, and maladjusted

Visiting teacher and homebound programs

Co-curricular activities programs

Special science and mathematics programs

Such programs reflect the school's concern to reach children and youth who have wide-ranging interests and capacities.

> 6. Interview a teacher or principal about the school's efforts to provide equal educational opportunity to all students. Make a list of specific programs which are designed to help the school reach all children and youth within it. Make a report to the class on these programs.

These programs, however, have little effect without teachers who are skilled in and dedicated to extending full educational opportunity to each child.

WHAT CAN THE TEACHER DO?

When Thomas Wolfe, the distinguished American novelist, was a student at Harvard University, he received a letter from one of his former teachers. Would he write a recommendation for her to the superintendent of schools? He was proud to be asked. This, in part, is what he wrote: [2]

> My friend and former teacher, Mrs. J. M. Roberts, has lately written me, explaining that some testimonial is desired as to her quality as a teacher, and asking me if I would care to record any opinion I have on that subject. I esteem it an honor and a privilege to do this, although I find myself in constant difficulties when I try to keep my pen from leaping away with a red-hot panegyric.
>
> But—with all the moderation and temperance and earnestness at my command I can do no less than consider Mrs. Roberts as one of the three great teachers who have ever taught me—this with all honor to Harvard, who has not yet succeeded in adding a fourth name to my own Hall of Fame.
>
> More than anyone else I have ever known, Mrs. Roberts succeeded in getting under my skull with an appreciation of what is fine and altogether worthwhile in literature. That, in my opinion, is the vital

---

[2] Claude M. Fuess and Emory S. Basford, eds., *Unseen Harvests* (New York: The Macmillan Company, 1947), pp. 437-38. Reprinted by permission of Paul Gitlin, administrator, CTA of Thomas Wolfe estate.

quality. That is the essential thing—the mark of a real teacher . . .

I have spoken of Mrs. Roberts merely as a teacher. This is perhaps the only testimonial you want. But I cannot stop before I speak of another matter that has been of the highest importance to me. During the years Mrs. Roberts taught me she exercised an influence that is inestimable on almost every particular of my life and thought.

With the other boys of my age I know she did the same. We turned instinctively to this lady for her advice and direction and we trusted to it unfalteringly.

I think that kind of relation is one of the profoundest experiences of anyone's life—I put the relation of a fine teacher to a student just below any relation of a mother to her son and I don't think I could say more than this . . .

Thomas Wolfe remembered two qualities above all others about Mrs. Roberts. She was first a good teacher who got under his "skull and appreciation of what is fine and altogether worthwhile in literature." Second, she was a fine person, taking a personal interest in each child, a lady to whom the children turned instinctively "for her advice and direction." She had the kind of concern which a mother has for a son. In a real sense equal educational opportunity begins in the attitude and skill of the teacher. If he feels deeply about our American educational creed and about the importance of developing talent wherever it is found, the chances are that he will find ways to do it.

Following are some practical ways in which classroom teachers can equalize educational opportunity within the classroom.

Use Group Work To Teach Democratic Values

Many classroom activities lend themselves to student group work. With guidance the teacher can structure these groups so that all the students have an opportunity to work with one another. Students who normally do not group together outside the classroom can learn to work together inside the classroom. Stereotyped ideas about one another will frequently disappear as students labor on common projects. The "not good looking child" can work with the "good looking" child, the "unpopular child" with the "popular child." The experience can be instructive for each. Such experiences can help considerably to teach democratic living and, at the same time, extend learning opportunities for many children. Students who plan and execute projects together are likely to gain a better appreciation of one another's abilities while increasing their own learning.

Provide For Individual Development And Expression

Each student in the class usually has a special contribution to make. Each has some unique talent, latent though it may be. A good teacher discovers these personal abilities and encourages the student to develop them. Many student abilities can remain invisible, especially in large classes. The teacher can help to make them visible, give some prominence to those students who, under normal circumstances, would be held in the background.

Such invisibility can be the lot of the bright student as well as the average student. Many bright children do not find sufficient challenge in the normal classroom program and need the stimulation of new experiences.

Individual differences in a classroom are great. The good teacher recognizes them and provides individual learning experiences to supplement the regular classroom program. Learning opportunities are thus extended.

Enrich The Curriculum

The curriculum itself should serve the needs of all children. If the curriculum is thought of as a fixed quantity which each child must master, some children will have difficulty. In Jonesville the curriculum has special appeal for those children equipped to handle it. Those who are not so equipped, experience frustration. If one believes that the school should serve the needs and abilities of all youth, then the curriculum must challenge all youth.

Develop Parent Contacts

In this chapter we aren't told much about the relationship between the teacher and the parents in Jonesville. In the case of Priscilla, in the next chapter, we shall learn more about this relationship. We may assume, however, that the Jonesville teachers would know more about the child's problems within the classroom if they had a good working relationship with the parents. The sense of isolation in school, which some children feel, is frequently reduced if they know that the teacher has a cordial relationship with their parents. Certainly the teacher gains a better understanding of the student through such a relationship. With this understanding the teacher is in a better position to help the student.

Maintain Community Cooperation

Taken together, the teachers of a school system constitute a powerful voice for interpreting the work of a school in the community. Each teacher has numerous contacts, professional and social, within the community. Citizens like to discuss school and civic affairs with teachers. The teacher is frequently in a position to help citizens understand what the school is trying to do. He can encourage their support.

The American school, as we have seen, has an historic mission to extend educational opportunity to all youth. Teachers can do much to keep this idea alive and growing in a community. Or on the other hand, they can reinforce class biases in education. Teachers can, by their silence or open approval of discrimination, defeat one of the purposes for which our schools came into being. The teacher must stand on the side of those who believe that the entire community is made richer and safer when the school extends an equal educational opportunity to every child within it.

The school is not for the few and the privileged. It is for the many, among whom are those who are struggling against great odds to achieve. The odds may be of many kinds. Whatever they are, it is the teacher's task to help the child over those odds and on to satisfying achievement. The teacher can do much to encourage community support of this historic and still-exciting goal in American education. In this effort he becomes worthy of the name teacher.

Good Follow-up Reading and Viewing

BOOKS

Burton, William H., "Education and Social Class in the United States," in *Readings in Education,* pp. 219-30, Arthur Foff and Jean D. Grambs, eds. New York: Harper & Brothers, 1956. The author's treatment of social class is directed toward educational workers and what they can do to help children and youth with varying values, beliefs, and attitudes.

Conant, James B., "The Cultivation of Talent in The 'Comprehensive' School," in *Crucial Issues in Education,* pp. 322-29, Henry Ehlers and Gordon C. Lee, eds. New York: Holt, Rinehart & Winston, Inc., 1959. This noted educator states that the introduction of special arrangements for the gifted pupil is one of the changes that marks the transformation of a satisfactory high school into a good high school.

Davis, Allison, "Status Systems and the Socialization of the Child," in *Social Foundations of Education,* William O. Stanley, *et al.,* eds. New York: Dryden, 1956. The author contends that many lower class children fail in school because they are humiliated and punished too severely in school and because learning reinforcements are denied them.

Educational Policies Commission, *Education for All American Youth.* Washington, D.C.: National Education Association, 1944. A comprehensive treatment of the challenge confronting educators in the effort to educate all American youth.

————, *Education for All American Youth—A Further Look.* Washington, D.C.: National Education Association, 1952. This revision of the 1944 publication reviews progress in the education of youth in the post-war years and points to future problems and prospects.

Embree, Edwin R., "Amazon of God," in *Thirteen Against the Odds.* New York: The Viking Press, Inc., 1944. The story of Mary Jane McLeod Bethune, her struggle against poverty to get an education and, finally, to found Bethune-Cookman College for Negroes.

Havighurst, Robert J., *Human Development and Education,* chap. 13, "A Boy Who Failed and What the School Might Have Done: The Case of Jed." New York: Longmans, Green & Co., Inc., 1953. The case study of a boy and his family, how he saw himself, how others saw him, how he failed in school, and what the school might have done.

Laidlaw, Clara, "The Little Black Boys," in *The Seas of God,* Whit Burnett, ed. New York: J. B. Lippincott Co., 1944. A short story describing a teacher's experience with two underprivileged brothers. Of special interest is the teacher's handling of social class differences within the classroom.

Thomas, Lawrence G., *et al., Perspective on Teaching,* chap. 9, "What Do Children Learn From Their Social Environment?" Englewood Cliffs, N.J.: Prentice-Hall, Inc., 1961. Some significant generalizations which can be drawn from the child's experience in five areas of social contact: family, playmates, social class, teachers, and organized school community.

Warner, W. Lloyd, Robert J. Havighurst, and Martin B. Loeb, *Who Shall Be Educated.* New York: Harper & Brothers, 1944. How stratification influences differences between schools, within schools, and social mobility. "Must" reading.

Whitney, Phyllis, *Willow Hill.* New York: David McKay Co., Inc., 1947. A government housing project brings Negroes into a previously all white neighborhood. Facing unfavorable community reactions, a group of high school students act constructively to combat racial prejudice in their school and community.

Yates, Elizabeth, *Nearby.* New York: Coward-McCann, Inc., 1947. A dedicated young teacher in a small school devotes her attention to all children, regardless of status, in the face of bitter class prejudice.

PERIODICALS

"Boys and Girls With Special Abilities," *NEA Journal,* October, 1958, pp. 467-74. A series of articles dealing with the identification and development of talent resources in English, mathematics, science, foreign language, social studies, and art.

Bucklen, H. E., "A Teacher Looks At Our Social Class Structure," *Educational Administration and Supervision,* Vol. 39, January, 1953, pp. 14-26. Constructive suggestions regarding what a teacher can do about social class influences.

Chamberlain, John, "Education Revolution," *The Wall Street Journal,* February 17, 1959, p. 14. This article describes what the school board of Shortridge High School, Indianapolis, is doing to improve the school. Included is a "multiple track" system in which the students are grouped in separate levels in accordance with their abilities, and the "differentiated diploma," reflecting the level of difficulty of the student's program.

Chapman, Helen, "What Have I To Give?" *NEA Journal*, Vol. 44, April, 1955, p. 230. Can help the prospective teacher appraise his personal qualifications for bringing educational opportunity to children of widely different backgrounds and interests.

Gordon, C. Wayne, "The Role of The Teacher in The Social Structure of The School," *Journal of Educational Sociology*, Vol. 29, September, 1955, pp. 21-29. The variety of roles carried out by a teacher and the frustrations experienced in doing so.

Harpen, Frances R., "The Guidance-Oriented Elementary Teacher," *NEA Journal*, Vol. 49, March, 1960, pp. 17-19. Helpful suggestions on how the elementary teacher can "look for talents, assets, and strong points within the individual child."

Neugarten, Bernice, "Social Class and Friendship Among School Children," *American Journal of Sociology*, Vol. 51, January, 1956, pp. 305-13. A comprehensive study of the social relations among children of different social class backgrounds.

Rich, John Martin, "How Social Class Values Affect Teacher-Pupil Relations," *The Journal of Educational Sociology*, Vol. 33, May, 1960, pp. 355-59. A good statement of some of the problems a teacher who honestly aspires to make the classroom a democratic microcosm confronts.

Wrum, Gilbert C., *et al.*, "Guidance," *NEA Journal*, Vol. 48, January, 1959, pp. 16-31. A series of articles dealing with guidance in both small and big schools. Illustrative of what schools can do when they are genuinely concerned about the welfare of learners.

FILMS

Americans All

Attempts to infringe on democratic rights of certain people because of racial and religious intolerance. Scenes in Springfield, Mass., showing how communities and schools can combat such injustice. (March of Time; McGraw-Hill Book Co., Inc., black and white, 16 minutes.)

Challenge of the Gifted

How the schools of Vallejo, California, meet challenge of gifted children without a change in basic curriculum through system of special classes. How students are selected; qualifications of teachers. (McGraw-Hill Book Co., Inc., color, 12 minutes.)

Counselor's Day

Shows a guidance counselor in his round of activities: interviews, consultations, classes, extracurricular activities, and professional writing. (McGraw-Hill Book Co., Inc., black and white, 10 minutes.)

Good Speech for Gary

Speech correction in public schools. Effect of speech defects on child's personality and benefits from remedial teaching. Suggestions for correcting poor speech. (McGraw-Hill Book Co., Inc., black and white, 22 minutes.)

Learning Democracy Through School—Community Projects

How schools teach democratic procedures as a part of their daily activities. Illustrations include student councils, student elections, youth centers, safety patrol, audio-visual service clubs, and other activities. (Educational Film Service, color, 21 minutes.)

Right Angle

A newspaper reporter sets out to examine the schools. He finds that they are doing a good job of educating all the children, regardless of their backgrounds and abilities. (National Education Association, black and white, 28 minutes.)

CHAPTER 17

THE STUDENTS WHO QUIT

The way a lot of us girls are treated at school no one can
blame us for the way we feel.

PRISCILLA

In the first chapter of this section we examined the American educational creed of equal opportunity for all. Our schools, we discovered, have played a decisive part in binding the nation together, in promoting democratic government and in spreading the good things of life to many citizens. In the second chapter we observed how the American creed has fallen short. Equal educational opportunity, for many reasons, is not extended to all our children.

Now we meet a student whose educational opportunity has been curtailed. What are such students like? How do they feel about the school? How did they come to feel as they do? What part did the teachers play in creating their feelings? How are they treated by other students? What part has the home played in their reactions?

Priscilla is a Jonesville high school student who quit school.[1] She is bright and fully capable of graduating from high school and, probably, college. In elementary school she did well, was liked both by teachers and fellow students, and gave promise of doing well in high school. Then something happened. Her attitude changed. She became bitter toward her fellow students and teachers. She quit. When she did, her opportunity for further formal education ceased.

It would be easy to blame someone—the girl, her parents, the teachers,

---

[1] W. Lloyd Warner, *Democracy in Jonesville* (New York: Harper and Brothers, 1949), pp. 78-81, 85-87, 88.

other students, the community. Probably all must share the blame. But we are not here to blame. Our purpose as teachers is to understand, to understand and help. Why did she feel as she did? Why did she behave as she did? What can the teacher do?

The story of Priscilla is presented as a case study, the examination of which can help us find answers to such questions as those above. The previous two chapters have given us some concepts to use in finding such answers. Therefore, no textual material is presented with the case. We shall pose specific questions for you to consider as we read the case. These may be used to sharpen your own perceptions. They should help you determine what you would do if you had a student like Priscilla in your own class.

PRISCILLA REPRESENTS MORE THAN ONE INDIVIDUAL

She represents all those young people who for some reason feel that the school does not have anything to offer them. Some actually drop out, as did Priscilla. Others stay in school, accept their diminished opportunity, and "just get by." Whatever the cause of their dissatisfaction, they are not getting full advantage of their educational opportunities.

Here are three questions posed by this case. How would you answer them?

> 1. Priscilla feels that she is being punished in the school environment. In what ways do you think a school environment can "punish" a child?
>
> 2. Priscilla makes a number of attempts to gain status in the school. She strives for prestige and acceptance. Had she won them, her story might have ended differently. If you were her teacher, how would you attempt to keep her interested in achieving?
>
> 3. When Priscilla's father wants to help her stay in school, he turns not to the school, but to a sympathetic lawyer. He has rejected the school as a source of help. Do you feel that this impasse in relations could have been avoided? How could a teacher help to avoid it?

THIS IS THE STORY OF PRISCILLA

Mr. Sellers, usually a heavy sleeper, was sitting straight up in bed, wide awake, listening. A strange sound had awakened him. It was like someone crying, someone in the back bedroom. He felt anxious and a little frightened, for none of the family should be home now. It was early in the afternoon, and his wife was down at the Volmers' doing the weekly washing for the boss's wife. Maggie and Bill were at work, too, and Priscilla should still be at high school. He continued to listen but could hear nothing. He lay down again and wondered if he could get a couple of hours' more sleep before he went on the night shift.

Then he heard the sound again. It was like the way the kids used to cry when they had been badly hurt and had run home to him and their mother for help. The sobbing increased and suddenly became unrestrained. Something certainly was wrong. He hurried out of bed, pulled some clothes on, and came out of the darkness of his room into the light of the small hallway which connected the girls' room with his. The door to the girls' room was shut. No sound could be heard. He knocked, but there was no answer. He waited a moment, wondering if he had been dreaming, started to go back to bed, when he heard the crying again. It sounded like Priscilla.

He opened the door and looked around. There was no one there. He looked in the closet and looked out the window into the yard, but could see no one. This frightened him even more. He was sure now that something was wrong. He heard a suppressed sob. It seemed to come from under the bed. In the dark beneath it he saw Priscilla's body, knees pulled up against her, head buried in her two arms, and all of her squeezed against the farthest and darkest corner.

"Priscilla, are you all right? What's the matter with you?", he asked. "Are you sick? What's the matter with you—have you been hurt?"

"No."

"Well, what's wrong?"

"Nothing."

"Priscilla, you come out from under that bed. You're acting like a baby. You used to get under there to cry when you were a little kid. Come on out now and tell me what's wrong."

After considerable coaxing, Priscilla came out. Her face was smudged, her eyes red, and her tears had made little marks like small dry pools on the powdered surface of her face. The sweater which covered her well-formed figure was smeared with spider webs, and her short, white socks were covered with gray dust. She held her head down and would not look at her father.

"Now, tell we what's wrong. What's happened to you? Maybe I can help you."

"No, you can't papa—no one can. I'm in the dog house again, and this time it's an awful big dog house. I can't stand it any longer. I'm going to quit that terrible high school. I want to get a job and go to work."

"Priscilla, I can't understand you any more. Why you used to love grammar school. You always had all A's on your report card, and now you're flunking and getting in trouble with your teachers.

I just can't understand it, Priscilla. You used to be such a nice kid, and I believe you still are. You liked school and had all those nice friends. What's happened? You don't want to quit school."

"Yes, I do, and I am."

"Look, Priscilla, I'd planned on your sister and brother going through school, but they quit and went to work. They had plenty of brains, but I let them quit because I thought they lacked ambition. I know it's hard to stick to it. I remember how my sister and I quit school, too. But you're the last, and I wish you would go on and give it a try."

"No, I'm never—absolutely never—going back to school again."

4. Priscilla's father had quit school. So had her brother and sister. What bearing do you think this fact has on Priscilla's attitude toward the school? Should the fact that her family did not complete high school be taken into consideration by the teachers who deal with Priscilla? How might a teacher help her to overcome this initial handicap?

Her father put his arm around her. Priscilla started crying again. After a while she said, "You and Mother just got to let me quit. I can't take it any more. Everyone up there hates me. No one likes me. The teachers hate me, and the kids won't have anything to do with me."

"That can't be true, Priscilla. Our family is okay in this town. We ain't rich, but I earn an honest living, and everybody thinks we are okay. No one can point the finger at us. Now, tell me what happened today. What did you do?"

"Well, I got caught playing hookey again. That old Swenson caught us. He's always snooping. He thought we were going down by the river to meet some boys, but honest we weren't. Florence, Ruth, Carol, and I just wanted to have a little fun. Just wanted to get away from all those snooty kids. And I'm not going back." Her voice became shrill and harsh. "I'm not going back. None of us is going back. We're all through with that school from now on.

"The way a lot of us girls are treated at school no one can blame us for the way we feel. There's nothing there for a lot of us but just coming to classes, listening to the teacher, reciting our lessons, and studying, and going home again. We're just pushed out of things."

5. Priscilla apparently gets no satisfaction from her classroom work. We have spoken about the importance of a curriculum that fits the needs of youth. What kind of classroom learning do you think would appeal to Priscilla?

"And I don't feel like I want to go to school. They snub us, and they won't talk to us. Some of them will speak to us sometimes, but most of the time they just ignore us. Now I know we're not rich. We're really poor people. I don't want the kids in high school to know that Mother takes in washing to get a little extra money to get some of the things that she needs. A lot of women take in washing here in town. There's nothing wrong with that. But they'd look down on me if they knew it.

"And we can't do the things they do. We have a large family, and I know, Dad, you're only a working man, and we can't afford to do a lot of things.

"But us girls would like to be in the school activities and school games—to go to the dances and things like that. We could do that without money. But they just make us feel like we're not wanted. I went to some of the activities when I first started to high school. But they just ignored us. Last year I was in home-making and in the Pep Club, but this year I'm not in anything.

"You know I don't go with the boys in high school. I just don't care to. I'd like to go with them, but most of the boys that I'd want to go with, they wouldn't ask me. I guess they just don't want to go with me. If you go to the football games, it's just the same way. Now, those Pep Club girls are supposed to sit together at a game and root together, and if you're not in one of the groups, you're left out. That's just the way it is."

Priscilla turned up both her palms and shrugged her shoulders and said, "Well, why go? We're made to feel out of place, and that's just the way it is.

"I want to graduate from high school, but I'll have to have English if I do. I flunked it last year. And I've been cutting it again this year—because there are just little kids in there, and they make me feel ashamed. I'm so much older and bigger than they are. Miss Jacobsen bawled me out for cutting, right in front of the class the other day because I didn't know the questions because I hadn't been there the day before. Well, that made me mad; so I cut the next day."

6. How do you evaluate Miss Jacobson's handling of this problem? Would you have handled it differently? If so, how?

While Priscilla spoke, Mr. Sellers looked at the floor. He said nothing. He knew what she said was true. His two older children had told him the same thing when they quit. He and the Missus had gone up to school and raised hell, but it didn't do any good. Now it was Priscilla's turn.

By God! It wasn't going to happen to her. But what to do? It wouldn't get him to first base to talk to Swenson or Lawson, those dirty so-and-so's. He'd go to see Oldham, the lawyer. He liked to raise hell. The big guys hadn't got a hold on George Oldham yet.

He gently patted Priscilla on the shoulder and kissed her on the forehead. "Look, honey, Daddy's going to try to help. We ain't going to take this without a fight. Mama will be home in a little while. Fix yourself up, Priscilla. Mama and I are going to do something about this. You'll see, we're going to help you."

He washed up and put on his coat. When his wife returned, they went down to Oldham's office.

Before Priscilla entered high school she was well liked by her teachers and classmates. She had had an outstanding record ever since she had been in grammar school. She had a reputation for being a nice child and for being intelligent and diligent as a student. All her playmates said she was a good sport. She went around with all the girls in her room, particularly "those nice girls who belonged to the best families" and who live over in the "Top Circle." Florence, Ruth, and Carol were also in that group. All of them came from Mill Town. Everyone knew it, but it didn't seem to make any difference. Their grammar school teachers said it showed what a good character, nice personality, and brains could do for anyone who really tried.

Now it was all different. She, Florence, Ruth, and Carol, and some of the others were no longer friends with the girls who came from The Circle. Only that morning Priscilla had put on her new pink sweater and plaid dress and gone to school almost happy. She looked just as good as anybody else. She had actually spoken to Sylvia Volmers, but Sylvia had turned her head and said something to Jane Eberhart and Judith Morrison and all three of them had laughed. Priscilla blushed, for she knew that they were laughing at her—particularly because they had been her friends in grammar school, and she had never learned why they had dropped her. When she got to her seat in the assembly hall, Mr. Scott had asked her to come to his office. When she got there, he told her he was sorry but she could no longer be a majorette in the band, an honor that all the girls competed for, because she had been skipping school and was behind in her studies. She knew when she walked into his office what he was going to tell her, for one of the girls who belonged to the corps said that the others were trying to force her out and get the Madison girl in. She went back to her seat. She saw Ruth and Carol and the others sneaking out. They had had a row with old lady Kennedy because they had been caught passing notes to the Gear boys. She decided to go with them.

Swenson had caught all of them. He brought them back to his office. They all attempted to lie out of it.

"I've had enough lies from you girls. Now just cut it out; get your story straight; I want the truth. I know that all of you are lying. And you're all trying to hide where you were. Do you want me to get your mothers down here again?

"I suppose I'll have to go out here and get a baseball bat and come in here and beat some brains into your heads. No, I guess that wouldn't do any good. Just nothing in you, nothing at all. Now I'm trying to save you girls, and you're just too dumb to know it. I think you're worth being saved, but if you won't let me save you, well, that's your own fault. I'm going to get your mothers in here, and we're going to try to save you."

7. Swenson's patience with the girls is obviously and understandably running out. How do you evaluate his handling of the problem?

It was late afternoon when Mr. and Mrs. Sellers arrived at Oldham's office. Oldham was alone.

"What can I do for you, Tom? You haven't robbed a bank, have you?"

"No, Mr. Oldham, but I wish I had. My little Priscilla has got into trouble at school with Lawson and Swenson. My wife and I thought you might help us."

"You see," said Mrs. Sellers, "It's like this, Mr. Oldham. We know her skipping school is serious. We realize that, and I think she realizes it. But the seriousness is not skipping so much as it is the situation in the high school. I'm referring to the discrimination among the students, by the superintendent, the principal, and the teachers. We noticed this same thing when my older daughter was in high school and we saw the same thing when my son was in school. And now, it's going on with the younger girls. Ever since we've been here, we have known that the sons and daughters of the members of the school board have an inside track. The same is true of the wealthy people here in town. The good grades seem to be given to the people that think they're a better class and have more money than we have. The same thing seems to be true of the class offices, parts in the plays, and things like that. Of course, it doesn't happen in every case, but that seems to be the way it works out most of the time. We're a large family. We have to watch the pennies to get along. Mr. Sellers is a workingman, and there are seven children in the family; so we have to be careful with our money. But this shouldn't make any difference in the school. But it actually does.

"The latest thing that has hurt Priscilla the most, but it's just like all the other things that have happened before, it's this majorette business. All the boys and girls pay for that course, and Priscilla was selected to be one of the majorettes. Her father and I thought she did as well as anyone else. At first, she did better, I think. But they did a dirty trick on her. Priscilla told me that band leader, Mr. Scott, told them to practice as much as they could outside of the school time. Well, the other girls used to get together and practice, but they would never tell her until it was all over. The only way she'd find out was when they all met at school, and the others had worked on one of the routines, and she couldn't do it. And then someone would say that was the way they did it at such and such a time.

"I think they were actually working to get Priscilla out of that group. Mr. Scott didn't find out what was going on until Lawson told Priscilla that she couldn't twirl any more. She came home and cried all afternoon and almost all night. I found it very difficult to get her to go back to school. Mr. Scott didn't want them to take Priscilla out. He felt that she could do as well as the rest if she only had the chance to practice. I'm sure that Mr. Lawson told Mr. Scott that he had to take her out of there. I believe the girls had a lot to do with Priscilla's being taken out."

8. We know that the total environment is important in learning. A good environment gives emotional and social rewards which reinforce learning. The majorettes gave Priscilla such needed reinforcement. What is the function of extra class activities? What should be the basis for determining who should participate?

9. Swenson is caught in cross pressures. Mr. Scott, the teacher, would like to keep Priscilla in the majorettes. The other girls, and their influential parents, want her out. He is disgusted with her behavior, as is the principal, Mr. Lawson. What should he do?

While Mrs. Sellers spoke, Mr. Oldham looked out the window. When she stopped he said, "It all sounds familiar, but I didn't think the kids were as class-conscious as their parents. Tom, I'd like to have you talk. What do you think about it? What do you think was back of all this?"

"Well, a number of things, Mr. Oldham. I can't say all of it. Swenson said she was dropped because she skipped school, but that isn't the whole thing. On my job, I run into a lot of things and talk to people a lot, and I hear a number of things. A lot of kids skip down there, and Swenson overlooks it. He just seems to land on certain ones. But if he gets it in for a boy or girl, he's very hard on them, and he always rides them. The school board's children and prominent people around town who have children there in the high school, their children always have the inside track. They seem to be in everything, and it's difficult for other students to get into activities and offices and grades and things like that. . . ."

On the way to his office next day, Mr. Oldham was stopped by Mr. Lawson.

"New travels fast around here, Mr. Oldham. A little bird told me that the Sellers were in to see you last night. I was wondering if they said anything about the majorette business?"

Oldham said, "Oh, a little, I think. It is still eating on Priscilla from what her mother said."

Lawson chuckled to himself and went on. "You know, she is so clumsy it was pitiful with her out there trying to throw the baton around. She just made the other girls look ludicrous. My, it was a sight to see her clumping down the street like an old truck horse. We just couldn't have her there, as it ruined the whole show for the other girls and made the band look bad. Scott did not want to take her out, as he thought she was doing a good job. The other girls did not like her in there. Don't you believe a word of it. Nice to have seen you. By the way, Louise's a remarkable girl. She's doing a fine job. Well, goodby."

10. Teaching is a profession, and teachers must learn to talk about students and their problems in a professional way. Assume that you were Lawson talking to Oldham. What would you say?

After a few telephone calls, Mr. Oldham asked for Swenson. "Hello, Dick. Mr. and Mrs. Sellers were in. They're considerably distressed about their daughter's quitting school. I guess the other parents are too. Could I see you? Why don't you come down to the house and have a drink?"

Their second drink was almost consumed. They had been talking about Priscilla's and the other girls' difficulties. Mr. Swenson said, "Hell, that's an old story. The Sellers, the Conways, and the Grunds were skipping school last year, and the year before, and I suppose they'll be skipping this year. I used to think that the Sellers girls, when they were in grammar school, were the sweetest little kids in town. But they've changed so much in the last year. The problem there with all those girls is lack of parental control. The Sellers let those kids run around like rabbits and never pay any attention to what the children do. The Conways are the same way. There's no parental control there, and so what can you expect from those kids?

"Old Tom Sellers just doesn't understand. He's just one of those sweet, loving souls who doesn't know what the hell it's all about. You know, I think the only appeal you can use on that girl is to take her down in the basement and beat the hell out of her. Of course, you hate to do that with a girl that old. But I've tried to reason with that girl; I've tried to threaten her; I've tried to talk to her; I've tried everything. But hell, there's no way to appeal to her. The only thing left is to beat the hell out of her. I think if she had the hell beat out of her a time or two, then she'd begin to see things.

"I think Priscilla and the other girls were all out with boys this morning. They were up town fooling around."

"But what about the majorette business? It sounds like that raised hell with the kid."

Swenson said, "Yes, I'm sure of that. That's what I gathered when I talked to her a few days ago. Her mother talked to me on the street the other day. I've almost reached the decision to put her back in there. If the other girls will let her come, and if Scott will let her in. I'm pretty sure that Scott will, but I just want to be sure that she can make her grades and that she doesn't cut school anymore. Really, the big thing, though, is that the girls are objecting to her being in there. The truth is that. Her skipping school was more or less an excuse to get her out of there. Lawson didn't want her in there because the other girls had been kicking about having her in there. The first time she did something, the heat was put on by some of the old families to get Priscilla out of there. Some of these old families around here really put on the pressure."

A few days later, Mr. Oldham saw Mr. Sellers on the street.

"It's no use, Mr. Oldham. She's quit. She's got a job over in Alexandria. She seems happy now and I guess that's what counts. I did hope, though, she'd go on to school and amount to something. I never had an education, and I wanted her to have a better chance in life than I had. Now she isn't going to get no place either. Nobody in my family ever wins. We don't have a chance. My sister and I tried for a good education but we dropped out; my two older kids came along and I sort of bet on them to come through, but they didn't. Then Priscilla, now she's out. It's like when I bet on the horses. I haven't got a chance. I can't win, can't place, can't show. I guess that's the way it goes in Jonesville."

Mr. Oldham looked at him, "Yes, that's exactly the way it goes here in Jonesville."

11. In the first chapter of this section it was suggested that you interview a fellow classmate about educational equality in his school. Now prepare a more detailed report on this topic: "How equal are educational opportunities in the school I attended?"

TWO STUDENTS REPORT

To stimulate your own thinking here are two student reports on equality of educational opportunity in the schools they attended. The reports are understandably autobiographical in approach. The first report expresses personal frustration in the school experience. The second report acknowledges the social class problem in the school, but points to the enriched program provided for students of widely different interests, abilities, and social positions.

If A Girl Intended To Be "In," She Had To Be Able To Wear Cashmere Sweaters

DORIS CAROLE MC CALL

Are there equal opportunities for education in our schools today? The school administrators and teachers might say "yes." As a student I would say "no." To illustrate, I would like to relate my experience in the seventh grade.

I was sent to a large high school in the middle of a wealthy school district. There were about 300 children in our class.

In this large student body, there were many cliques. These cliques were not just groups of children who chose to pal together and still associate with others. They were separate classes of children competing with each other for the most recognition from the school, and were thrown together because of their economic status in the community.

There were three major divisions of children. At the head of the groups were the students who wore the best clothes, held the class offices, were chosen for special class functions, and generally received the best grades. These were the economic "betters."

Then there were the so-called "middle class" children that were more or less popular, had average grades, took part in a few activities and dressed (according to standards in this school) fairly well. Between this group and the first, there was much competition for offices, special duties, and better grades.

Then there were the children from poor homes. These children dressed very poorly and did not participate in class activities, were not elected to offices, made the worst grades generally, and were completely ignored by the others.

To give you some idea of the standards set up for popularity, let's take the dressing standard for this school. If a girl intended to be "in," she had to be able to wear cashmere sweaters and wool skirts, nice jewelry, and perfume. She could never wear the same outfit more than once a week or she was not fit to be "accepted." The required attire for boys was wool slacks and sweaters or white shirts with sports jackets. If the student could not meet these standards he was not accepted socially.

The economic pressure was so strong and so much a part of the classroom that the poorer class student, or the shy student, felt so hurt and left out he did not concentrate on his studies. He felt insecure, and did poorly in his school work.

The teachers in the school favored the more wealthy students generally, and the other children were not given the special help and recognition they needed. The classroom atmosphere was formal and the discussions were totally monopolized by the "better" students.

There was much gossip and rumor-spreading in the school as well as a high rate of drinking and smoking, swearing and gambling. These were the "smart" things to do. (The seventh graders were participants also.) If a student could not accept these things, then he had no place in student society.

There was a very high rate of drop-outs in the tenth and eleventh grades. These occurred totally among the middle and the poorer classes of students. The school did not offer counseling and guidance for these students, and few teachers were willing to help the students solve their problems.

I feel that the main reason so many drop-outs occurred was because of the tremendous social pressure put upon these students; it never for a moment let up. These were the children who were left out—left out of friendship and left out of any sort of recognition. They had developed a bitter, rebellious attitude because of the pressure put upon them. They were not considered good to anyone, not even to themselves, and as soon as they were able they sought release from the pressure.

My personal experience in this school was an unhappy one. I wanted more than anything to be well liked, and tried very hard. It seemed to me that most of my efforts were frustrated. I tried out for our class play; I tried out for a talent show and many other activities, but never seemed to be selected from among all of the other students.

I never felt dressed well enough no matter how nice I looked; I felt sure everyone was talking about me because I had heard gossip so often. I became terribly self-conscious and shied away from many friendships. Because of the pressure I made myself miserable.

My unhappiness showed up in my grades; they became poorer and poorer. I became bitter toward the school and the teachers and did not try. I found many who felt the same as I did, and so did not get any better.

My parents were beginning to worry, and fortunately helped me to overcome enough of my bitterness to get better grades. I still did not like the school any better, and the social system did not change. The next year I moved.

There were many children in my class whose parents were not as interested in them as mine had been in me, and they did not improve. They continued to be unhappy and receive poor grades.

I am sure that this school is only one example of many where social discrimination hinders the chance for each student to have equal educational opportunities. Perhaps some other schools do not have such a problem as this one. Or perhaps their problem is racial prejudice or something else, but many schools have some force that makes it difficult to have equal educational opportunities.

I feel that it is wrong for people to discriminate against one another in anything, but especially in education. When one person or group of people take away the right of another group to improve themselves, they are only helping the forces they dislike so much to breed and grow stronger. In the school I went to for the seventh grade, the social discrimination not only took happiness away from the students while they were at school but kept them from being able to attain the happiness and satisfaction and chance for improvement they were entitled to and could have achieved through education.

I know that not all schools are like the one I just described. The school I moved to and graduated from was very friendly and was interested in helping the individual student learn to his full capacity. The difference in the two schools showed in my grades and in my attitude.

Many Of The Teachers In My School Helped All The Students
SARAH LITOWSKY

When I had finished reading the case history of Priscilla, I realized how lucky I had been in going to a high school in which everyone, no matter how poor he was, had an equal chance to succeed.

During my elementary and junior high school years I was in a clique where all my friends were in the middle class, as I was. All of us, being in the group, shared the same luxuries and things that we could afford. When I found that I was going to high school, I was sort of skeptical about what was going to happen to my life, since the majority of the student body came from wealthy families.

During my first few days at M. H. S., I was on guard, expecting to find snobs everywhere I went and to a certain extent, I did; however, there were enough kids who weren't of this type that I found friendly.

I found the story about cliques was true. In order to belong, you had to own at least thirty cashmere sweaters, and it was said that if you didn't belong to these cliques you would never amount to anything in school activities. These stories, I found, were not entirely correct. It was true that you needed thirty sweaters to join certain cliques, but the idea of not getting anywhere in school if you didn't belong to a clique was wrong. There were other organizations, such as religious or school clubs which allowed everyone, no matter what their religion, economic status or race, to join.

Everyone had an equal chance to hold office. Of course, many times those from the wealthy group became officers, but usually, I found, they had the ability to hold these offices and to lead the students in our school.

Also, everyone had a chance to work on the school paper and year book. This way I got to know many people from all income brackets, and also to know the way they lived and felt about different things. I could go on and on to mention all the various activities available to *everyone* in our school.

I was shocked when reading about the discrimination of the teachers in Jonesville. Many of the teachers in my school helped all the students, no matter what race or economic level they may have been in. Many times, I would spend a good two hours after school, receiving help from my teachers. Besides getting help on my school work, many times these teachers were willing to help me with my personal problems, and, getting impartial advice from them, they helped mold my life.

Another reason why I was lucky to go to M. H. S. was my gaining an understanding of people of other religions and races. I know of many people who have prejudices against negroes and some religions because they, themselves, had never had a chance to associate with these people. I learned how wonderful these people are, and was able to understand how they feel towards the many discriminations they face today.

I think I was very fortunate in my high school years. Priscilla had to quit school because of the environment presented at her school, but I was impelled to forge ahead and become a part of the school activities. Of course, many times, the wealthier students showed their superiority, but instead of quitting, I wanted to show them that I could be as good as they were no matter how great they thought they were.

Through the help of my teachers, and being able to join activities that weren't partial to the color, religion, or economic bracket, I feel that I am a better person than many who come from high schools where there is discrimination. I can now judge people and not take for granted, as I did when I entered M. H. S., that all people are one way. I only hope that eventually every high school will be the same as mine.

EACH TEACHER HAS A CONTRIBUTION TO MAKE

Americans have taken the lead in spreading educational opportunity among the people. The early colonists set the pattern and correctly foreshadowed our great faith in education. In education Americans found the means of making democratic government workable, of giving the poor a chance to compete for the good things of life, of Americanizing thousands of foreign born persons, of unifying them in common purposes.

In carrying out their historic mission, the schools have had good friends when they needed them most. Each new extension of educational opportunity has been won against stubborn opposition. But influential men in our past and present have come forward to reaffirm the necessity of full educational opportunity. As historian Commager reminds us: "The schools have served the nation well."

They have also fallen short. The battle for equal educational opportunity is a continuing one and each teacher has his own contribution to make. We hope that Jonesville is not typical of American schools today. We do know that the problem remains in many communities. The problem might be large or small. As long as it is there, teachers will be called upon to seek out ways of helping that child whose educational opportunity is being curtailed. In this effort he invests teaching with its finest meaning.

Good Follow-up Reading and Viewing

BOOKS

Ambrose, Edna, and Alice Miel, *Children's Social Learnings*. Washington, D.C.: National Education Association, 1958. Reviews research on the influence of social environments on children and the practical implications of this information for teachers.

Davis, Allison, *Social-Class Influences Upon Learning*. Cambridge, Mass.: Harvard University Press, 1948. A plea that curriculum and teaching methods be suited to the needs of children of all social classes.

Davis, Billie, "I Was a Hobo Kid," in *Readings in Education,* pp. 11-19, Arthur Foff and Jean D. Grambs, eds. New York: Harper & Brothers, 1956. An underprivileged migrant girl tells of her experiences while transferring from school to school. Her experiences with friendly and understanding teachers and administrators illustrate what the schools can do to extend educational opportunity to all students.

Havighurst, Robert J., *Human Development and Education,* chap. 14, "A Girl Who Succeeded and How the School Helped Her: The Case of Roberta," and chap. 15, "A Girl Who Failed and What the School Might Have Done to Help Her: The Case of Elsie." New York: Longmans, Green & Co., Inc., 1953. The influences on each are identified and described, especially that of the school and teachers.

Hollingshead, August B., *Elmstown's Youth,* chaps. 8-12. New York: John Wiley & Sons, Inc., 1949. These chapters describe how the youth of five classes in a small midwestern town are treated in high school and how they react.

Pressey, Sidney L., and Francis P. Robinson, *Psychology and the New Education,* chap. 8. New York: Harper & Brothers, 1944. This chapter, on the characteristics of the adolescent, points out the importance of the school in his social development.

Taba, Hilda, *School Culture: Studies of Participation and Leadership.* Washington, D.C.: American Council on Education, 1955. An excellent review of the results that measure how school cultures influence student participation and leadership.

PERIODICALS

Becker, Howard S., "Social-Class Variations in the Teacher-Pupil Relationship," *Journal of Educational Sociology,* Vol. 25, 1952, pp. 451-65. Reports Chicago research on teacher's attitudes toward children of different social classes.

Havighurst, Robert J., "The Hard-to-Reach Adolescent," *The School Review,* Vol. 46, Summer, 1958, pp. 125-33. A descriptive statement of the "hard-to-reach" youth, two brief case studies, and an analysis of the reasons for their behavior.

————, and Lindley J. Stiles, "National Policy for Alienated Youth," *Phi Delta Kappan,* Vol. 42, April, 1961, pp. 283-91. A far-reaching proposal for helping those youths who have not found a satisfactory channel of growth toward adult competence. Should be read by every teacher and prospective teacher.

Horton, Robert E., "The Ten Imperative Obligations of Youth," *Phi Delta Kappan,* Vol. 41, December, 1959, pp. 100-01. A statement of the goals of public education regarding youth responsibility.

Hunt, Paul R., "Job-Upgrading: Rehabilitation for the Drop-Out," *Phi Delta Kappan,* Vol. 40, February, 1959, pp. 219-20. A teacher-coordinator describes a large city school system's program for rehabilitating the drop-outs between the ages of sixteen and twenty.

Livingston, Hugh A., "High School Graduates and Drop-outs—A New Look at a Persistent Problem," *The School Review,* Vol. 46, Summer, 1958, pp. 195-203. This article presents a list of characteristics of the drop-out, and suggests ways to understand the pattern of drop-out behavior.

Pellman, Maurine, and Gordon P. Liddle, "A Program for the Problem Child," *Phi Delta Kappan,* Vol. 40, January, 1959, pp. 174-78. A report of the Quincy Youth Development Project in which the University of Chicago is attempting to help this midwestern community of 45,000 learn to educate problem children more adequately.

"Student Mental Health," *NEA Journal,* Vol. 49, September, 1960, pp. 17-31. A valuable series of articles for the prospective teacher who wants to learn more about this important aspect of teaching.

Yoshino, Roger, "The Classroom Teacher and the Pre-delinquent," *The Journal of Educational Sociology,* Vol. 33, November, 1959, pp. 124-30. A discussion of how the classroom teacher can identify and work with the pre-delinquent.

FILMS

Citizenship in Action

Opportunities that are offered high school students to participate in citizenship activities through the student council. The function of the student council as it relates to citizenship practices within the school. (University of Indiana, black and white, 25 minutes.)

Education for Democracy

Sets forth the purposes behind current methods and practices of the public schools at all levels. (Missouri State Teachers Association, color, 22 minutes.)

Group Needs

Teen-age cliques. Problems arising within teen-age groups. (University of Michigan, black and white, 30 minutes.)

Mike Makes His Mark

A skillful school counselor helps a teen-ager who is in trouble. (National Education Association, color or black and white, 29 minutes.)

Problem of Pupil Adjustment
Part I—The Drop-Out

Cause of drop-outs suggested as the lack of purposeful, concrete, interesting experiences in the school; too much emphasis on repetitious drill, memorization and regimentation. (McGraw-Hill Book Co., Inc., black and white, 20 minutes.)

Problem of Pupil Adjustment
Part II—The Stay-In

A school which adapted its program to pupil needs and thereby reduced the drop-out rate. More meaningful learning experiences; greater student interest; real life applications of things learned. (McGraw-Hill Book Co., Inc., black and white, 19 minutes.)

Social Development

Characteristic social behavior of children from infancy to adolescence. Negativeness; shyness; the "impossible" four-year-old; development of group consciousness; the gang age; and the "princess" stage. Need for parental understanding. Methods of dealing with difficult behavior. (McGraw-Hill Book Co., Inc., black and white, 16 minutes.)

PART 8

THE PERSONAL AND PROFESSIONAL LIFE OF THE TEACHER

Chapter 18: The Decision To Teach

CHAPTER 18

THE DECISION TO TEACH

Search for some investment for your humanity, and do not be
frightened away if you give yourself as a man to man.

ALBERT SCHWEITZER

The decision to teach should not be made lightly or hastily. Nor
should teaching be entered for the lack of other things to do. Teaching
is an exciting and demanding profession, a way of life for those who are
suited to it and prepared for it. For those who are not suited to it, unhappiness is their lot. Far too much is involved in this decision; it should
be made only after most careful and personal consideration.

The decision to teach is more than a personal one. It involves many
other lives. The choice of some professions is quite strictly a private
affair. Teaching is somewhat different. While the decision to teach is a
personal matter, that decision must always be made with the welfare of
children and youth in mind. Their futures are also involved.

In this chapter we look at the personal and professional side of teaching. We ask: What is the teaching profession like? How can you test
the decision to teach? What about salaries and working conditions?
Finally, we present four interviews of teachers, conducted by students
who wished to get first-hand information about the personal and professional life of a teacher.

WHAT IS THE TEACHING PROFESSION LIKE?

Teaching is a service profession. What, we should ask, is a service
profession? And, how does it differ from other professions?

Our society is held together by the performance of many vital services.

Society is dependent upon these services and when they are not performed, people suffer. Services connected with food, clothing, health, housing, transportation, government, and education are vital to all of us. Not all persons, of course, performing these services are considered to be professional. Three things usually characterize a profession. First, there is a high degree of skill required to carry out the profession. Second, the period of preparation is usually an extended one. Third, the preparation is usually taken in an institution of higher learning.

A service profession has a further distinguishing feature. Those entering a service profession do not do so primarily for personal or financial gain. Personal gain may come, but the rendering of service is the primary reason for carrying on the task. Such persons, we say, are service motivated.

Teaching is this kind of profession. Teachers perform the vital function of educating the young primarily because they are committed to the importance of this function in society and enjoy rendering this vital service.

We do not imply, of course, that only those in service professions render vital service. Most people who are engaged in what are usually called gainful occupations fill vital needs. Further, these people frequently find satisfaction in stepping outside a gainful role in order to perform, voluntarily, vital and necessary community services. As we shall see in a moment, Albert Schweitzer commends this kind of behavior and believes that it is a part of our obligation to our fellow man. In teaching, however, the service function is built-in. The teacher does not have to search "for some investment for his humanity." His profession affords in full measure the opportunity for such investment. Some persons, of course, may teach all their lives without ever realizing what it means to make such an investment. Teaching itself does not guarantee that a person will find satisfaction in service to others. That depends upon the particular teacher.

HOW DOES ONE GET THE MOST FROM A SERVICE PROFESSION?

Let's turn to the experience of Dr. Albert Schweitzer to help us find an answer.

Albert Schweitzer: You Must Show More Than Average Devotion.

Albert Schweitzer achieved eminence both as an interpreter of Bach and as a theologian, before taking up his medical studies in order to become a missionary. His long years of service in Lamberene, Africa, have been marked by no great imposing physical monuments. There is no elaborate and antiseptic hospital in the jungle as a result of his labors, just a tin roofed dispensary where natives feel at home. Around the dispensary there are huts where the families of the sick live while their ill ones are regaining health under the care of Dr. Schweitzer and his staff. The sick recover faster in the company of their families. Near the edge of the clearing, against the backdrop of the jungle, is a grove of fruit trees which has a special significance for Dr. Schweitzer. Although Dr. Schweitzer had treated their sick for many years, the natives still persisted in "appropriating" fruit from the hospital trees. So Dr. Schweitzer planted this grove where all comers could help themselves.

What is Albert Schweitzer's special contribution to an understanding of teaching? It doesn't lay in the "things" of teaching, but rather in its spirit. Teaching is more than an occupation. Great teachers have always enjoyed giving service to others, without which teaching is dull, for both teacher and student. Dr. Schweitzer has broadened this concept of service to include all occupations. Man achieves his very best when he gives himself as man to fellow man. In his formulation of this belief, Dr. Schweitzer illuminates the heart of teaching.[1] Here are his own words:

> Slowly we crept upstream, (on one of the long African errands of mercy), laboriously feeling—it was the dry season—for the channels between the sandbanks. Lost in thought I sat on the deck of the barge, struggling to find the elementary and universal conception of the ethical which I had not discovered in any philosophy. Sheet after sheet I covered with disconnected sentences, merely to keep myself concentrated on the problem. Late the third day, at the very moment when, at sunset, we were making our way through a herd of hippopotamuses, there flashed upon my mind, unforseen and unsought, the phrase, "Reverence for life." The iron door had yielded: the path in the thicket had become visible.

What does "reverence for life" mean for Dr. Schweitzer?[2] He explains:

> Just as a wave cannot exist for itself, but is ever a part of the heaving ocean, so must I never live my life for itself, but always in the experience that is going on around me. It is an uncomfortable doctrine which the true ethics whisper in my ear. You are happy, they say: therefore you are called upon to give much. Whatever more than others you have received in health, natural gifts, working capacity, success, a beautiful childhood, harmonious family cir-

---

1 Albert Schweitzer, *Out of My Life and Thought* (New York: Henry Holt and Company, 1949), p. 156.
2 Albert Schweitzer, *The Philosophy of Civilization* (New York: The Macmillan Company, 1959), pp. 321, 322-25.

cumstances, you must not accept as being a matter of course. You must show more than average devotion of life to life . . .

But to everyone, in whatever station of life he finds himself, the ethics of reverence for life do this: they force him without cessation to be concerned at heart with the human destinies and all the life destinies which are going through their life course around him, and to give himself, as man, to the man who needs a fellow man. They will not allow the scholar to live only for his learning, even if his learning makes him very useful, not the artist to live only for his art, even if by means of it he gives something to many. They do not allow a very busy man to think that with his professional activities he has fulfilled every demand upon him. They demand from all that they devote a portion of their life to their fellows . . . What he has to bring as an offering is the secret of each individual. But one with another we have all to recognize that our existence reaches its true value only when we experience in ourselves something of the truth of the saying, "He that loseth his life shall find it."

Teaching is a "giving" profession, requiring that the teacher give himself as a human to other human beings. It is in this process of "losing" himself in the destinies of his students that he finds greatest satisfaction. Can we test our ability to succeed in such a profesison? There are some questions we can ask ourselves to help us determine our suitability for teaching. Let us examine some of them.

HOW CAN YOU TEST THE DECISION TO TEACH?

It is possible to test one's decision to teach against certain requirements of the profession? You can ask yourself questions about the work of a teacher and see how you react. You can use your reactions to test your own suitability for teaching. How do you answer these queries which relate to the service nature of the profession of teaching?

Do You Genuinely Enjoy Working With Boys And Girls?

There are many different ways of rendering service to others. It can be forced and grudgingly given. Or the giving can be spontaneous, fresh, and exciting. Students, of course, quickly sense the spirit in which teaching is given. How teaching is given may in the long run be more important than what is given. Teaching that is spontaneously given because the teacher loves his work will always be more powerful than that which is given from a sense of duty. In the presence of genuinely devoted teaching the student might say this: "My teacher cares about me and my fellow students. He loves what he is teaching and he thinks it important in our world. He wants us to learn and grow, and I can depend upon him for help."

Karl Menninger vividly describes how these two contrasting approaches toward helping others influence teaching.[3] One example is of the teacher who does not genuinely enjoy, or love, helping students to learn.

> One teacher faces her school room in the morning with some such attitude as this: "Here are twenty students, the offspring of twenty taxpayers who have hired me to tell these children that $6 \times 6 = 36$. They could find it out for themselves in time, but they will never get to long division and the computation of interest rates if I do not hurry them up and make them take this for a guaranteed fact right now and remember it forever. They may not see why $6 \times 6 = 36$, and I don't know why it is myself; they may not see why they have to learn it and I can't make it seem very reasonable to them, so I will just tell them they *have* to learn it. They haven't anything else to do; they won't have the courage to defy me and refuse to believe it; I am bigger than they are, and I am the teacher, and so I can make them say it, and if I make them say it often enough it will stick. Later they will be grateful to me. Maybe, in the meantime, their parents will consider me a good teacher and not complain to the principal."

By contrast, here is a teacher who teaches spontaneously and with true devotion.

> Another teacher might face her class with some such attitude as this: "These children love me. They think I know lots more than I do. I tell them that 6×6 is the same as 3 tens plus a 6, called "thirty-six" by agreement, and I must tell them that this is one of those conveniences that people have agreed upon in order to save time. I will show them that they could count this up for themselves every time if they liked, and I will do it for them once, to show them how one *does* save time by remembering it instead of having to count it up. I will show them how much fun multiplication is, and I can tell them how 6 is one of the numbers that always show themselves again when they are multiplied by themselves. I will tell them how the numeral came to assume its present form. I will show them how much easier it is to multiply with an Arabic 6 than with a Roman VI. I will make 6 have a personality for them different from the personality of 7 or 3. I realize that the personality of 6, 7, 3 and all other numbers I tell them about will be reflections of my

---

[3] Karl Menninger, *Love Against Hate* (New York: Harcourt Brace and World, 1942), pp. 249-251.

own personality. And, because they love me and because they want so much to please me, they will be interested in my numbers, and in all that I tell them, and they won't have to *try* to remember anything. They will remember it automatically, just as they will remember me. Then, later, when someone tells them that $6 \times 6 = 40$ or that one can spend money and still have it, they will not be impressed or misled. They will remember, not that Miss Jones made them learn the multiplication table, but that there was a Miss Jones once who knew them and loved them, and knew the world too and loved it—and showed them the 6's in the world and what the 6's do to one another."

This is the kind of teacher who stimulates the love of learning. Learning depends upon this kind of stimulation which springs from one who genuinely enjoys giving it.

Do You Enjoy Helping Boys And Girls Regardless Of Their Personal Responses To You?

The teacher who extends love and devotion to his students will usually have it returned. But what if it is not? What if the student rejects or simply ignores it? That is the test of a true teacher. What he does then determines the real nature of his commitment to the profession.

Return for a moment to Albert Schweitzer's statement. Why did he call for showing "more than average devotion of life to life"? Was it because the devotion would be returned? Dr. Schweitzer does not even mention that possibility. Rather, he says that one ought to practice "reverence for life." He comments, "Just as a wave cannot exist for itself, but is ever a part of the heaving ocean, so must I never live my life for itself, but always in the experience that is going on around me." This can be an "uncomfortable" doctrine which says that you are called upon to give much because you have received much.

A good teacher, therefore, does not give himself to his students because he expects them to give to him in return. His own giving is not dependent upon their giving. His own devotion to his work is independent of their response. It springs from his own feeling that what he is doing is worthwhile and adds value and dignity to the human family.

This is a crucial matter, for the teacher whose devotion to students is dependent upon the student's devotion to him is surely headed for keen disappointment and possible failure. Some students will simply not respond to a teacher in this way.

Nor should the teacher expect it. Consider, for example, the vast difference between the student and the teacher roles. The teacher is an adult; the student, a child or adolescent. The teacher represents authority, making continuous demands upon the child who is constantly expected to respond in a favorable way. The teacher has much to say about the child's future in terms of promotions, evaluations, and recommendations. Teachers' and students' values are different and they consider different things to be important. Considering these real differences, the teacher should not expect that his devotion to his students will be reciprocated in the same way that it is given.

Further, the teacher deals in futures. The child's immediate responses to the teacher may not be a reliable clue to his future responses. As the years pass, students frequently change their estimates of the impact of a teacher upon them. Teachers who were popular with the students may be downgraded with time. Other teachers may be upgraded as the value of their contribution becomes more apparent. The teacher is more like a sower than a harvester. As H. G. Wells said, the teacher is a "sower of unseen harvests." His primary job is to sow well, knowing that if he does, others can harvest well. A teacher who is dependent upon the student's affection frequently causes students to be dependent upon him. He teaches so that students must constantly seek his favor and guidance. He finds great satisfaction in having his students so completely dependent upon him that they cannot produce work without him.

But the good teacher encourages students to become independent, to grow away from him, to be individually resourceful. In a sense the teacher trains the student to forget him. "My son is coming to do without me," Emerson once wrote in his Journal, "and I am coming to do without Plato." The good teacher disappears out of the life of the student. He is remembered as a person. The student will not remember exactly what it was the teacher has contributed to his understanding. He has made it his own, just as the teacher hoped he would.

If a teacher does not expect that his devotion should be reciprocated, what should he expect of students? He should expect that students will show their regard for him by taking seriously what he teaches. This is the way Karl Menninger explains it.[4]

> For the teacher must constantly live as if to say "I love you; I will show you this by my genuine attitude and by the patience and honesty and vividness with which I communicate to you the information you are scheduled to receive. That you love me in return I will infer from the extent to which you accept my teaching." It is the art of teaching to obtain love in this sublimated form instead of through a direct expression.

---

4 *Ibid.*, pp. 254-55.

Are You Interested In Helping Boys And Girls To Want To Do And Be Something?

There is a difference between just helping someone and helping someone in a particular kind of way. The teacher has some definite aims in mind. These aims differ from the aims of other professions and occupations. The teacher, for example, is not a promoter of a product or idea. He does not seek to profit from his operations. He does not deal in tangibles which can be weighed and counted.

Yet, his aims are specific. He wants children and youth to want to do and be something. He seeks no favors in return. His job is to assist youth to realize its full potential. In carrying out his task, the teacher points to higher standards of achievement and helps children to discover their own full potentialities.

Carl L. Becker has written about one of his former teachers, Frederick Jackson Turner, historian of the American Frontier.[5] Before going to the University, Becker had learned about Turner from a young lawyer in his home town who had taken work from him. This is the way Becker remembered their conversation about "old Freddie Turner."

> "Is he old?" I asked, picturing the long gray locks of a Faust before the devil comes in the spotlight.
>
> "Oh no, not *old*. We just called him that, I don't know why—just a rough way of showing boyish admiration without being sentimental about it, I suppose."
>
> "What does he teach?"
>
> "Well, he teaches American history. But it's not what he teaches, the subject I mean. The subject doesn't matter. It's what he is, the personality and all that sort of thing. It's something he gives you, inspiration, new ideas, a fresh light on things in general. It's something he makes you want to do or be. I don't remember much American history, but I'll never forget that man Turner, old Freddie Turner."

After Becker entered the University, he confirmed at firsthand his friend's impression of Turner. "I was infected by the desire to study history," he said. "This, of course, was Turner's fault and not mine—for it was true, as my lawyer friend said, that Turner had a singular capacity for making you want to do and be something."

Good teachers are like that. They stir students to set higher goals for themselves.

---

[5] Carl L. Becker, "Wisconsin Historian," in American Masters of *Social Science,* ed. Howard W. Odum (New York: Holt, Rinehart and Winston, Inc., 1927). Reprinted by permission.

Can You Set A Worthwhile Example?

The student studies first the teacher and then the subject. If he likes what he finds in the teacher, the chances are he will like what he finds in the teacher's subject. If he does not like the teacher, the matter may end there, and the subject will not be studied. What the teacher is becomes a crucial matter.

Carl L. Becker [6] remembered Frederick Jackson Turner in this way:

> He made his students want to do what he was doing and to be, if possible, what he was. And what was he? And what was he doing? Fascinated by the man, I attended to his every gesture and expression, listened to everything he said, less at first for the content than for the voice, the intention, the implication. The implication of the whole performance was of something vital being under consideration, something that had in itself only incidentally to do with students "taking a course." The implication was that we (all of us together, if *we* chose—that was our affair) were searching for something, ferreting out hidden secrets. Facts there were, plenty of them, and as a matter of course to be known; but that wasn't the end. There was something concealed there, in and behind the facts, some problem that concerned humanity at large waiting to be solved. The implication was that we might, on our own account, turn over the dead facts once more, on the chance of finding something, something that others had missed.

Perhaps this matter of seeking a worthy example is even more important for the teacher of young children. The young child likes to identify closely with his teacher. He likes to feel that he may some day be like his teacher. In fact, many teachers use as their example a former teacher whom they admired and respected.

Oksana Kasenkina was a Russian teacher who was employed in the foreign service of the Russian government. Wanting to escape Communism, she leaped from a window of the Russian consulate in New York. In her autobiography, *Leap to Freedom,*[7] she tells of the influence upon her of one of her teachers of pre-communist days in Russia. Her narrative reminds us of the importance of the example which is set by the teacher.

> Madame Mazurenko was one of those blessed people who not only have a great gift but are fortunate enough to exercise it. She was

---

6 *Ibid.,* pp. 234-35.

7 Oksana Kasenkina, *Leap To Freedom* (Philadelphia: J. B. Lippincott Company, 1949), pp. 24, 25-26.

more than a teacher. Endowed with the wisdom and an ability which transcends training, she was a rare person, an educator . . .

I remember my last conversation with her especially well. She had surprised me in my nook in the ramp which led to the boys' building. The ramp was a quiet and a sweet-smelling place because of the many plants which grew there.

"So!" she exclaimed with a smile. "This is where you study. I wondered where you always disappeared."

"Somehow it is easier for me to study here."

Madame Mazurenko looked about her and nodded. She was a small woman with dark hair and vivacious eyes, and looked much younger than her fifty years. Now, however, she suddenly looked grave, and sat down next to me.

"I shall be losing you soon, and we have not had a chat for a long time. Tell me, what do you plan to do after you are graduated?"

"My father has always wanted me to be a teacher," I replied. "I should like to be as fine a teacher as you are."

I said the words without guile. Then, taking my hand, she asked, "What would you like to teach?"

"Everything about Nature," I said. "I should like to go to the Cossack *khutors,* where there is everything I like: the steppe, orchards, forests, meadows and all their living creatures."

She patted my hand.

"You will be a good teacher," she said slowly, "if you always remember two things. One, to teach with your heart more than with your head. The head harvests too many things which wither and die; but the heart harvests only love, which is the greatest and which is deathless.

"Two, remember that you will always receive more from the children than you can give them. Plant the seed of love within them and they will teach you the meaning of life."

Madame Mazurenko had kissed me then, and left me.

Are You A Good Student?

"It makes no difference to me," Comenius once said, "whether I teach or am taught." A good teacher is first of all a good student, and in the act of teaching he also learns; the more he shares ideas, the more he keeps. The good teacher likes to deal with ideas and is sensitive to the significant ideas around him. He enjoys good reading and is constantly replenishing his stock of ideas. He seeks out friends who have similar intellectual interests and discusses topics of mutual concern. He keeps feeding new ideas into his classwork, and he stimulates his students with new thoughts. The teacher who lacks this scholar's interest in new ideas is like a water cistern which eventually runs dry for the want of a fresh supply. The teacher who is a good student is like a well that taps deep veins of water upon which it can constantly draw. Students are entitled to teachers who are up-to-date in their own fields of interest, and who have lively interests generally in the world about them.

We have raised five questions which can help you test your decision to teach. Each question tells us something about the requirements of teaching. To teach well, a person must enjoy helping children and young people, regardless of their personal responses to help. He must enjoy helping them to become the best that they can become. A teacher is a living example who can either invite the student to learning or drive him from it. Most of all, the good teacher is a good student who loves to expand his intellectual horizons. He is thus able to lift the horizons of his students.

Almost two thousand years ago, Quintilian summed up the professional requirements for teaching.[8] It is surprising how much meaning his thoughts have for us today. Here is the way Quintilian described his ideal teacher:

> Let him, above all things adopt the attitude of a parent toward his pupils and consider that he is taking the place of those who entrust their children to him.
>
> He must have no vices himself and tolerate none in his pupils. Let him be stern but not melancholy, friendly but not familiar, lest in one case he incur dislike, in the other contempt. He must constantly dwell upon the honorable and the good; for the more he admonishes his pupils the less he will require to punish them. He must never lose his temper, yet he will not pass over what deserves correction; he must be simple in his teaching, and able to endure hard toil, persevering rather than exacting.

WHAT ABOUT SALARIES AND WORKING CONDITIONS?

A great deal has been written about teachers' salaries and working conditions. The published data indicates clearly that salaries continue to move steadily upward and that working conditions are continually improving. Salaries are still not at all what they ought to be, and working conditions for some teachers are definitely substandard. The overall picture, however, continues to brighten.

It is hard to generalize about working conditions and salaries for teachers. Education in America is essentially local business, run by the

---

8 William M. Smail, *Quintilian on Education* (New York: Oxford University Press, 1938), pp. 73-74.

individual states, with large responsibilities delegated to local school boards. Consider the fact that there are fifty states and more than 35,000 local school boards, and you get some idea of the difficulty of generalizing about the welfare of teachers.

This section, therefore, will not give detailed figures about salaries and benefits which may not apply in the area where you would like to teach. We shall, however, give some generalizations which are valid in most places. We shall also indicate how you can learn what you want to know about a specific school system and what you can look for in seeking an attractive teaching position. Also, the selected references at the end of this chapter present valuable data on salaries and welfare matters. For our discussion, we shall separate working conditions and salary, although in practice they are hard to separate.

LOOK FIRST AT THE TEACHER'S WORKING CONDITIONS

Consider security. Teaching generally is a secure profession. It is not subject to seasonal highs and lows. Capable teachers may be assured of employment year in and year out, regardless of fluctuation in the economic cycle. While teachers salaries are slow to respond to periods of prosperity, they tend to withstand periods of recession.

There is another kind of security that goes along with the teaching profession. It relates to geographic location. Jobs in some professions are available only in certain locations. Teaching positions are available practically everywhere. Teachers may decide in what regions they would like to teach, with reasonable assurance that they can find a position. This advantage has special appeal to a woman teacher whose husband's work requires him to live in a particular place. It has appeal to all who have personal reasons for wanting to live in a particular section of the country.

While there is security within the profession, there may not necessarily be security within a particular school system, and this is what interests you when applying for a job. How can you tell how secure a particular school system is? Here are some guidelines.

Does The School System Have A High Or Low Rate Of Turnover Of Teachers?

The rate of teacher turnover can tell you much about the school system's ability to attract and hold good teachers. If, for example, you discover that fifty percent of the teachers who taught in the school last year are not returning for the coming year, you may wish to inquire why they are not returning. The cause could have nothing whatever to do with the quality of the school system. The cause could be just a combination of purely personal reasons. On the other hand, the exodus could be due to poor working conditions within the system. How can you find out? Some discreet inquiries within the community or with teachers will probably bring you the information you need in order to make your own determination.

Does The School System Have Tenure?

Teacher tenure is a device for giving security to competent teachers and protecting them against irresponsible pressure. You may wish to inquire whether or not the school system in which you would like to teach has teacher tenure. Some tenure systems are statewide. Others are on a local option basis. Tenure usually works this way. The new teacher is hired for a probationary period of two or three years. If his work is satisfactory during this period, he may be offered further employment which qualifies him for tenure. If his work is not satisfactory, he may be discharged before he is given tenure. Once given tenure, he may be discharged only on charges of incompetency or for moral reasons, and then only after "due process" before some official body with judicial powers to make a decision in the case.

How important is teacher tenure to the teacher? Such programs give security in law to the teacher's position. This does not mean, however, that systems without tenure are not secure places to teach. Many other factors are involved in determining security. School traditions, the community, and the regard for teachers are all to be considered. Again, if you wish to test the matter, speak with the teachers in a particular system about the security which they do or do not enjoy.

Turn Now From The Security Of The Profession To The Security Of The Particular Subject You Are Teaching

Teachers of some subjects are more in demand than others. You may wish to consider this fact in selecting your teaching area. Don't, however, select a teaching area solely because the teacher demand in it is high. Consult your own interest and abilities first. If you really want to teach in a particular area and are capable and well educated in it, the chances are that you will find a suitable position.

The demand for particular teachers shifts from time to time. How can you find out about areas of greatest demand? There are four good sources: your own college or university educational placement director, the superintendent of schools where you think you might like to teach, the State Department of Public Instruction in your capital city, and the National Education Association in Washington, D.C. The Director of Educational Placement is close to the situation and can tell you in which areas he is receiving the most and the least requests for teachers. Local superintendents of schools can tell you what their own greatest needs are. The State Department of Public Instruction can tell you what the situation is in the state. And the National Education Association in Washington can tell you about national trends.

Generally speaking, the demand for elementary school teachers continues to be high, and the supply is short of the demand. The shortage is more critical in early elementary school. More men are now being attracted to elementary school positions and they are in great demand. High school teachers of foreign language, science, and mathematics are in short supply. But there are more teachers seeking positions in social studies than there are positions to be filled. There are more men trained to be athletic coaches than there are coaching positions. The same is true of men's physical education. Women's physical education teachers, however, are in short supply. It is wise for men who are interested in coaching or in teaching boy's physical education to have strong academic teaching areas. Junior high school teachers are in great demand, especially those who have taken some special training for this level of work. The supply of music, art, and commercial teachers tends to be about equal to the demand. Vocational agriculture and industrial arts teachers are in short supply. There are more people trained to be counselors and guidance directors than there are positions. And the same holds true for those who have taken advanced work in school administration. Classroom teaching experience is considered a prerequisite to gaining positions in either guidance or administration.

Teaching is a secure profession because of the increasing demand for teachers. Some school systems are more secure places to teach than others, and certain subject areas offer more assurance of employment than others. When you seek employment it is wise to consult people who can inform you about the conditions in the school or schools of your choice.

Physical Surroundings And Equipment Are An Important
Part Of Working Conditions

Teachers for the most part work in pleasant surroundings. Modern schools with their bright colors and open spaces provide a work setting which is superior in many ways to other working situations. Tremendous progress has been made in school architecture, especially since the Second World War, and advances are continuing. These new schools consider the teachers' needs as well as the students' needs. Teachers' lounges, dining rooms, and work and storage areas are built into modern schools to help the teacher work more efficiently and under more pleasant conditions.

Instructional materials and aids are a part of the teacher's working environment. The teacher's effectiveness is determined in part by the instructional resources available to him. Books, films, television, laboratory and shop equipment, and supplies help to make for good working conditions. Most schools are putting increasing amounts of money into such worthwhile educational investments. When you apply for a position, you may wish to ask about the building in which you would be working and about instructional supplies available to teachers.

People, Above All, Affect Working Conditions

More important than physical surroundings or the instructional resources are the people with whom the teacher works. Students and colleagues are an important part of the teacher's working environment.

We have talked a great deal about the relationships of students and teachers and we need not extend the matter here. The one common theme that binds teachers and student teachers together is their love of working with boys and girls. They find special challenge in working with young people in an area where things are not set or static, but where people are always in the process of "becoming." As teachers know, boys and girls can be the most exasperating creatures on earth. They can also be the most fun. They keep the teacher's work ever new and changing. If a teacher's work becomes boring it probably indicates that he needs to take a fresh and deeper look at his students. The teacher who looks deeply into the unexplored realms of boys and girls can never be bored.

There is a question you should ask yourself in the job-hunting process: With what kinds of boys and girls can I work best?

Many schools accommodate boys and girls with widely different backgrounds. This is apt to be true of the metropolitan high school that draws its students from widely-scattered sections. On the other hand, some high schools, and especially elementary schools, serve only a local community and are apt to have more or less homogeneous student bodies.

Some teachers who come from a particular background find it difficult to work with children with varied backgrounds. Generally speaking, we can understand people better who are "like us." This should not deter you, however, from launching your teaching career with children who have backgrounds different from your own. You should give some consideration, however, to the kinds of boys and girls with whom you feel you would like to work.

The teacher's colleagues are a vital part of the working situation. For the most part, teachers enjoy working together and are apt to develop a strong in-group feeling, especially in the particular building where they work, and to a lesser extent in the school system of which the building is a part. Colleagues are especially important to the new teacher in helping him adjust. They can also be of valuable assistance to the new teacher when he encounters new and unexpected problems. Most teachers are generous with their help to the new teacher, and the new teacher is wise in learning all he can from his more experienced colleagues.

The Teacher's Status Affects Working Conditions

What is the teacher's professional status in the community? Again, it is hard to generalize about the teachers' status because it fluctuates from time to time and place to place. Further, different groups within a community will hold different opinions about the teacher's professional status. Recent studies [9] of the teacher's professional status would seem to indicate the following:

(1) Nearly all citizens regard teaching as a profession.

(2) In terms of importance to the community, citizens rate teachers above almost every other group.

(3) In terms of status in the community, citizens rate teachers in the middle range of occupational groups.

Certain Benefits Enhance Working Conditions

Teachers have always cited certain benefits which go with the teaching profession. Many of them list the summer vacation and frequent holidays as a part of the benefits of teaching. The summer provides time for extra and different employment, travel, or study, and it always provides a break in the year's occupation. Occasionally teachers like to do teaching during the summer. Such opportunities are on the increase in those school systems which are expanding their summer programs.

---

[9] National Education Association, *Public Opinion Polls on American Education* (Washington, D.C.: The Association, 1958).

Frederic W. Terrien, "Who Thinks What About Educators," *The American Journal of Sociology*, Vol. XIX (September, 1953), p. 154.

Lloyd W. Warner, Robert J. Havighurst, and Martin B. Loeb, *Who Shall Be Educated* (New York: Harper and Brothers, 1944).

Other benefits have been added to teaching in recent years. One such benefit is the leave of absence granted by many boards of education. Such leaves may be granted for various reasons, for example, illness, advanced study, foreign education service, pregnancy, or military service. In addition, "business" and "sick" days are granted by many boards of education.

TURN NOW TO SALARY CONSIDERATIONS

It is generally recognized that teacher's salaries are not as high as they ought to be, and persons considering the teaching profession should scrutinize closely their standard of living aspirations to see if they can live within the teacher's income. It is true that the teacher's salaries have made dramatic increases in recent years and that this upward trend is continuing. Here are some general considerations about teachers' salaries:

(1) Salaries tend to be higher in metropolitan than in rural areas (as does the cost of living).

(2) Salaries tend to be higher in the North and West than in the South (again, so does the cost of living).

(3) Compared with other salaries available to the two sexes, a teacher's salary is more attractive to women than to men.

(4) Teachers' salaries in a particular community tend to reflect the general income level of that community; that is, the higher the general level of income, the higher the teachers' salaries; and the lower the general level of income, the lower the teachers' salaries.

(5) Teachers of special subjects or subjects requiring extra time tend to be paid higher salaries. For example, workers in practically all areas of special education—school psychology, men's and women's athletics, and some areas of music—are apt to be paid more than the regular salary schedule. Latin teachers, because they are in short supply, command attractive salaries.

(6) Most boards of education now use a single salary schedule. The single salary schedule pays the same salary to teachers at all grade levels of the school system. The teachers, however, must have had the same training and experience. (This assumes, of course, that they are not teaching in one of the special areas mentioned previously.) Thus, those teachers with the most training and experience rank highest on the salary schedule, regardless of teaching level.

(7) Most salary schedules provide for an annual increment, which may

range from $100 to $400. The top of the salary schedule may be reached in different periods of time, depending upon the particular salary schedule. On some schedules the top may be reached in as few as eight years, on others in as many as fifteen years.

(8) Most salary schedules provide for added increments for teachers with advanced training and degrees. Usually $200 to $300 extra per year are given those who hold advanced degrees beyond the bachelor's degree.

(9) Most boards of education pay teachers on a nine or ten months' basis, depending upon the length of the school year. Many boards of education, however, will distribute the pay over a period of twelve months to assure a regular income, if the teacher so desires.

(10) A few salary schedules provide for merit increases for exceptional service. These increases are given beyond the regular increments provided for in the salary schedule.

(11) A common beginning range of salaries for new teachers with the B.A. degree is from $4,000 to $5,000 for the school year. Some beginning salaries, it should be remembered, are below this range, while others are above.

(12) A common top range for salaries of experienced teachers is from $7,000 to $8,000. Here, too, certain top salaries fall outside this range, some below, others above.

Fringe Benefits Are A Part Of Salary

Many states have retirement plans in which the teacher's contribution is matched by state or local board of education contributions. Most teachers are now covered by the provisions of the Social Security Act. Group insurance is available to teachers in many areas, and a few school boards provide hospital insurance for teachers.

As we said earlier, education is largely a matter of local and state determination. For this reason, practices regarding salaries and benefits differ greatly from locality to locality. You should, therefore, investigate conditions which exist in the locality of your interest. If you have a particular school system in mind, interview or write the superintendent of schools and ask him for a copy of the salary schedule and the board of education personnel policies. From these two documents you will be able to determine what you may expect by way of salary or other financial benefits.

1. Collect salary schedules and personnel policies from several different school systems in different geographical areas. Prepare a report on the similarities and differences in them.

TEACHERS CAN ADVANCE THEIR OWN WELFARE

In this chapter we have been concerned with the personal and professional side of teaching. It is well to keep in mind that the teacher himself can do much to advance his own personal and professional welfare. These matters are not irrevocably fixed. They change, and the teacher can influence the direction of the change.

The teacher's welfare begins in his own classroom. The teachers who teach well are devoted to their work. They inspire learning and advance the welfare of all teachers. Conversely, poor teaching can harm the welfare of all. Boards of education and citizens are more apt to support increased salaries and benefits for teachers if they feel that the children of the community are being taught well.

Teachers can do much to advance their welfare by helping interpret the work of the school to the community. Teacher contacts with parents and citizens' groups all help to bring greater understanding of the role of the school in the community.

Teacher organizations are dedicated to advancing the welfare of teachers and the cause of education. Local, regional, state, and national educational organizations give visability to the work of the teacher. Each teacher can contribute to his own welfare and that of the other teachers by joining these organizations and working actively in them.

The decision to teach, as we have said before, is a personal one which can only be made by you. It calls for serious thinking about one's personal and professional aspirations. Your period of preparation should provide you with opportunities to gain new insights into teaching and to develop skills in the profession.

2. Sketch out on a single piece of paper your own personal and professional aspirations. Then interview several teachers and find out what their personal and professional lives are really like. Compare your aspirations with what you have found in your interviews.

FOUR STUDENTS INTERVIEW TEACHERS

Let us now turn to four interviews conducted by students who were seeking to learn first-hand about the teacher's personal and professional life. Four such interviews, of course, cannot give us a representative picture of teaching. They can suggest, however, some of the items you can explore when you talk with teachers. These particular interviews were selected because they illustrate some of the factors which we have discussed in this chapter. You will notice certain items of interest in these interviews:

(1) These teachers choose to teach because they enjoy working with children and young people, and they stay in the profession for the same reason.

(2) The teachers believe that they enjoy personal freedom, both with their students and in the community. The "teacher stereotype is leaving the classroom."

(3) They enjoy staff relationships.

(4) They feel they are respected as citizens in the community, not as "socialites" but as "good and useful members of the society."

(5) Living on a teacher's salary and raising a family requires thrift.

(6) The teacher's working conditions have both good and bad aspects. Summers and holiday vacations are listed on the positive side, while large classes, inadequate facilities, and outside responsibilities are listed on the negative side.

(7) The beginning teacher gains confidence and skill with experience.

(8) It is common for women to combine a teaching career with marriage and a family.

Let us now turn to the students' interviews with teachers.

Mr. R. B. Said He Can Walk Into The Class Exhaling Smoke And The Children Don't Run Home And Tell Their Mothers.

Interviewed by MARILYNNE BROWN

For this report I interviewed a husband and wife who have both been teaching for three years. In this way I was given both the man's and woman's point of view on the teaching profession.

Both Mr. and Mrs. B. went into teaching for two reasons. They enjoyed working with people, and they wanted a profession which offered security. As Mr. B. pointed out: "There is no better insurance policy than a teaching certificate." For a man, there is prestige in the community, and a great deal of respect. Further, teaching offers a stepping stone into school administration. Mr. B. said that his secondary teaching would help him prepare for a high school principalship, and that eventually he would like to go into higher education.

Mrs. B. said that there is a tremendous amount of prestige and that the pay is excellent. After a woman has a family she can always return to teaching.

Both Mr. and Mrs. B. said that teaching was what they had expected, except that the social relationships with the staff were better than they had been led to believe. They said that they were surprised how the teacher stereotype is leaving the classroom. The children accept the teachers on the same level as they do their own parents. Mr. B. said during his gym hour he can walk into the class exhaling smoke and the "children don't run home and tell their mothers, or whisper among themselves about their teacher." Both teachers agreed that the situations they encounter and the student and staff relationships are what they enjoy most about teaching.

Then we turned to the problems of teaching. Mr. B. said that a major problem for a man is the insufficient salary which he receives. However, for a woman this is no problem, because she receives a "better than average salary." Other problems were listed in this manner: Large class loads, inadequate facilities (such as books, audio-visual equipment, and necessary supplies), overload duties such as unexpected secretarial-type duties, outside responsibilities such as P.T.A., committees, parent-teacher meetings, and keeping records for the state.

Both teachers said that they were overloaded in college with theory and short-changed on practice, even though they had had student teaching. There were many problems like, "How do I grade?" and "How do I give assignments?" for which they felt they were not prepared. Also some principals refuse to accept teachers as professionals. One other problem is that of Board of Education policy. If there is an extension of the school year, the teachers have to drop their own plans and stay in school to teach. Mr. and Mrs. B. also said that when a teacher returns for advanced work beyond the bachelor's degree he gets inadequate reimbursement for hours accumulated. For instance, Mr. B. is taking two credit hours toward his Master's degree and receives only $14, while Mrs. B. receives only $10 for the same amount of time.

Then we turned to personal requirements for teaching. The teacher's own personal requirements are first and foremost, a good sense of humor, ability to get along with all types of people, and the ability to organize oneself and make quick decisions.

In general, by interviewing these two teachers, I have become much more aware of the benefits, rewards, problems, and expectations of a teacher. This interview was a profitable experience and made me realize just what makes up a career in teaching.

Mr. C. S. Said That A Man With A Family Can Live Quite Comfortably On A Teacher's Salary, And With Summers Off It Is A Good Occupation.

Interviewed by DOUG BALOGH

Mr. C. graduated from a State University and has been teaching in a metropolitan system for four years. He was a math major and teaches the sixth grade in elementary school. He is now working on his master's degree.

Mr. C.'s reactions to teaching can be summed up quite accurately in three words: satisfactions, summers, and salaries. One of the first responses he made did not surprise me at all after I read about the one hundred student teachers. He spoke of the great amount of satisfaction he receives when he watches a child learn through his teaching stimulus. He was quite modest in saying that any teacher can produce this learning, but he finds a special sort of reward when he realizes his efforts are not going to waste. He said he saves the student papers throughout his association with them and then at the end of the year he goes through them and notes the progress each child has made. He says that knowing that you have helped a child write a better sentence and express himself more clearly adds satisfaction to the teaching profession.

Mr. C. feels quite strongly about the self-contained classroom. He feels the teacher gets to know the child much better and learns the students' strong and weak points. This understanding helps the teacher to gear the classroom work to each student's needs in such a way that all students are kept busy and at work on what they need most. "If one knows potentials, then you can develop them," he says.

Mr. C. enjoys the summer and holiday vacations, and also the salary. He said that a man with a family can live quite comfortably on a teacher's salary and with the summers off, it is a good occupation. He feels that after a few years in teaching, a teacher earns enough to live comfortably, though not extravagantly. He says that the summer and holiday vacations are sort of a supplement to his salary, which he appreciates.

Some of Mr. C.'s other comments were related to his original plans for teaching and to how he chose this field. He originally wanted to teach high school, but after being placed in elementary education, he found he enjoyed it enough to stay with it for good. He said that his family had many teachers in it and that he had been closely associated with it throughout his life. This was one of the reasons he went into the profession. He did mention that he entered teaching without an idealistic attitude; still he discovered that there was more work to it than he had anticipated.

Mr. V. S. Feels A Sense Of Service To The Community Which Can Be Equaled In No Other Form Of Livelihood, And This Is Not A Static Feeling, But One That Increases With Each Year One Teaches.

Interviewed by SAM WEBSTER

The subject of my interview, Mr. V. S., has been teaching at the secondary level for twenty years. He is the father of four children and a very respected member of faculty and community. His formal education includes a B.A. degree in education and an M.A. in administration, plus many additional hours of training in the particular fields in which he teaches. This is what teaching means to him:

"I feel that teaching has given me a feeling of self-satisfaction which I could not have experienced in any other occupation. I feel that I am respected as a citizen in the community, not perhaps as a socialite, but definitely as a good and useful member of society."

At this point, I quickly injected this question: "Don't you feel that you are somewhat inhibited by society as to what things you can and cannot do?"

Mr. S. replied, "I can see where some teachers might perhaps feel that they are somewhat apart from the community and inhibited by it, but for me personally the answer is no." He went on to say that he feels a sense of service to the community which can be equaled in no other form of livelihood, and this is not a static feeling, but one that increases with each year one teaches. As a teacher grows older and has more and more years behind him, former students grow up and become adult members of society. It is because of this that a teacher's sense of service and respect in the community increase as the years progress.

When I asked Mr. S. if he could have raised his family of six on his salary alone, he awarded me a prompt "no." His wife also teaches school and it is because of this double income that he can support his family of six. He adds that he probably could have gotten by, that is existed, on his salary alone, but could never have afforded the things a teacher wants for his family, such as college educations. He then summarized humorously by stating, "A teacher has champagne tastes but must manage on a beer pocketbook."

My subject felt that the working conditions are very pleasant in the teaching profession with the nine-month year and the daily hours and conditions. However, he added that a good teacher must always be willing to devote time to counseling with his students about personal problems. "This," he went on, "can lead to many complications within one's self. That is because a teacher must have an interest in his students above and beyond this professional interest, but still must be careful only to stimulate the student and not directly to advise him. There is a fine line between counseling and discipline, and one must be careful not to cross this line and become involved with the opinions of the students' parents."

Mr. S. points out that although teachers are in a somewhat abstract way apart from the community, they have a society within themselves, and this society is generally a very happy one. He is also of the opinion that, in general, teachers' families are happier than most.

In summation, Mr. S. feels that despite the financial restrictions, teaching is to him the most rewarding and fulfilling course of life he could have chosen. He feels that he has accomplished something good with his life and that he is a respected member of society. His closing statement was, "I've never been sorry."

Mrs. L. J. B. Knew That Being Around Children Would Always Offer Interesting Situations And Not Be Dull Routine.

Interviewed by STEPHANIE WALSH

I would like to introduce Mrs. B., age 28, happily married, and having an unwavering devotion to teaching. At the present she is expecting her second child and has not been teaching this past year. However, she plans to resume teaching within the next two years.

Mrs. B. graduated from a liberal arts college and has taught first grade for four years in four different schools. Each school was not only in a different state but it was also in a different type community. I am interviewing her with regard to this past experience and shall be comparing her first year of teaching with its problems to her fourth year and its fulfillments.

"Why did you choose the teaching profession, Mrs. B.?"

"Most of all, I enjoy working with children. I knew I could satisfy this desire by teaching. Then, too, I knew being around children would always offer interesting situations and not be dull routine. I had also thought of the opportunities of teaching abroad and had planned to do so after two years here in the states."

"Did your first year of teaching fulfill your expectations and satisfy these desires?"

"Hardly! My first position was in a first grade class on an Army base. Over a period of a year I had come in contact with sixty children coming and going as their fathers were transferred and assigned. I was frightened and felt unprepared. No course of study was available and no special help was offered. I had children from all over the world, including two Puerto Rican children who could neither speak nor read English. I felt the job was overwhelming and did not feel it was fair to the children to have an inexperienced teacher their first year. I have always felt that a first grade teacher makes a lasting first impression on their students which will continue through their school years.

"By the end of the year I felt less incompetent but my main concern was still subject matter, and had I prepared these children for the second grade? Concerning the two Puerto Rican children: One had learned to read and speak English very well, while the other, who was far less intelligent and had an emotional problem, had not learned to do these things. At least one accomplishment!"

"By the fourth year did you find your teaching position more satisfactory, and in what ways?"

"I found by this time that as you develop competence and self-confidence, you gain more satisfaction out of your teaching. The first year I was very concerned about subject matter and the way in which it was presented. By the fourth year my concern had shifted to the children as individuals and to helping them develop. I had confidence in my subject material and knew this was adequate, but now the emotional and discipline problems were of greater importance.

"For example, Robert was one of my problem students at my last school here in the city. He feigned helplessness from the very beginning. He dawdled, was uncooperative, and had an intense feeling of inferiority. With the cooperation of his mother and her frequent conferences with me, we were able to build Robert's self-confidence. Ignoring his dawdling and giving him a little extra attention without forcing it helped Robert in school. He is now doing very nice work in the second grade."

Mrs. B. began her teaching career with a feeling of inadequacy in material preparation and self-confidence. By her fourth year of teaching she felt better prepared in subject matter but had a deeper concern for her pupils as individuals. Mrs. B. knows that she will return to her teaching because now she has found satisfying fulfillment in working with "her" school children.

THE GOOD TEACHER ASSISTS DISCOVERY

The theme throughout this book is contained in its title: *The Discovery of Teaching*. The book ends now, but the discovery of teaching goes on. The teacher, as he assists discovery in others, is ever-discovering teaching himself. His is the act of being taught as he teaches. On the frontispiece of this book Mark Van Doren remarks: "The art of being taught is the art of discovery, as the art of teaching is the art of assisting discovery."

It is our hope that this book has assisted you in some way to discover teaching. Even more hopefully, perhaps it has helped to increase your enthusiasm for making further discoveries about teaching. The quest is a large and worthy one, and can light your professional path for years to come.

Good Follow-up Reading and Viewing

BOOKS

Burrup, Percy E., *The Teacher and the Public School System,* chaps. 12 and 14. New York: Harper & Brothers, 1960. Chapter twelve treats the professional status of teachers and teacher organizations. Chapter fourteen discusses teacher welfare: salaries and salary schedules, retirement, social security, sick leave, and tenure.

Chandler, J. B., *Education and the Teacher,* chaps. 10, 14, and 15. New York: Dodd, Mead & Co., 1961. Chapter ten views national, state and local teacher organizations, and discusses professional obligations and benefits. Chapter fourteen treats in detail the social, economic and legal status of teachers. Chapter fifteen reviews job opportunities and career patterns for teachers.

Cressman, George R., and Harold W. Benda, *Public Education in America,* chaps. 7 and 8. New York: Appleton-Century-Crofts, Inc., 1961. Surveys the professional requirements and benefits of teaching. Describes professional organizations. Reviews job opportunities, salaries and benefits. Sample salary schedule included.

Elsbree, Willard S., *The American Teacher.* New York: American Book Company, 1939. Describes the development of the teaching profession in America.

Fund for the Advancement of Education, *Teachers for Tomorrow.* New York: 1955. An exhaustive analysis of America's need for teachers.

Hamrin, S. A., *Planning for Your Career.* Chicago: Science Research Associates, Inc., 1956. This book is designed to help you analyze your interests and abilities.

Haskew, Laurence D., *This Is Teaching,* chaps. 10 and 11. Chicago: Scott, Foresman & Company, 1956. These two chapters pose cogent questions for the person who is considering teaching and spells out what is involved in preparing to teach.

Hepner, Harry W., *Psychology Applied to Life and Work,* chap. 11. Englewood Cliffs, N.J.: Prentice-Hall, Inc., 1952. Suggests methods of choosing a vocation: self-analysis, tests, other devices. Answers the question: How do occupational misfits happen?

Kearney, Nolan C., *A Teachers Professional Guide.* Englewood Cliffs, N.J.: Prentice-Hall, Inc., 1958. This book explains how teachers can help themselves, care for their professional interests, and adjust to the wide vareity of conditions they find in their work.

Kitson, Harry Dexter, *I Find My Vocation.* New York: McGraw-Hill Book Co., Inc., 1954. An interesting feature of this excellent book on career choice is a list of biographies of successful persons in many different occupations.

Leacock, Stephen, "The Lot of the Schoolmaster," in *Essays and Literary Studies,* Fourth Edition. New York: John Lane Company, 1916. Leacock, humorist and satirist, examines the condition of the secondary teacher.

Lieberman, Myron, *Education as a Profession,* chaps. 8, 9, and 14 and pp. 214-25. Englewood Cliffs, N.J.: Prentice-Hall, Inc., 1956. These chapters discuss the teacher's characteristics and occupational status.

Miller, G. F., *Letters From a Hard-Boiled Teacher to His Half-Baked Son.* Washington, D.C.: Daylion, 1935. A rollicking and satiric series of letters from teacher-father to teacher-son, covering advice on a multitude of details in teaching.

National Education Association, *A Manual on Certification Requirements for School Personnel in the United States*. Washington, D.C. This biennial publication gives a detailed description of certification requirements for all public school positions in different states.

———, *Economic Status of Teachers in 1958-59*. Washington, D.C.: 1959. A comparison of teachers' earnings with those of other occupational groups.

Perry, Bliss, *And Gladly Teach*. Boston: Houghton Mifflin Company, 1935. A classic statement on a happy forty-nine year career as a teacher at Williams, Princeton, and Harvard.

Smiley, Marjorie B., and John S. Diekhoff, *Prologue to Teaching*, Part 1, "The Vocation of Teaching." New York: Oxford University Press, 1959. A valuable collection of readings dealing with the teacher as a person, his professional functions, social and economic status, and certification.

Stinnett, T. M., *The Teacher and Professional Organizations*, Third Edition. Washington, D.C.: National Education Association, 1956. A series of units on teachers' professional organizations for use in pre-service education courses.

Thomas, Lawrence G., *et. al., Perspective on Teaching*, chap. 14. Englewood Cliffs, N.J.: Prentice-Hall, Inc., 1961. A good survey and description of job opportunities in education.

Van Dalen, Deobold B., and Robert W. Brittell, *Looking Ahead to Teaching*, chaps. 2 and 3. Boston: Allyn and Bacon, Inc., 1959. Chapter two is a comprehensive discussion of professional status, ethics, and organizations. Chapter three presents factual data regarding salaries, tenure, and working conditions.

Wynn, Richard, *Careers in Education*, chaps. 1, 6, and 7. New York: McGraw-Hill Book Co., Inc., 1960. Chapter one discusses factors which contribute to happiness in a career and how to choose an occupation. Chapter six surveys job opportunities in education and reviews the situations in particular areas. Chapter seven discusses common misconceptions about teacher's salaries. Informative treatment of salary schedules.

PERIODICALS

Best, John Wesley, "A Study of Certain Selected Factors Underlying The Choice of Teaching as a Profession," *Journal of Experimental Education*, Vol. 17, 1948, pp. 201-58.

Blum, Lawrence P., "A Comparative Study of Students Preparing For Five Selected Professions Including Teaching," *Journal of Experimental Education*, Vol. 16, 1947, pp. 31-65. This study is concerned with a comparison of the personal characteristics and interests of students training for the professions of education, law, medicine, journalism, and mechanical engineering.

Jewett, Robert E., "Why The Able Public-school Teacher Is Dissatisfied," *Educational Research Bulletin*, Vol. 36, October, 1957, pp. 223-34, 244. A realistic discussion of the able teacher's problems in handling large classes and excessive clerical and managerial work.

"Merit Rating," *Phi Delta Kappan*, Vol. 42, January, 1961, pp. 137-63. A series of seven articles on merit rating and pay. Gives history, pros and cons, and examples.

National Education Association, "The Status of the American Public School Teacher," *Research Bulletin,* Vol. 35, no. 1, February, 1957, p. 41. This bulletin reports on the social status of the men and women who were serving as public school classroom teachers in the school year 1955-56.

National Education Association, *Biennial Salary Survey,* Washington, D.C. (Published biennially.) This up-to-date salary survey is conducted every other year by the NEA.

―――――, *Teacher Supply and Demand in Public Schools,* Washington, D.C. This annual study of teacher supply and demand by the NEA includes different teaching levels in different states. The most comprehensive study of supply and demand available.

Palmer, R. Roderick, "Is Teaching a Profession?" *Phi Delta Kappan,* Vol. 34, January, 1953, pp. 139-40. The author lists the characteristics of a profession and the problems of professionalizing teaching.

Redefer, Fredrick L., "Factors That Affect Teachers Morale," *The Nation's Schools,* Vol. 63, February, 1959, pp. 59-62. Redefer reports the responses of 5,000 teachers to questions relating to job satisfaction and morale. Factors which relate to both good and poor morale.

Stiles, Lindley J., "Security Isn't Enough," *The Nation's Schools,* Vol. 58, December, 1956, pp. 43-44. Dean Stiles proposes that "to solve the teacher crisis, we need to pay competitive salaries to all teachers and give better salaries to better teachers."

"Ten Years of Change in Teacher's Salary Schedules," *NEA Research Bulletin,* Vol. 29, No. 2, May, 1961, pp. 52-57. This research study of teacher's salaries demonstrates the dramatic rise in salaries during the last decade.

Terrien, Frederic W., "Who Thinks What About Teachers?" *American Journal of Sociology,* Vol. 59, September, 1953, pp. 150-58. This study measures public attitudes toward educators by sampling the registered voters of a small community.

U. S. Office of Education, *Teaching Opportunities,* Circular 589, Washington, D.C., 1959. Practical information about teaching positions in public and private schools, overseas schools, and colleges.

Whitcomb, Mildred, "Eyes on Winnetka," *The Nation's Schools,* Vol. 61, June, 1958, pp. 40-42. In this interview, the superintendent of schools of Winnetka, Illinois, tells how the salary schedule was developed and how it affects teachers in that system.

Wynn, Richard, "Teachers Are Entitled to Job Satisfaction," *The Nation's Schools,* Vol. 55, May, 1955, pp. 43-45. Discusses the teacher's various needs in relation to job happiness. Demonstrates that remuneration does not rank first among persons seeking job satisfaction. Lists other important factors making for happiness in teaching.

FILMS

Appointment with Youth

A dramatic presentation of the work of a teacher. The film concludes that teaching is a good profession, not just for its good working hours, salary, and vacations, but more importantly, for the deep personal satisfaction it gives. (McGraw-Hill Book Co., Inc., black and white, 26 minutes.)

Choosing Your Occupation

Methods of self-appraisal, occupational possibilities, preparation, requirements, and guidance facilities in choosing an occupation. (Coronet Instructional Films, black and white, 10 minutes.)

How To Investigate Vocations

High school boy starts out to investigate possible vocations by taking tests to determine his aptitudes; reading books on different vocations; listing questions he wants answered; talking to people in various occupations. Shows him in summer job picked to help in final selection of occupation. (Coronet Instructional Films, black and white, 11 minutes.)

Personal Qualities for Job Success

Three young people in interviews for positions. Qualities important for holding a job. Initiative; personal appearance; work habits; willingness to accept criticism; ability to get along with people. (Coronet Instructional Films, black and white, 11 minutes.)

Planning Your Career

Important considerations for choosing a career. How to learn about yourself through such tests as: verbal meaning, special ability, reasoning, number, and fluency. How to learn about vocations. (Encyclopaedia Britannica Films, Inc., black and white, 16 minutes.)

Teaching

Importance aand advantages of teaching; personal and professional qualifications; stresses the responsibilities and opportunities of teaching. (Vocational Guidance Films, black and white, 10 minutes.)

Tips for Teachers

Teaching efficiency from the standpoint of selling ideas. Such items as dress, personal appearance, and the "you" attitude stressed interestingly and valuably. Primarily concerned with the teacher as an individual dealing with other people. (Jam Handy, black and white, 19 minutes.)

INDEX

A

Activities:
  class, extra, 283-287, 291
  co-curricular, 271
  learning promoted by, 116-117, 123, 125-126, 129-131, 134
Adult education, 238
Agassiz, Louis, 147-149, 163, 175, 181, 187-188
  compared with Rousseau, 170-171
  laboratory of, 164-171
  quoted, 162, 164-165, 167-169, 171
American Universities Field Staff, 193, 196
Americanism, education and, 256-257
Anstine, Richard, quoted, 136-137
Antin, Mary, 256
  quoted, 247
Apprenticeship, learning through, 127-131
Arithmetic, 91-92, 115
Arnold, Matthew, 67-68
  quoted, 64-66
Art teachers, 28
Association, learning by, 130-131
Attitudes:
  problems in, 9-11
  toward school, 183-184
Authority:
  submission to, 178
  of teacher, 97-98

B

Balogh, Doug, quoted, 317-318
Basford, Emory S., 271n.
Basic knowledge and skills, teaching of, 227
Becker, Carl L., quoted, 304-305
Behavior:
  classroom, 24-27, 181-185
  new, learning and, 109

Behavior (*Cont.*):
  of non-directive teacher, 255-256
  problems in, 9-11
  reputation and, 266
Brown, Marilynne, quoted, 316-317
Brown v. Board of Education, 246n.
Buck Harbor, Maine, 74-78, 145
Byas, Earlynn, quoted, 237-238

C

Carskadon, T. R., 244, 258
  quoted, 243
Charleston, 80-81
Chase, Mary Ellen, 83, 89, 96, 145, 188
  quoted, 73-78
Cheating, 11
Chicago, 89
Children:
  emphasis on, in teaching, 98-101
  experience in working with, 43-44, 69-70
  kindness toward, 90
  respect for, 90
  understanding of, 26
  (*See also* Students)
Cicero, 58-59, 63-64, 67
  quoted, 68
Citizens, participation of, in school affairs, 212
Class activities, extra, 283-287, 291
Class bias, influence of, on learning, 267-269
Classes, informal, 123
Classroom instruction, good, 31-32
Classrooms, 122-123, 148
  class bias in, 267-269
  composition of, 262
  ideal, 135
  social class structure of, 264-267
  teacher-dominated, 179, 181-185
Cliques, 282-284, 288, 290

Date Due

JAN 18 '63			
JAN 19 '63			
JUL 17 '63			
JUL 31 '63			
FEB 12 '64			
APR 21			
JUL 6 '6			